The Amasian Way

A Practical Guide to

Asian American Leadership

Bartholomew S. Jae

Orchard Fire Publishing • Gloucester, Massachusetts

First Printing: April, 2026

ISBN: 978-1-968961-16-9 (Paperback)

OFP-0522-01P

Published by Orchard Fire Publishing

Jonathan Feist, Publisher and Editor in Chief
Gloucester, Massachusetts, USA
Printed in the USA

For more information and additional titles, visit:
www.orchardfire.com

Contents

Acknowledgments

To begin, I express my gratitude to God for everything I am and all that I possess.

This book is primarily dedicated to my parents, who made countless sacrifices to give my brothers and me better opportunities. I also dedicate it to my supportive wife, Amasian Grace, whose encouragement helps me improve every day, and to my beloved children, Matty and Bethany, who continually keep me grounded.

My heartfelt thanks go out to all those who supported me as an immigrant boy navigating life in a new country, to my colleagues and fellow volunteers for being such exceptional partners, and to the mentors and advocates whose guidance has fostered my professional growth.

Lastly, I dedicate this book to the pioneering Amasians whose efforts paved the way for me and so many other AAPI professionals to thrive in corporate America.

Introduction

The Amasian Way serves as a leadership development framework tailored for Asian American and Pacific Islander (AAPI) professionals. It intentionally shapes others' perceptions of you over time and helps turn consistent performance into a strong reputation. This approach emphasizes being deliberate, engaging in continuous learning, taking proactive action, and constant improvement. It presumes dedicated effort and holds participants accountable. The main goal is to establish lasting credibility, which can, in turn, lead to greater leadership roles and expand your influence.

The Amasian Way is a framework for shaping experience.

The term "Amasian" is a play on words. It blends the terms *amazing*, *Asian*, and *American*. This book is intended for AAPI professionals who navigate both Eastern and Western cultural influences and want to lead with both substance and visibility. However, the lessons of the Amasian Way can help anyone who feels the pull of multiple identities, is caught between cultures, and straddles tradition and nonconformity.

I acknowledge that the terms "Asian" and "AAPI" are both broad and encompass numerous countries and cultures. I am aware that various abbreviations have been employed to refer to Asian Americans. For the sake of consistency, I will use the abbreviation AAPI throughout this book.

The Amasian Way distinguishes itself from other leadership models by facilitating the translation of multicultural instincts, strengths, and experiences into leadership behaviors that are clear, trusted, and valued within diverse environments. The approach encourages intentional leadership while maintaining authenticity, rather than conforming to external expectations.

The Amasian Way empowers you to lead as the ultimate you.

The Amasian Experience Principle

When most people think of Dwayne "the Rock" Johnson, they do not begin with his background. They begin with his presence, discipline, consistency, and impact. His Samoan and Black identities are real and meaningful, but they are not the primary lens through which the public experiences him. His body of work shapes his narrative.

That did not happen by accident. It happened through repeated, visible performance across different platforms, job roles, and interactions. The "Dwayne Johnson Experience" became a global phenomenon through hard work and consistent performance.

You don't need to be famous to benefit from this approach. The same idea works at work. Trust grows when your brand promise is well defined, and you consistently demonstrate strong leadership. The more people come to trust you, the more new opportunities will arise.

At its core, the Amasian Way is about how people experience you as an AAPI leader.

People may initially notice your background, your identity, or your differences. Ultimately, what determines trust, influence, and opportunity is how you are experienced over time. Your consistency. Your judgment. Your contribution. Your reliability under pressure.

This is the lever the Amasian Way is designed to help you pull.

The book's main idea is straightforward: real-life experience challenges bias. Stereotypes persist when our experiences are limited or shallow, but they fade when we encounter rich, repeated, and undeniable experiences. Eventually, these experiences build your reputation, which in turn defines your *leadership brand promise*.

People will trust you and follow you repeatedly because of how you made them feel under your leadership.

WHY THIS, WHY NOW, WHY YOU

The more things change, the more they stay the same.

Asian American and Pacific Islander (AAPI) professionals are not struggling to get hired. We are struggling to advance. According to the Ascend Research Foundation, over the years, the data have consistently shown that Asian men and women are still among the most likely to be hired, but the least likely to become executives. Across industries and organizations, the pattern is consistent: representation is strong at entry and individual contributor levels, then drops sharply as roles become more senior. This gap has persisted for decades, and it cannot be explained by work ethic, education, or capability alone.

This issue is not unprecedented; it stems from longstanding societal patterns. The current context has evolved, but discriminatory practices persist. Historically, Asian Americans have faced systemic and overt discrimination, as evidenced by legislation such as the Chinese Exclusion Act of 1882, the Immigration Act of 1924, the establishment of War Relocation Centers for Japanese Americans in 1942, and post-9/11 actions targeting South Asian, Muslim, and Sikh Americans. Following the COVID-19 pandemic in 2020, hate crimes against Asian Americans have reached record levels. The complex legacy of both discrimination and allyship continues to affect parity for AAPI executives.

Perceptions regarding substandard manufacturing quality and lack of respect for intellectual property in certain Asian countries are occasionally extended to Asian Americans. These views, combined with traditional stereotypes associated with Asian Americans—such as the model minority myth, high risk aversion, and limited communication skills—may contribute to unconscious biases hindering the advancement of AAPI professionals.

Diversity concepts have evolved over the years. Racial tolerance gave way to political correctness and affirmative hiring practices. Equity and belonging were added to diversity and inclusion after the call for fair treatment following the horrific murder of George Floyd. The narrative has moved from intolerance to tolerance, to embracing diversity and inclusion, and then to building fair and equitable workplace cultures. For a period, diversity, equity, and inclusion efforts acted as a stabilizer. They created language, visibility, and in some cases protection.

However, the challenges of increasing representation and upward mobility for AAPI professionals are enduring. Even when diversity, inclusion, and equity had greater momentum, progress was slow. Now it is slowing further. Diversity efforts were often strategically centered on other groups, namely women, Black, and Latinx professionals, because AAPI professionals were viewed as "doing just fine" under the model minority myth. Women were closest to executive parity, so gains could be made with less effort. Traditionally underrepresented minorities were at the bottom of representation, so improvements were easier to point to as visible wins. AAPI professionals sat in the middle of the pack and received the attention that a middle child gets at home. I know, because I am both AAPI and a middle child.

Broad-stroke diversity training attempts to improve inclusion in the workplace. They called out unconscious bias and systemic discrimination that show up quietly and repeatedly at work. You are passed over for stretch assignments or high-visibility opportunities without explanation. Decisions are made behind closed doors, and you learn about them after the fact. Your ideas are ignored until someone else repeats them. You are interrupted, talked over, or treated as the executor rather than the owner. Outside the room, assumptions about your ambition, confidence, or readiness form without your voice present to challenge them.

Often, these moments are not driven by malicious intent. They are the product of norms that have long gone unquestioned. When behaviors are normalized, they rarely feel harmful to those who benefit from them, even as they limit those who do not.

Over time, these moments accumulate. They shape access, visibility, and trajectory. They influence how you are experienced long before they ever appear in a formal performance review.

In these moments, the unspoken question is rarely whether you are competent. The question is whether you belong. That pressure shifts your energy from doing the work to defending your right to be in the room. When belonging feels conditional, thriving becomes difficult. You may be delivering, but you are not operating with full psychological safety, full risk tolerance, or full voice.

Now, efforts and progress made over the past decade to improve respect and fairness in the workplace are weakening. Opposition is gaining strength, shifting corporate priorities. Budgets tighten. Commitments soften. At the same time, anti-Asian sentiment has become more overt in public discourse. Visibility has increased, but protection has not.

The shift led some colleagues to overtly express their resentment and belief that inclusion efforts created unfair advantages. Even when unspoken, that belief changes behavior. Skepticism replaces trust. Scrutiny replaces curiosity. You are measured more harshly, credited more slowly, and forgiven less often. AAPI professionals find themselves defending against constant criticism that they were "DEI hires" versus merit hires.

This dynamic imposes a burden on professionals' energy and mental well-being. The effort that could otherwise be dedicated to learning, leadership, and development is instead diverted toward self-protection. Over time, such demands can inhibit growth and have negative psychological effects.

Many AAPI professionals respond by working harder, staying patient, or trying to out-communicate stereotypes. Each approach has value. None directly addresses the day-to-day mechanism through which bias shapes opportunity.

You may say to yourself, "I am very Americanized. I identify as an American. I do not fit into any of the stereotypes attributed to Asians. I probably will not get much out of this book." There are two things that I would say in response to this.

Whether you are Americanized or not, your diversity is evident. As a result, people initially judge you by your appearance until they truly get to know you, and that's often when stereotypes come into play. For instance, when I was growing up, people would compare my dad to Mr. Miyagi from *The Karate Kid*, and strangers would approach him saying, "Wax on!" Many of my classmates just assumed I practiced Kung Fu, often mimicking Bruce Lee's war cries to provoke me. It was also common for people to think I would end up working in a Chinese restaurant or a laundromat. When people lack familiarity, they tend to fill in the gaps with stereotypes—so it helps to understand them and figure out how to overcome them.

In my thirties, I would have described myself much the same way, until I realised that my Eastern upbringing was affecting how I interacted with a particularly significant group: senior executives. As a consulting director, I needed to be more assertive than I was being when dealing with them. Therefore, readers who see themselves as "Americanized" might find valuable insights here.

Corporate business books may not resonate with certain groups, such as small business owners or leaders of non-profit organizations like parish churches or community centers. Consider the relationships you have with local regulators, Chambers of Commerce, potential funders, and those influenced by your leadership. Understanding your leadership brand promise and experience is essential for these interactions. The insights provided here offer valuable benefits for you as well.

This Is the Amasian Way

It is important for AAPI professionals to cultivate leadership abilities that highlight their multicultural advantages and position their brand promise as the central message, rather than focusing solely on diversity. Developing these skills enables AAPI professionals to distinguish themselves as leaders, regardless of prevailing attitudes toward diversity in workplace environments.

Bias is rarely defeated by explanation.
It is disrupted by experience.

Your demonstrated experience across various situations and under pressure is a more reliable indicator of trustworthiness, credibility, and future opportunities than personal descriptions or others' initial perceptions.

The Amasian Way is a leadership development approach designed for AAPI professionals, transforming results into experience and experience into opportunity. By combining the strengths of Eastern and Western cultures, you create a powerful authentic leadership style that helps you reach your ultimate potential.

It is built on a simple premise: *If you deliver a clear brand promise and people consistently experience you as a leader, then experience becomes the dominant narrative.* Over time, your brand promise travels faster than assumptions. It earns you increased scope, sponsorship, and followership. It becomes a practical way to rise without denying bias, erasing identity, or waiting for systems to change.

Traditional leadership frameworks frequently do not address the unique challenges encountered by AAPI professionals. These frameworks tend to emphasise general leadership traits without adequately considering their applicability within real-world contexts that may reinforce or counter prevailing assumptions. This highlights the complexity involved in navigating diverse cultural backgrounds and identities simultaneously. As a result, conventional guidance often omits essential components and actionable strategies required for substantive leadership development.

The Amasian Way does not overturn leadership frameworks prevalent in Western corporate cultures. Instead, it recognizes how multicultural influences shape AAPI professionals and supports them in adapting and growing as leaders. By embracing their genuine and multicultural strengths and identities, those who follow the Amasian Way are empowered to create distinct leadership experiences and make a meaningful impact.

You Are Ready to Get Uncomfortable

Comfort, complacency, and compliance remain powerful deterrents. AAPI professionals take comfort in staying heads-down, avoiding visibility and risks, or believing that patience and hard work will eventually prevail. It often feels like psychological safety. In reality, it is frequently stagnation in disguise.

Doing nothing, being complacent, and being subservient are still choices. However, silence is still interpreted, and not standing out is still labeled. Being agreeable is not the same as being trusted. Being busy is not the same as being impactful. Waiting for permission when you have agency is seen as a lack of initiative rather than loyalty.

In environments not designed for you, comfort rarely works in your favor. Some fear losing their working visa if they stand out. The opposite is true if you are standing out for the right reasons. Those who stand out by delivering a strong impact and experience are more secure than those who do not stand out at all.

You must get uncomfortable if being comfortable is not getting you where you want to go.

This book is not written for everyone. It is not written for people who want validation without effort or progress without accountability. It does not promise fairness, safety, or guaranteed outcomes. Bias is real. Systems are imperfect. Some doors will remain closed no matter how prepared you are.

Leadership itself is also not for everyone. The higher up you go, the more scrutiny you will be under, and more critics will use racist language to derail you. Former PepsiCo CEO Indra Nooyi was caught up in a politically charged controversy in 2016. Some critics referenced her Indian background in their rhetoric. Boston Mayor Michelle Wu represents very liberal policies. Some of her critics refer to her as the "Mayor of Wuhan" and a Chinese national communist, even though she is the daughter of Taiwanese immigrants. Similarly, Elaine Chao, who served as U.S. Secretary of Transportation and the wife of Senator Mitch McConnell, was referred to as "Coco Chow" and "China-loving," despite being born in Taiwan and having been a U.S. citizen for decades. There is no end to the ignorant call for AAPI leaders to "Go back to where you came from." These three AAPI women leaders have done an outstanding job of standing up for themselves, but not everyone can.

This book targets professionals committed to high-quality work and thoughtful improvement. It speaks to individuals who analyze their experiences, seeking not just to understand events but also to extract meaningful lessons. It's designed for those who candidly assess both their strengths and areas for growth, who are curious to expand their knowledge and challenge conventions, who show resilience in overcoming difficulties, and who maintain the discipline to persist in learning, growing, and leading. More importantly, this book calls on AAPI professionals to step up and lead, despite the risk that their exposure could lead to unwanted biases.

Let's play a game of "Would you rather?" When faced with a moment when diversity is challenged, would you rather be heads down, hoping things will change, or stand up to lead despite the pressure to stay below the radar? There is an old saying, "In life, a person is either making things happen, watching things happen, or wondering what happened." You are here to learn how to make things happen.

If you have ever felt capable of more than your current role allows you to demonstrate, if you have sensed your impact could be greater with the right clarity and preparation, this book was written with you in mind. Not because you are owed something, but because you are willing to earn it.

"Leadership," as the word is used in this book, is not a title or a destination. It is a practice. A repeated choice to take responsibility for your growth, your impact, and your influence, especially when conditions are not ideal.

Dr. Martin Luther King Jr. is attributed to saying, "It is always a good time to do the right thing." I believe it is always a good time to lead yourself, others, organizations, and societies to do the right things. The more leadership reps you *choose* to make, the more you will improve your leadership skills and impact.

Here is what you will build as you move through this journey:

- Self-awareness and identity strength, so you can lead without shrinking or performing a persona.
- A growth engine built on reps, not wishful thinking.
- Communication and connection skills that make your work and your point of view legible.
- Strategic focus, so you stop living in reaction mode and start moving outcomes.
- Leadership behaviors that earn followership from any seat.
- A service mindset that expands your impact beyond your job and strengthens your purpose.

There is a path forward. It is not easy, but it is learnable.

If you are still here, the question is no longer whether you are capable. It is whether you are willing and ready.

JOURNAL ACTIVITY

There are a number of journal activities throughout this book. You may want to start a physical or online journal to capture your responses to them all. You may also want to capture yourself on video in place of a written journal entry.

Complete the following sentences:

1. My leadership journey is:

2. I wish I was more:

3. I want to lead because:

4. People should follow me because:

Reflection Questions

- How are you feeling about where you are today in your leadership journey?
- Where do you perceive challenges are coming from?
- What is your conviction or purpose for leading?
- What is your promise to those who follow your lead?

DISCOVER MORE

A Discover More section appears at the end of each chapter. This section will list terms, concepts, and resources from the chapter that you may want to learn more about. For example:

The Diversity-Equity Gap in the Fortune 500: Too Few Racial Minority Executives (Ascend Research Foundation)

THE AMASIAN WAY FRAMEWORK

The Amasian Way framework is organized into eight interconnected practices:

1. **Introspection.** Leaders are self-aware. They believe in their purpose and ability. Amasian leaders can find alignment and balance across multiple cultural identities and discover their purpose and ambitions.
2. **Plan.** Leaders are intentional planners. They create a vision, develop a roadmap, and plan. Then they actively manage, work, and evolve that plan. Amasian leaders are disciplined in planning and execution.
3. **Curious.** Leaders are lifelong learners. They tackle things they do not fully understand because they are resourceful and have a network to rely on. They connect ideas to innovate and create something more. Amasian leaders combine book and street smarts to be the head of the class.
4. **Show Up and Move.** Leaders show up and step up consistently, and they have a bias for action and results. They forge ahead and blaze a trail for others to follow. They find the courage to be bold and resilient. Amasian

leaders can summon their experiences to move when others stand still.

5. **Communicate and Connect.** Leaders inspire others to take action. They communicate and build relationships with impact and purpose. They elicit rational and emotional responses and align everyone towards common goals. Amasian leaders can flex and bring a diverse group together.
6. **Grow.** Leaders have a growth mindset. They recognize they must continually improve themselves and their organization to remain relevant. Amasian leaders can adapt and innovate in new environments.
7. **Lead.** Leaders need to show up and lead others. They understand that their title alone will not inspire performance and results. They must draw on a variety of leadership skills to succeed. Amasian leaders lead for *we* before *me*. Their ambition aligns with the organization's, customers', and society's success.
8. **Serve.** Leaders give back and pay forward. They lend their time, talent, and treasure to the betterment of society. Amasian leaders are upstanders who advocate for the AAPI community and serve society.

The framework presented here aligns with widely recognized leadership models. It represents the culmination of my experience in leadership development and my professional growth. The Amasian Way encourages a thorough exploration of these practices through an AAPI perspective. This approach enables a comprehensive understanding of Western leadership success factors, supports the reframing of perceived challenges, and leverages the strengths inherent in a multicultural identity. Mastery of all elements is not expected immediately. Rather, the framework guides, defines, and structures your ongoing leadership development. Each chapter offers both conceptual insights and practical actions for career-stage-appropriate application in real-world settings, which are essential for building authentic confidence through meaningful practice rather than hypothetical preparation.

HOW TO USE THIS BOOK

Leadership is about how you prioritize, what you say, and how you lead, especially when the stakes are higher. It is something you learn, develop, and practice early in your career and continue to refine and improve throughout the remainder of your career.

This book is both a journey and a reference.

You can read it straight through or return to specific chapters as needed. Each chapter includes reflection and action prompts applicable to different career stages.

You are not expected to agree with everything in these pages. You are expected to think, test, and adapt. The Amasian Way is not a doctrine. It is discipline.

Progress requires commitment and consistent effort. Some experiments may not succeed, and certain risks might not yield the anticipated outcomes; these are inherent to the process. It is essential to remain focused on advancement and to methodically document accomplishments. In practice, the objective is not perfection, but rather continuous improvement and persistent effort.

I cannot promise fairness, safety, or guaranteed success. Bias is real. Systems are imperfect. Some outcomes will always be beyond your control. But instead of lying still and lamenting the situation as a victim, this book challenges you to make progress within your control: how you prepare, how you learn, and how you move.

There are a few things I want to acknowledge upfront.

- **Stereotypes.** *Asian American and Pacific Islander* is a monolithic label that encompasses many different cultures and lived experiences. Not all AAPI fit stereotypes, and not all stereotypes apply universally. Please be open to the discussions in this book, even if you do not initially relate to the stereotypes described.
- **Run with it.** This book is intentionally light and practical. I will not provide exhaustive research, case studies, or academic theories. If you encounter unfamiliar terms, be curious and look them up.

- **"Fixing the victims."** Some may ask why this book focuses on preparing professionals rather than fixing systems. I agree that organizations can do better and must do better. This book exists to help you lead regardless of whether systems change fast enough.
- **My voice, your prerogative.** I wrote this book as myself. You may disagree with me. That is fine. Take what is useful, adapt it, and make it your own.

Key features of this book include personal stories, AAPI- and career-stage-specific lenses on leadership concepts, journal activities, chapter summaries, suggested topics for further discovery and active learning, and a clear "So What" for each chapter.

I hope you find the lessons I learned on my AAPI leadership development journey helpful. What happens next is up to you. Own your development.

Now is the time for you to step up and lead our future the Amasian Way.

LOOKING AHEAD

The chapters that follow translate this framework into practice. They focus on the behaviors and decisions that shape how you are experienced in real environments, with real constraints. The next chapter focuses on discovering yourself through introspection and understanding the influence of your multiple identities. This is not about becoming someone else. It is about becoming more intentional about how you show up as yourself.

CHAPTER 1

Discover the Ultimate You

The initial phase of the Amasian Way involves gaining clarity about one's identity and purpose. Engaging in thorough self-reflection is essential for enhancing self-understanding and clarifying how one presents oneself. This process of self-discovery can help individuals overcome inhibitions and minimize distractions from code-switching across different identities. It is vital to cultivate self-acceptance before seeking meaningful relationships or making impactful contributions in a professional environment.

For AAPI professionals, this challenge is often amplified by the need to reconcile multiple identities shaped by contrasting cultural influences, namely Eastern and Western traditions. Nevertheless, successfully navigating these complexities and achieving internal harmony empowers individuals to learn, grow, and develop as effective leaders.

THE AMASIAN WAY calls for you to believe in yourself first.

In this chapter, we will explore the following introspection concepts:

- Navigating multiple identities and code-switching
- Eastern and Western cultural influences
- Personalities, values, beliefs, and feedback
- Discovering harmony, unique multicultural strengths, and purpose

SIMULTANEOUS EQUATION OF IDENTITIES

Every individual is characterized by various statistical categories, such as gender, race, religion, or sexual orientation. However, no single classification fully encapsulates one's identity. In reality, each person embodies multiple intersecting identities. For example, within my family life, I assume the roles of father, son, and uncle, while professionally, I fulfill responsibilities as a leader, manager, and direct report. Socially, I may also be perceived through physical attributes or demographic factors. At any point, we all navigate the complexities of multiple identities. The ongoing negotiation of these diverse aspects is a universal experience that connects all people.

I rarely pause to consider if my Asian heritage should influence how I act at work. Most of the time, my managers, colleagues, and coworkers see me simply as myself, not specifically as a Chinese American. For example, since I don't have a Chinese accent, an acquaintance once remarked that she wouldn't know I was Chinese if she couldn't see me. Still, for those unfamiliar with me, my Chinese identity is immediately apparent from my appearance.

People might not expect that I'm a practicing Catholic, an American citizen, or a fan of the Boston Celtics. These are examples of my invisible identities. Aspects like sexual orientation, religious views, experiences with abuse, relationship or family status, and financial hardship all represent invisible identities that can strongly shape how someone thinks and acts.

Everyone must negotiate their visible and invisible identities. No one is exempt. In America's diverse society, levels of acceptance for these identities vary. Some are widely embraced while others face discrimination. While certain individuals support all kinds of identities, others may exclude or judge. If more people recognized that the challenge of managing our many identities is a shared experience, it could lead to greater understanding and less prejudice worldwide.

The Amasian Way calls us to find harmony among our multiple identities.

Balance and alignment come with embracing who you are as a person of multiple identities. It sacrifices nothing. It takes advantage of everything. It is about making *all* your visible and invisible influences work for you. It is about embracing and flexing those identities to realize the ultimate you.

THE PROBLEM WITH CODE-SWITCHING

We have all been conditioned to "code-switch" to fit in. In other words, many of us compartmentalize our identities, and we switch between them when we move from one setting to another. I recall being taken aback when I overheard a black employee being told to keep their Ebonics on the streets. I was even more surprised to learn that "assimilation" or "check your diversity at the front door" is still commonly given as career advice.

Today, five generations are in the workforce for the first time. Earlier generations still believe in assimilation, while newer generations believe in acculturation. Cultural *assimilation* occurs when a minority fully adopts the dominant culture's values, beliefs, and practices to the point of losing most or all of their own culture. *Acculturation* is the idea that a person should retain their cultural identity while also adapting to a new culture.

Coaching for success can be contradictory and inconsistent, depending on whether the advice comes from someone who favors cultural assimilation or acculturation. I recently heard dated coaching advice delivered to minority professionals, telling them to essentially hide what makes them culturally diverse and adopt the American culture to fit in at work. "Do not invite co-workers to your homes or take them to an ethnic restaurant." This cultural assimilation advice may have helped the speaker's career many years ago, but it did not resonate with a young professional audience that felt American society had moved beyond that way of thinking.

People who navigate multiple identities may expend a lot of energy. Many minorities code-switch to fit in. This may be a constant facade. It can be exhausting to always be on our toes, recalling how to behave with different audiences. Code-switching also intensifies the stress that comes with "imposter syndrome."

Historically, minorities were encouraged to erase their "Asian passivity," "Black aggression," and "Latino heat" so they would be more like their American counterparts at work. The more they assimilated, the greater their acceptance and maybe even success. Asian Americans who assimilated were rewarded with the "model minority" stigma because they worked hard and did not complain about their place in the pecking order.

Much has been written about the harm done to the AAPI community. It positively reinforced our subjugated position in American corporations and instigated jealousy from other minorities towards us.

Please note that it would be impossible not to rely on stereotypes when discussing diversity. Some people are 100 percent assimilated and never feel conflicted. For me and many other AAPI professionals that I have encountered, assimilation led to not feeling whole. I always felt that the more people acknowledged my Americanized personality, the more I felt ashamed that I was losing my Chinese identity. Code-switching can also feel like constantly waiting to be caught in a lie.

Many AAPI individuals adopt Americanized names to make their identities easier for others to remember and pronounce in professional and social contexts. While this practice is generally low-risk, it raises important questions about identity and cultural assimilation. Personally, because I was given both an English and a Chinese name at birth, choosing between them doesn't feel like a sacrifice. However, as a parent, I would be disappointed if my children ever felt pressured to abandon their names just to blend in. Opting for an Americanized name can sometimes lead to more frequent code-switching, which might eventually result in letting go of additional aspects of one's cultural heritage. Over time, this could even include working instead of celebrating major cultural holidays.

When I was younger, I experimented with acting in theater and remember how much effort it took to truly embody a character from a script. Each time I played a different role, I noticed that pieces of those characters stuck with me afterward. Code-switching feels similar; it's like acting "in character" in certain circumstances. The energy spent suppressing or pretending can drain your ability to make a meaningful impact. Over time, behaving differently from your authentic self might cause you to lose parts of yourself. These are the hidden costs of code-switching: reduced energy and a gradual loss of authenticity.

This dynamic operates in both directions. The discomfort experienced when one suppresses their ethnic identity in the workplace, or their Western influences at home, reflects this tension. As an AAPI individual, you are shaped by both an Eastern upbringing and a Western environment. Suppressing either set of influences can be energetically draining and counterproductive. As a paraphrased Chinese proverb states, "A person who uses one chopstick to eat rice will go hungry."

Code-switching refers to the practice of individuals modifying or concealing aspects of their identity to assimilate within a particular environment. This process often results in a diminished expression of one's authentic self. In contrast, communication *flexing* is a strategic skill that involves adjusting communication styles to enhance mutual understanding. Flexing may also involve deliberately highlighting certain facets of one's personality to address specific challenges. Whereas code-switching may limit personal authenticity, flexing demonstrates situational awareness and aims to facilitate more effective interactions.

Here is a table to help you better understand the difference between code-switching and flexing.

Code-Switching (to Assimilate)	**Flexing** (to Acculturate)
• Does not feel belonging • Suppresses part of self • Pretends to fit in to surrounding • Amplifies feeling of the imposter syndrome	• Feels belonging, does not feel pressure to pretend to fit in • Brings whole and authentic self into the conversation • Flexes communication style to create a connection

Picture living a life where your thoughts, feelings, words, and actions are all in sync. You simply embrace who you are, free from guilt or any sense of being an imposter. There's no need to juggle different roles or loyalties. You're completely at ease with yourself. You trust in your own personality and abilities. This marks the first step of the Amasian Way: achieving harmony through self-understanding.

"WHO AM I ANYWAY?"

"Who Am I Anyway" is a song from the musical *A Chorus Line* that has stuck with me my whole life. It questions whether a resumé and headshot are the true representation of an actor, or a person. This question still plays in my head all the time, to this day, ever since college. It has become the anthem of my "imposter syndrome."

Imposter syndrome is a common experience that many professionals encounter throughout their careers. Individuals may question their own abilities and whether they are truly qualified for the responsibilities assigned to them. This sense of self-doubt often persists even as one advances into leadership positions. Typically, imposter syndrome arises from heightened awareness of our own limitations compared with how others perceive us. In reality, developing deeper self-understanding may help alleviate these feelings of inadequacy.

Our cultural upbringing plays a significant role in shaping our beliefs. Like other minority groups, AAPIs frequently navigate the intersection of their heritage and American society. In many cases, their ideologies and religious views contrast sharply with those of the mainstream culture. This often results in challenges when trying to reconcile these differing perspectives in daily life. For AAPIs, the journey to find a sense of belonging can be especially complex.

During the 2022 Winter Olympics, Zhu Yi, a Chinese American figure skater representing China, faced harsh criticism on Chinese social media over her performance, with some expressing that she should not have replaced homegrown athletes. In contrast, Eileen Gu, who won gold for China, engaged openly with the media about balancing her American and Chinese identities; this story continued in 2026. I understand their sense of disconnection—feeling too American to be considered truly Chinese in China, yet too Chinese to fit in as an American in the United States. For many AAPI individuals, this experience serves as a persistent reminder of not fully belonging anywhere.

> *The Amasian Way calls us to find harmony between our Eastern and Western identities.*

THE YIN AND THE YANG (EAST MEETS WEST)

Our cultural upbringing, including religion or lack thereof, greatly shapes our values and beliefs. Therefore, let us explore the polarizing influences of Eastern and Western cultures that shape us. Again, I recognize these are stereotypes and may not immediately resonate with everyone.

- **We versus me.** Eastern cultures often emphasize collective identity and community well-being, fostering a welcoming, humble attitude. Western cultures place greater emphasis on individual achievement, reflected in differences such as socialism versus capitalism or team versus self-advocacy at work. I advise international students to use "I" instead of "we" when sharing experiences in interviews.
- **Traditional vs. Progressive.** Eastern cultures often value tradition, while Western cultures tend to challenge it. This generally results in more conservative traits in the East and greater risk-taking and innovation in the West. However, many Asian countries balance modern, innovative lifestyles with longstanding traditions.
- **Voice versus presence.** Leading training sessions in Italy was a completely different experience from leading them in China. In Italy, lively debates could easily keep you on the opening slide for an hour. In contrast, participants in China typically listened quietly throughout the entire session. This reflects the "model minority" stereotype of professionals who work diligently without complaint. Unfortunately, this percep-

tion may lead to the mistaken belief that AAPI professionals lack social or communication skills to express their perspectives.

- **Creative versus industrious.** Another model minority stigma that is applied to Eastern culture is that they are hard workers who will do everything they can to get the job done. Western cultures are encouraged to be creative and to find a work-life balance. This also shows up in stereotypes of Asians as more technical and not suited to be expressive artists.
- **Iterative and validation.** The stereotype suggests that Eastern workers prefer to share work only when it is complete, while Western workers seek ongoing feedback through iteration. However, widespread use of "likes and comments" features in both social media and workplace tools has made immediate validation a global norm.

There are *so many* loopholes in these stereotypes. I am sure many of you were as triggered by them as I was while typing them. Most of the Easterners that I know are entrepreneurs who are more street-smart than book-smart. They are constantly looking for innovative ways to get the job done faster and easier. The youth of every culture break tradition. So while these stereotypes exist, we should acknowledge that newer generations of more globalized citizens are slowly evolving them.

The positive aspect is that this section is titled "East *Meets* West." AAPI professionals embody a blend of Eastern and Western cultures. In traditional Eastern philosophy, harmony and balance are fundamental values. We have the capacity to draw from both cultural backgrounds. Straddling these worlds allows AAPIs to adapt easily and move fluidly between different perspectives. Additionally, we prioritize overall wellbeing and seek benefits that benefit everyone. This ability to understand multiple viewpoints enables us to unite people with differing opinions and help them achieve success together. As someone who loves good food, I'm reminded of Ming Tsai's *East Meets West* television program, where he crafted incredible dishes by merging cooking styles and ingredients from both the East and the West. I view AAPI professionals in much the same way—a unique blend of traditions that leads to remarkable outcomes.

The challenge presented by the influence of multiple forces on our values and beliefs is that our behaviors, decisions, and actions may become inconsistent or subdued. This can result in less distinctiveness, as there may not be a pronounced inclination toward a particular perspective. My results on the DISC personality assessment placed me at the center, indicating the capacity to exhibit traits from all four dominant personality types. Consequently, individuals who typically associate specific dominant personalities with particular people may find it challenging to recall my profile. Furthermore, this versatility could lead some to hesitate before collaborating with someone perceived as having variable personality traits.

We should leverage the distinct advantages offered by our integration of Eastern and Western perspectives. It is also important to remain mindful of the differing influences and to seek effective methods to reconcile them, ensuring we present ourselves consistently.

JOURNAL ACTIVITY

What motivates you? Consider the following. Where do you lean?

	How do I behave at work?		
Motivation	I am motivated by my personal success.	I am motivated by my team's success.	I am not motivated by success.
Advocacy	I am more likely to advocate for my performance.	I am more likely to advocate for my team or company.	I neither advocate for myself or my team.
Work Habit	I challenge traditional methods and drive change.	I have strong work ethics and get the job done.	I work as directed; my priorities are outside of work.
Hierarchy	I influence others and voice my opinion regardless of my role.	I know my place in the pecking order and waiting for my turn.	I do not pay attention to hierarchy nor aspire to be promoted.

Reflection Questions

- What did you recognize in your responses?
- What surprised you?
- Is it obvious if your behavior at work leans towards Eastern or Western influences?

Things to keep in mind as you evaluate your answers:

- There are no right or wrong outcomes. You are who you are.
- Your response may change over time with more work experience and career maturity.
- The more difficult it is for you to commit to an answer, the more likely both Eastern and Western cultures simultaneously influence you.
- It would be interesting to evaluate similar behaviors in your personal life to see if you change behaviors (code-switch).
- Context *always* matters. For example, I am an immigrant who grew up in a Caucasian community and was raised by less traditional Chinese parents. My wife is second-generation and lived in Chinatown, raised by very traditional parents. We were both baptized Catholics as infants. Our values and beliefs are both similar and dissimilar because of the contexts in which our multicultural influences showed up in our lives.

YOU ARE THE ANSWER TO SIMULTANEOUS EQUATIONS

Have you ever read a description of yourself based on your Zodiac sign and thought, "That's sort of true, but not all of it." Have you ever had difficulty completing a behavioral test, such as Myers-Briggs, because it felt like you could answer the question multiple ways? Zodiac and Myers-Briggs are both based on stereotypes. When we have trouble relating to written descriptions of ourselves, we are navigating several identities at that moment.

An engineer colleague recently reminded me of the concept of simultaneous equations. He said we all learned it in school, but most forgot. It is the concept in which you must factor in multiple equations to fully appreciate the problem. For example, it would be too simple to contribute a string of nor'easters to global climate change. There are likely other things involved that also made that weather pattern possible.

This conversation got me thinking about how sometimes the KISS concept—keep it simple, stupid—may not be the best path regarding diversity and inclusion. Most awareness programs focus on simple unconscious biases and stereotypes based on a single aspect of a person.

The truth is, we are all products of numerous potential simultaneous equations. For example, when we assume a middle-aged white male is of the majority, we may be overlooking his sexual preference or his psychological disability, etc. When we learn that a Chinese woman is an immigrant and assume that she may have a language barrier or will exhibit stereotypical behaviors of a woman raised in China, we may be overlooking that she was a baby when she moved to the U.S. and was raised as a Mormon in Utah.

Even people with the most check-the-box attributes of the "majority" in America constantly navigate multiple identities based on where they grew up, their upbringing, their alma mater, their income and career stage, age, ability, etc. Imagine the executive who was an all-star quarterback in college with a full scholarship but grew up in a trailer park with alcoholic and abusive parents. All those factors may contribute to his decisions and behavior at work.

We are all navigating several identities. We are all complex creatures who usually behave a certain way based on beliefs and cultures, and sometimes based on mood swings. If we are all solutions to simultaneous equations, there may be common ground that can be leveraged to address diversity and inclusion problems worldwide.

Therefore, you must consider all the influences that make up your simultaneous equation in search of the ultimate *you*. Your multicultural upbringing provides a foundation of values and beliefs that influence your decisions, behaviors, and actions. That foundation will evolve as you are exposed to influences beyond your family, such as friends, life and work experiences, and trauma.

VALUES AND BELIEFS

Despite advances in scientific understanding of the causes of illness, many people still believe that exposure to cold can cause a cold. During my childhood, my parents frequently advised me to cover my midsection while sleeping, because many Chinese believe that wind can get into the navel and cause stomach aches. Even now, I habitually ensure my stomach is covered at night, regardless of the temperature. Such behaviors often persist due to long-standing conditioning that shapes our thoughts and actions. As someone with both Eastern and Western cultural influences, these diverse perspectives shape how we approach life and the workplace.

Values

We place value on things daily. We choose how we spend our time, talent, and money based on what we value most. There are some assessments that will help you discover what you value most. Most of these assessments will ask you to prioritize family, friends, work, money, charity, success, and other factors. Based on the previous discussion, you can see how your cultural influences can shape your values' priorities.

Personal values significantly influence individual choices and behaviors. For instance, I observed a colleague who consistently prioritized returning home promptly to care for his dog, placing this responsibility above working overtime or engaging in after-work networking activities. This reflects differences in personal values and priorities. Similarly, many parents choose to set aside career ambitions to focus on raising their children, demonstrating a greater emphasis on family than professional advancement. Emerging generations often place greater importance on work-life balance and community involvement than on career progression and salary. Ultimately, personal values play a crucial role in guiding individuals in determining their primary commitments.

Beliefs

Beliefs shape our actions by establishing behavioral boundaries. As mentioned, I have noticed that AAPI job candidates often prefer "we" to "I" when discussing their work experiences. This can make it challenging for interviewers to pinpoint the candidate's specific contributions to a project's success. This pattern frequently stems from a belief in collectivism, which values group wellbeing and harmony over individual recognition.

Faith and religion have significantly shaped my perspectives, guiding my behavior and decision-making processes. Having been raised in the Catholic tradition and educated in Catholic institutions, I remain active in parish life. In challenging circumstances, I consistently draw upon my religious beliefs for guidance and resilience. Additionally, I have developed a set of personal principles based on my faith, which inform my conduct and choices.

I may find it difficult to work in a culture where corporate objectives and methods conflict with my religious beliefs. For instance, I would not work for a company that intentionally harms innocent people to make a profit. Leaders will often check outcomes against their moral compass and make decisions accordingly.

Exploring your values and beliefs will help you understand your thoughts, behaviors, and actions, as well as your identity.

JOURNAL ACTIVITY: Values and Beliefs

Values

- List five things that you value the most
- Reorder them in the priority of importance to you

Reflection Questions

- What do you recognize in your list and priority?
- What surprised you?
- How might Eastern or Western cultures have influenced your list and priority?

Beliefs

- List five beliefs that you accept as universal truths that guide your life.

Reflection Questions

- What do you recognize in your list of beliefs?
- What surprised you?
- How might Eastern or Western cultures have influenced your list of beliefs?

HOW DO I SHOW UP? Personality Tests

Many assessments can help you better understand who you are on the surface (of the iceberg), including Myers-Briggs, DISC, and Hogan. While they can be oversimplifying and stereotyping, understanding their approach and method can be very insightful in explaining your tendencies, and they can help you express, in a common language, your personality with others who have taken similar assessments.

Some popular personality tests that you may want to do more research on:

- **Myers-Briggs Type Indicator (MBTI).** This widely used personality test categorizes individuals into 16 personality types based on four dichotomies: extraversion vs. introversion, sensing vs. intuition, thinking vs. feeling, and judging vs. perceiving.
- **DISC Assessment.** This assessment categorizes individuals into four primary behavioral styles: dominance, influence, steadiness, and conscientiousness.
- **StrengthsFinder.** This test is designed to identify an individual's unique strengths and talents, categorizing them into 34 distinct themes.
- **Hogan Personality Inventory (HPI).** This personality test assesses an individual's potential for success, categorizing them into one of seven personality dimensions: adjustment, ambition, sociability, interpersonal sensitivity, prudence, inquisitiveness, and learning approach

Rather than viewing assessment results as absolute truths about yourself, it's helpful to see them as just one perspective. While these assessments are grounded in scientific methods, their accuracy can be affected by factors like test analysis biases towards certain population groups, your mood during the exam, or even skepticism that might influence how you answer. Additionally, some people interpret results so literally that they begin to align with them, much like those who closely follow horoscopes or the Chinese zodiac, regardless of their actual personalities.

I have found it fun to describe myself using the intersection of my Myers-Briggs and DISC results, my being on the cusp of two horoscope signs, and my being born in the year of the rat as a middle child.

Taking advantage of these assessments and naming some of your tendencies is a helpful part of the introspection journey. You can access personality tests at school (Office of Counseling or Career Services), at work (HR, Learning, or Leadership Development), and on the Internet.

JOURNAL ACTIVITY

Personality Tests

- Research and identify a personality test
- Complete an assessment
- Review the assessment results and analytics

Reflection Questions

Record in your journal (written or video):

- What did you recognize in yourself
- What surprised you
- How does this inform your relationships
- How does this inform your work performance

Feedback

To understand how others perceive you, gather feedback either informally from coworkers, supervisors, and customers, or formally through a *360-degree feedback* assessment. You can also use the *Net Promoter Score* by asking, "Would you recommend me to someone else?" on a 10-point scale, ensuring it relates to your service.

Gathering feedback provides you with insights tailored to your individual experience, rather than comparative information based on other test takers. As such, these findings may be more directly applicable to your personal development. It is important to approach the results objectively; unexpected items may arise that were previously unknown to you. The feedback is intended for reflection and growth, not for dismissal, justification, or adverse reactions.

My first executive coaching experience began with a personality test and 360-degree feedback, which provided a baseline and areas for improvement. The feedback surprised me, especially learning that my Saturday inbox management came across as an unprioritized information dump to my team. I realized I needed to set clearer expectations and communicate my priorities more effectively.

At work, we often say, "Feedback is a gift." Staying open to feedback shows us how others see us and, if left unchecked, shapes our reputation.

JOURNAL ACTIVITY: NET PROMOTER SCORE

1. If necessary, learn about the NPS method for collecting and rating feedback.
2. Depending on your role, identify a group of peers, teammates, customers, supervisors, and direct reports.
3. Ask them to evaluate you on a 10-point scale (10 being most likely) of whether they would recommend you to someone else for _____.
4. Also, ensure they can provide free text feedback to support their rating.
5. Collect and analyze your results.

Reflection Questions

- What did you recognize in the feedback?
- What surprised you?
- What feedback energized you?
- What feedback was particularly difficult for you?
- What would you stop, start, and continue based on the feedback?

DISCOVER HARMONY, AMASIAN POWERS, AND PURPOSE

So far in this chapter, you've reviewed the main elements of introspection: your various identities, code-switching challenges, East-West cultural tensions, values, beliefs, personality, behavior, and feedback from others.

This is where those threads converge.

By reconciling our various identities and gaining clarity about the values and beliefs that shape our actions, we can move forward purposefully as our genuine selves, rather than wasting energy on inner conflict.

For AAPI professionals, deeper self-reflection is essential. Navigating multiple demands can lead to significant unresolved tension, which consumes considerable energy. By recovering this energy, individuals can intentionally direct it toward greater impact, leadership, and purpose.

> *The Amasian Way calls us to channel our energy to win through harmony, reframing and flexing, and purpose.*

Harmony: Consistency, Energy, and Focus

Harmony starts with self-awareness and understanding your own habits. Feeling at ease with yourself means you waste less energy pretending to be someone you're not. This allows others to see a steady, authentic version of you, which also helps you perform more reliably.

Harmony also means being comfortable with your strengths. It allows you to lean into what you do best to improve performance and productivity. For example, if you knew you were better at shooting three-point shots in basketball than making layups, you would shoot from beyond the arc more often to increase your probability of winning.

What gives you harmony does not have to be written in stone. You will evolve whether you want to or not. You will change for many reasons, including natural maturity, increased experience, and major life or career transitions. Immigrating to the U.S. was one of the biggest shake-ups in my life. The birth of my children changed my purpose. Turning fifty changed my ambition. Each of these moments temporarily put me in disharmony.

You can also intentionally put yourself in disharmony—by realigning your values and beliefs and changing your behaviors—to grow. Harmony is restored once the transition is complete.

Individuals may also purposefully introduce a period of disharmony by reassessing their values and beliefs and modifying behaviors to facilitate personal growth. Harmony is re-established upon completion of this transitional process.

At its core, harmony is finding the balance that reflects your true self. It allows you to break free from code-switching because you no longer have to suppress parts of who you are. When you achieve harmony among your multicultural influences and identities, your thoughts, words, and actions align. Your energy stops leaking, and you can fully focus on winning.

Once harmony is achieved, you are ready to reframe and flex your Amasian strengths.

Why Harmony Is Hard for AAPI Professionals

For many AAPI professionals, one of the biggest obstacles to stepping into leadership is deeply rooted cultural conditioning: be quiet, speak only when spoken to, don't make waves, don't lose face for the family by making mistakes. These may sound like stereotypes, but they are precisely that because many of us grew up hearing them repeatedly.

As a result, we often struggle to be bold and brilliant in environments where leadership is associated with visibility. I have observed that most AAPI professionals have a threshold at which they are bold and brilliant, often with siblings, close friends, or within AAPI circles of trust. Once the environment extends beyond that circle, many retreat into humility, heads down, hard work.

The issue is not a lack of ability or potential. It is conditioning.

I have had many Asians, especially Chinese, tell me they do not initially recognize me as Asian. Dim sum waitresses and in-law aunties are often surprised when I speak Cantonese. Occasionally, this works to my advantage. I once overheard a Cantonese-speaking staff member articulate thoughtful, strategic ideas about work—what could be improved and what he would do if he were the boss. I walked over, introduced myself, and asked him why he had never raised those ideas. After being surprised that I understood Cantonese, he told me quietly that he did not think it would matter. He assumed he would not be taken seriously.

What I heard was the mindset of "冇用" meaning no use. No use trying, because nothing will change. A sense of powerlessness in the face of what feels institutional.

There are two forces at work here. One is external: stereotypes, systemic inequities, unconscious bias, microaggressions, and non-inclusive cultures. The other is internal: unvalidated assumptions of powerlessness, lack of confidence or visibility, limited networks, or the absence of mentors.

This book focuses primarily on the internal factors because those are within your control. As your influence grows, so does your ability to shape external conditions.

Reframing and Flexing Without Losing Yourself

If we do not break out of the conditioning that keeps us the "model minority," it can become a self-fulfilling prophecy.

To break out, we need to systematically break the mold by being bold and brilliant until it becomes our leadership habit. The benefit of navigating multiple identities and cultures is that we can do so in a way that incorporates our risk-averse nature, managing risk thoughtfully while still stepping forward. Rather than thinking of your leadership journey as giving up yourself and becoming someone else (cultural assimilation), think of it as building a bridge that takes you from where you are to where you want to go. You can reframe what holds you back as fuel for becoming an even better leader.

There are some concepts I try to impress upon my children through repetition and conditioning. I ask them, "Why shouldn't you give up on something that is difficult at first?" They respond, "Because we can get better at it over time." Then I ask, "How do you get better at something?" They respond, "Practice."

That simple exchange is more than parenting; it's leadership development. Practicing boldness outside our comfort zones helps it feel natural over time. In this book, we'll call these efforts "reps," a term borrowed from the world of exercise.

The following are some ways to reframe the challenges that may hold us back from leading others.

The Team and You

Coming from a collectivist culture to one that rewards people who stand out may feel uncomfortable, especially when advocating for yourself. Try starting where you are already strong: advocate for the team's impact (collectivism) and then incorporate where you made a difference by using the word "I." This helps you begin to draw attention to your narrative without feeling like you are abandoning your values or becoming self-centered. You are clarifying the contribution rather than taking credit.

Find Your Voice

Reframe speaking up from being disruptive or disagreeing to speaking with purpose. Silence can be interpreted as a lack of contribution. Speaking without substance can weaken your brand. The goal is not to talk more. The goal is to be heard when it matters.

More junior professionals can find their voice by volunteering to recap the previous meeting's minutes or summarizing action items at the end of a meeting. This is a low-risk way to build presence and demonstrate leadership behaviors without needing to "win the room."

More seasoned professionals can sharpen their voice by practicing improv methods, such as "yes, and..." to advance a conversation without putting others on the defensive. For example, if you have a reservation about a plan, instead of saying "but...," you can say, "yes, and...we should minimize the risk of ___ by ____." This keeps momentum while still demonstrating rigor.

Presence Over Speech

Generation Z and Alpha talk about the "Sigma." They may prefer the leader who is present and decisive—even a lone wolf—over an "Alpha" who is loud and charismatic. You can turn humility into a powerful presence by speaking when it matters, rather than constantly speaking without substance.

Compare someone who swears all the time to someone who never swears. Which one stops you in your tracks when he or she drops the "f-bomb?" The power is not in frequency. It is in timing. Your strength is in your substance, and your presence is in your confidence. You do not have to show off to be seen. You can "drop the mic" when it has the most impact.

Network Your Way

If going to a bar, golfing, or watching the game isn't your cup of tea, invite others to try something you enjoy, such as Vietnamese coffee, dim sum, or karaoke. It is better to be in environments where you can feel comfortable and be authentic. If you must decline an invitation, find another way to show up. If large crowds drain you, network in smaller groups or one-on-one. You never know. Once you become more comfortable with networking, you may even be open to trying something new.

You Matter

One of our biggest challenges is that we sometimes convince ourselves we are not interesting or valuable to others. That mindset keeps us from networking, seeking mentors, and advocating for what matters to us. The reality is: you matter in many ways.

The fact that you have unrealized potential matters to someone seeking to leave a legacy. To a company-funded pension owner, your success supports their future retirement. To someone who loves developing others, your growth is the reward of their effort. You will never fully understand how valuable you are until you engage people and learn what matters to them. If you show up and deliver, you become invaluable.

Flex Without Losing Authenticity

Due to the interplay of Eastern and Western cultural influences, individuals may demonstrate greater adaptability across these perspectives. In contrast, those shaped primarily by a single dominant culture might have greater difficulty adopting traits associated with other traditions. It is important to acknowledge that these generalizations are not absolute; an individual's upbringing informs their values and beliefs through a complex array of factors. For instance, one may be raised in a Western context yet maintain a strong orientation toward collectivism, depending on environmental circumstances.

The trick is to flex without losing yourself. Losing yourself turns flexing into code-switching, and that costs energy. When you flex well, you are not suppressing who you are. You are drawing from what is already in you to bridge a gap.

Here are steps to help you flex:

1. **Name the pain.** Identify the moment where your default approach is costing you the outcome.
2. **Understand your behavior.** Recognize the cultural influence or instinct driving your response.
3. **Reframe and flex.** Borrow from the opposing trait to achieve the goal without abandoning authenticity.

4. **Eye on the prize.** Focus on long-term outcomes: readiness, influence, results, trust.
5. **Practice. Practice. Practice.** Start in low-stakes situations, build up, seek feedback, and improve.

Flexing and reframing are tools. They are not meant to replace your authentic self. When you can flex between cultural influences, your leadership becomes authentic, dynamic, and balanced.

LEANING INTO YOUR EASTERN CULTURAL INFLUENCES

Your Eastern cultural influences are not a crutch, nor are they something to hide in order to assimilate into American culture. They are assets. When understood and embraced, they can help you become a more holistic, grounded, and effective leader and professional.

Below are some common Eastern cultural influences that many AAPI professionals may recognize in themselves. These are not absolutes or prescriptions. They are tendencies that, when acknowledged, can be intentionally leveraged.

Collectivism

You are a collaborator who values team success. This inclination helps you be inclusive, build consensus, and earn buy-in from others. Your focus on the collective win lifts people around you and makes them feel valued and seen. Your community is more vast than work. You bring together the collective multiplier of all of your social circles.

Discipline

You have a strong work ethic and are willing to grind to get things done. You value doing things right rather than doing them fast or haphazardly. You take time to evaluate risks and act thoughtfully. You are steady and sturdy. You care about studying a subject deeply and being prepared before you speak or act.

Respect

You respect others and are willing to consider different points of view and perspectives. You demonstrate emotional intelligence by caring about how others feel. You take time to read the room and recognize when it is appropriate to listen, support, or mediate conflict rather than dominate the conversation.

Hustle

You carry the entrepreneurial instincts of someone who had to figure things out to survive or help their family get ahead. You are resourceful, innovative, and agile. When faced with obstacles, your default mindset is simple and powerful: you will find a way.

Patience

You see the forest for the trees. You are willing to play the long game rather than chase short-term wins. You think in terms of durability and sustainability, and you develop strategies that may take longer to pay off but deliver greater impact over time.

These cultural influences play a crucial role in shaping your values and beliefs. By intentionally embracing them, you become a leader who works diligently alongside your team, perseveres, when necessary, innovates with care, and focuses on long-term strategic goals rather than short-lived recognition. These qualities set you apart; although they are appreciated in Western business culture, they are comparatively rare. While these traits may come naturally to you, those without similar cultural backgrounds might need to develop them deliberately.

REFRAMING RISK TAKING

Eastern cultures are often risk-averse and tend to avoid the limelight for fear of failure and losing face. Leadership, however, comes with a heavy burden: constant visibility, judgment of every decision and action, and full exposure when things go wrong. The higher the leadership position, the greater the exposure. For many, this reality is difficult to bear.

Many AAPI professionals grew up in households that reinforced messages such as "keep your head down," "be silent," "don't make waves," and "don't bring shame to the family." Some of this conditioning can be traced to histories of authoritarian rule, where stepping out of line could have severe consequences. In old movies, crossing the government often meant the entire family paid the price. Some of this conditioning was passed down through generations of parenting. Some of it comes from collectivism, where one person's failure is felt as a burden on family, friends, coworkers, the organization, and even customers.

A significant part of this dynamic is fear—fear of shame and fear of failure. The phrase "losing face" is loosely translated from the idea that you cannot go out in public because you are so ashamed. Your family, by association, is also too ashamed to show its face.

AAPI children experience considerable stress due to expectations of academic and professional achievement, as well as concerns about family reputation. Suicide represents the primary cause of death among AAPI youth. These issues are not theoretical; they reflect the actual experiences of this community.

Each time I stumble, my natural reflex is to think about how much shame I have brought upon myself and my family. My instinct is to retreat and be alone because I do not feel I have a "face" to see people: "冇面 見人."

Reframing Risk Without Losing Yourself

To overcome this fear, the work begins with perspective. Focus on the long-term goal. Leadership requires taking calculated risks, managing them thoughtfully, and building alignment and accountability across the organization. It requires resilience, agility, and innovation.

Some of this growth will require borrowing intentionally from Western cultural influences. This does not mean abandoning who you are. It means expanding how your strengths show up.

You can be *bold and brilliant* while remaining grounded and substantive.

This reframing often requires conversations beyond the workplace. Reconcile with your loved ones. Help them understand that you are stepping into the light carefully and thoughtfully. Assure them that if you stumble, you will bounce back and climb even higher. Lean on their love and support. Use their fear and caution as fuel to be grounded, prepared, and planful.

Reconciling Identity into Leadership Strength

Reconcile your multiple identities so you become the best version of your authentic self.

- Use your strong work ethic to lead by example.
- Use your fear of shame to deliberately manage your brand and narrative.
- Use your humility to remain curious, sensible, and practical.
- Use your discipline to learn, develop, move, and grow steadily.
- Use your long-term, big-picture orientation to think strategically.
- Use your respect and collectivism to deliver results that benefit everyone.

If your cultural influences make you more grounded and humbler rather than loud and charismatic, let that be your strength. Leadership does not require razzle-dazzle. Many people deeply admire leaders who are strong and steady, with a proven track record and the ability to speak with substance.

Your consistency, discipline, and results become credibility. Your credibility becomes trust. You are not a performer enamored with the sound of your own voice. You are not someone faking it until you make it. You are a truth teller whose presence carries weight.

Becoming Magnetic Without Becoming Someone Else

You can be magnetic by becoming the people's champion.

Use your sense of collectivism to show appreciation and acknowledge others' efforts. Support those around you as you move forward, instead of advancing at their expense. Aim to be friendly and approachable, avoiding arrogance. Command attention with quiet confidence and presence, rather than with showiness or excessive flair.

Be seen for your brand promise, your results, and your impact. Build trust rather than fandom. Be authentic rather than aloof.

When you take the time to be with people and lead for them, you build deeper, more durable relationships with those you lead.

Reframing Politics, Networking, and Allyship

Films and television frequently portray office politics in an exaggerated manner, suggesting covert and questionable activities. In practice, productive outcomes in government and corporations rely on effective political strategies to achieve objectives through consensus-building, influence, and strategic partnerships. Even small businesses can become stronger by organizing into a Chamber of Commerce. I recently attended an anniversary reception for the AAPI Civic Action Network, which brings together dozens of smaller AAPI community-focused nonprofits to multiply their impact.

Think back to childhood. If you wanted something badly and knew your parents would not approve, you probably appealed to your siblings to side with you and strengthen your bargaining position. That instinct was political but not unethical. It was human.

Communication Is the Missing Link

More importantly, communication is essential for gaining support and approval. We cannot rely on actions and results alone to speak for themselves.

Many AAPI professionals trust that people who matter will notice their body of work and reward them accordingly. In doing so, they may be missing a critical success factor: the ability to communicate and advocate for that body of work.

That communication rarely happens solely in formal meetings. It usually happens in smaller, more intimate conversations behind closed doors. These conversations shape decisions before they are ever finalized.

I recently observed an advocacy group relying solely on public appeals rather than engaging with committee members individually before the meeting. As a result, they lacked sufficient support and were unable to advance their position. The group perceived direct stakeholder engagement as political maneuvering, when it should have been recognized as an essential aspect of effective stakeholder management.

This Is Not New Territory

The need to engage in personal conversations to advocate for what you need or want is not unfamiliar. We have all done this throughout our lives. Yet, for some reason, many of us decide that this behavior becomes inappropriate or taboo at work.

Consider this paradox: many AAPI professionals originate from barter cultures, where negotiating openly with vendors is expected and respected. Yet in professional settings, the same individuals avoid direct confrontation and hesitate to negotiate compensation, scope, or recognition during performance reviews or job offers.

Similarly, most of us grew up navigating group consensus and appealing to individuals one-on-one to gain buy-in before addressing the group. At work, however, this same behavior is often mislabeled as "shady" or "underhanded."

This is where reframing matters. Office politics, networking, and allyship are mechanisms for achieving outcomes.

Reframing the Work

Build support by communicating and advocating before meetings, using conversations to create alignment rather than viewing them as a matter of politics.

Stakeholder management is a core leadership skill. Meetings become far more predictable when you have already spoken with attendees individually, listened to their concerns, understood their priorities, and incorporated their perspectives.

These conversations allow you to socialize your point of view and gather feedback on how to gain broader support. When people feel heard beforehand, they are far more likely to publicly support you.

Networking offers significant advantages. Consider your personal life. It is generally preferable to have established relationships with professionals such as plumbers, electricians, or contractors whom you can contact in urgent situations, rather than resorting to an impersonal online search.

Networking at work operates the same way. Every time I meet someone at a party and learn what they do, I instinctively evaluate whether this is someone I might one day turn to or help, in a moment of need. In the workplace, your network becomes a source of allyship, coaching, insight, and opportunity.

As your network grows, so does your leverage.

Forming alliances is crucial for both survival and success. Taking inspiration from the realty TV show *Survivor*, where alliances are openly discussed, it's clear that, just as on the show, people in organizations also seldom achieve success entirely on their own, even if this is not always openly acknowledged.

Think of your allies as the community you are both serving and benefiting. This aligns naturally with collectivist cultural values. Alliance-building is not self-serving when the outcome benefits the group.

Practice Makes This Normal

Like everything else in this chapter, reframing politics, networking, and allyship requires practice.

The book "Never Eat Alone" by Keith Ferrazzi offers practical insights into relationship-building at work. Every time you eat alone or only with close friends, you may be giving up an opportunity to build meaningful professional relationships.

Many AAPI professionals may find it more effective to share ideas and refine their perspectives in smaller, more private settings than in larger meetings. Leveraging this preference can serve as a strategic asset when seeking to influence others in such settings.

AMASIAN SUPERPOWERS

When you learn how multiple cultural influences shape you and reframe challenges, you begin to recognize a powerful advantage: you are not confined to a single stereotype or operating system. Instead, you live in the grey space between Eastern and Western norms.

That grey space is not a weakness. It is where your advantage lives.

Achieving harmony between Eastern and Western identities through introspection, reframing, and flexing provides individuals with distinct capabilities that are not universally accessible. These attributes are developed through practical experience rather than as mere theoretical concepts.

Amasian Superpowers and Where They Come From

We all come at our multiple identities differently. I recently had lunch with someone who arrived from mainland China at the age of 18. His Chinese heritage influence is much stronger than mine because I moved to the U.S. at the age of 10.

Parenting may also differ, as I have Chinese American co-workers whose parents never celebrated any Chinese festivals or holidays, while a Caucasian couple that I know go out of their way to expose their adopted Chinese daughter to Chinese culture. I know several Korean American professionals who grew up in white American families in the Midwest and have discovered their Korean heritage on their own.

So, we all come at cultural influences differently. As I mentioned before, it is difficult to discuss this topic without some form of perceived stereotypes. However, if you have both Eastern and Western cultural influences, you may be able to tap into the following synergistic "super powers."

Trait	Why You Have This
Agility	You have been exposed to multiple cultures and ways of thinking. You are open-minded, adaptive, and comfortable adjusting course as context changes. You are capable of reframing and flexing.
Universal Appeal	You can see both sides of an argument and bridge opposing viewpoints. You naturally seek harmony and shared wins rather than zero-sum outcomes.
Curiosity	You value learning. You are humble enough to seek external perspectives, benchmarks, and better ways of doing things. You are resourceful by necessity.
Loyalty	You are loyal to your organization, stakeholders, and team. You want collective success and are motivated by winning together rather than winning alone.
Substance	You possess both book smarts and street smarts. You take calculated risks, value execution, and prioritize results over theory or optics.
Value Orientation	You carefully evaluate investments and trade-offs. You understand true value and are willing to negotiate firmly when it matters.
Results-Oriented and Biased for Action	You have a strong work ethic and a pension for execution. You focus on outcomes and consistently ask, "So what?"
Persistence and Resilience	You are willing to grind through adversity. When you fail, you recover, adapt, and move forward stronger.

These are not the only Amasian superpowers you will uncover. As you continue this journey, you will likely recognize others shaped by your specific experiences, environments, and challenges. We will return to this topic in later chapters.

By recognizing your strengths and understanding their origins, you can confidently embrace them rather than undervaluing them.

PURPOSE

Why do you want to lead? What will drive you to put in the hard work to discover alignment and develop Amaisan Leadership skills?

Bruce Lee said, "Do what you believe, and deeply believe in what you do." This captures how purpose arises from conviction and action.

In recent years, the corporate world has moved beyond simply defining vision and mission statements. Organizations now articulate purpose statements that guide decisions, behaviors, and priorities. Purpose answers the question not just of what an organization does, but why it does it.

Here are a few examples:

- Campbell Soup: "Real food that matters for life's moments."
- Coca-Cola: "Refresh the world. Make a difference."
- Target: "To help families discover the joy of everyday life."

Purpose statements give meaning to strategy. They serve as a north star when trade-offs must be made.

Purpose at the Individual Level

Executives have increasingly adopted this same concept to articulate their leadership purpose. You may encounter this described as a leadership brand statement or personal brand statement. Regardless of the label, the intent is the same: a clear and compelling expression of why you lead and how you intend to show up.

I once went through an introspection exercise to develop my own purpose statement and shared the process during a keynote presentation. The purpose statement I arrived at was simple:

"I make people happier."

That statement forced me to reflect deeply on how and why I show up for my family, friends, colleagues, customers, and community. It became a lens through which I evaluated decisions, priorities, and trade-offs.

Purpose does not need to be grandiose. It needs to be true.

Purpose as the Anchor

At this point in the chapter, purpose is not an abstract exercise. It is the logical outcome of everything you have examined so far:

- Your multiple identities
- Your values and beliefs
- How you show up
- How others experience you
- The cultural influences you reframe and flex
- The superpowers you earn through harmony

As the final step of this introspection, you are now ready to answer a critical question: *What is your purpose?*

If you cannot answer why you want to lead and why anyone should follow you, then others will struggle to answer those questions as well.

Purpose Becomes Brand

The Amasian Way calls you to project your purpose, value, and impact as your personal brand. Your brand promise should become the narrative people associate with your performance and leadership.

The Amasian Way begins with believing in your abilities and your purpose.

When your purpose is clear and consistently reinforced through results, it becomes increasingly difficult for others to judge or define you by anything else. Your purpose will also provide solid footing for the rest of your Amaisan Way journey.

JOURNAL ACTIVITY: WRITE A PURPOSE STATEMENT

1. Research the concept of purpose statements.
2. Review your company's purpose statement, if applicable.
3. Review the purpose statements of three brands you admire.
4. Identify and review the personal purpose statements of three executives.
5. Write your own purpose statement using insights from this chapter.
6. Share ("shop") your purpose statement with trusted advisors for feedback.

Reflection Questions

- How did your introspection help you arrive at your purpose?
- How does your purpose statement resonate with others?

THE AAPI LENS

AAPI professionals must reflect not only on their skills and goals but also on cultural expectations, identity challenges, belonging, and the greater consequences of failure.

Without deeper introspection, AAPI professionals risk:

- Expending energy managing perception rather than impact
- Confusing harmony with compliance
- Defaulting to code-switching instead of intentional flexing

This chapter encourages AAPI professionals to focus on building on existing strengths rather than repairing perceived flaws. By aligning identity, values, actions, and purpose, leaders can achieve enduring, prominent, and impactful leadership.

CAREER-STAGE LENS

Early Career/Individual Contributor

- Focus on self-awareness and energy management
- Identify where you are code-switching unnecessarily
- Practice low-risk flexing (voice, visibility, framing impact)
- Begin defining why you want to lead—not just advance

Mid-Career/People Manager

- Use introspection to clarify leadership identity and brand
- Reframe Eastern strengths into visible leadership behaviors
- Seek feedback intentionally to understand how others experience you
- Articulate a purpose that guides trade-offs and prioritization

Senior Leader/Early Executive

- Resolve internal identity tension to lead consistently under pressure
- Use harmony to model grounded, authentic leadership
- Anchor decisions in purpose when stakes and visibility are high
- Prepare to translate purpose into strategy and planning

Regardless of career stage, the work is the same—the context changes.

CHAPTER SUMMARY

Self-awareness is one of the defining characteristics of effective leadership. Knowing yourself allows you to leverage your strengths, address gaps, and direct your energy toward a meaningful purpose rather than wasting it trying to fit into expectations that were never designed with you in mind.

AAPI professionals often face internal conflict from balancing Eastern and Western cultural influences, which can result in fragmentation and reduced effectiveness if not addressed.

Key Takeaways

- As AAPI professionals, we are shaped by both Eastern and Western cultural influences.
- Navigating multiple identities is not unique to AAPI professionals. It is what unites all human beings.
- Code-switching between identities carries an opportunity cost that drains energy and impairs performance.
- Eastern and Western cultural polarities shape our values and beliefs, which in turn drive our decisions, behaviors, and actions.
- Your Eastern cultural influences are not a weakness or something to hide in order to assimilate; they are assets that can make you a more holistic leader.
- Introspection helps uncover your tendencies, build harmony across identities, and reduce the need to code-switch.
- Knowing yourself allows you to show up consistently, spend less energy pretending, and focus more energy on impact.
- Personality assessments and feedback provide useful perspectives but they are inputs, not absolute truths.
- Reframing and flexing your multicultural identity enable you to advocate, influence, and build networks without losing authenticity.
- Once you achieve harmony and learn to flex between leadership skills, you are ready to define a purpose that will carry you forward.

JOURNAL ACTIVITY: PUTTING IT ALL TOGETHER

To move from insight to action, focus on one behavior you want to change based on what you learned in this chapter.

- Identify one behavior you want to improve based on feedback or self-reflection.
- Identify personality traits that may be influencing that behavior.

- Review assessment insights to determine what adjustments are required.
- Identify the value(s) or belief(s) driving the behavior.
- Determine whether those values or beliefs need to be realigned.
- Identify cultural influences shaping those values or beliefs.
- Identify an opposing cultural influence you can reframe or flex to support change.

Reflection Questions

- What did you learn about yourself?
- How do your multiple identities influence your decisions and actions?
- Where do you feel harmony—and where do you feel tension?
- What can you reframe and flex moving forward?

DISCOVER MORE

Explore the following topics to deepen your understanding:

- Simultaneous equations
- Code-switching vs. flexing
- Imposter syndrome
- Cultural assimilation vs. acculturation
- Freud's Iceberg Analogy
- Myers-Briggs Type Indicator (MBTI)
- DISC Assessment
- KISS (Keep It Simple, Stupid)
- Values and beliefs
- StrengthsFinder
- CliftonStrengths
- Hogan Personality Inventory (HPI)
- 360-degree feedback
- Net Promoter Score (NPS)
- *Never Eat Alone* (Keith Ferrazzi)
- Purpose statements

PUT IT TO WORK

Things that you can do to get started in the next 30 days:

- Take a personality assessment
- Seek 360-degree feedback
- Write a purpose statement

SO WHAT

Successful leaders regularly practice introspection because they understand that leadership must be built on a foundation of character, clarity, and conviction.

For AAPI professionals, engaging in this process is essential. Without thorough self-reflection that extends beyond conventional leadership frameworks, there is a risk of diminished cohesion, increased energy spent on code-switching rather than effective leadership, and a reduced capacity to reach one's full potential.

By exploring how Eastern and Western cultural influences shape your instincts, decisions, and behaviors, you can reclaim that energy. Embrace your multiple identities. Reframe and flex to find harmony. Unleash your Amasian superpowers. Anchor yourself in purpose.

Only then are you ready to lead with intention and invite others to follow.

LOOKING AHEAD

With a clearer understanding of who you are, why you want to lead, and how your cultural influences shape your instincts, the next responsibility is direction. Introspection without intention can stall momentum, and purpose without a plan remains aspiration. The next chapter focuses on Planning—how to intentionally invest your time, energy, and Amasian superpowers so your leadership journey moves forward with clarity rather than chance.

CHAPTER 2

Plan Your Journey

In the preceding chapter, you undertook the significant task of introspection. You examined your identity, values, beliefs, cultural influences, and purpose to establish a foundation of alignment and direction. Building upon this groundwork, the next step is to broaden your perspective by analyzing the systems, regulations, and practical realities that will influence the trajectory of your leadership development.

If you're working hard but not progressing, the issue is likely strategy, not effort. Understanding the rules and how success is measured helps turn energy into results. Focus on what's most important now, take action with a simple next step, and remember: progress requires planning, not just hope, luck, or patience.

In this chapter, we will discuss the following concepts:

- Understanding what success looks like for you, others, and your organization
- Creating a roadmap for your leadership development journey
- Working and updating your plan along the way

KNOW THE GAME

Before coming up with a game plan for your career, you need to first be a student of the game. You need to understand both what you are up against and what will help you succeed along the way. Knowing the game allows you to strategize, navigate, and level up with intention. This section is about understanding how success actually works in the environments where you want to advance.

I recently watched a stage production of *Hamilton*, by Lin -Manuel Miranda. With writing this book on my mind, the lyrics from the song "The Room Where It Happens" jumped out at me. It used a game as a metaphor and reminded the audience that they cannot win a game if they do not play. That lyric captures a hard truth about careers: progress rarely comes from waiting to be noticed. You must step into the game, even when the outcome is uncertain.

Certain individuals object to using the term "game" in relation to work, as they associate it with concepts that are trivial or lacking seriousness. Nonetheless, it is important to recognize that gaming mechanics serve as a relevant analogy for strategy, performance, and continual improvement in professional contexts.

Games are a universal phenomenon, with individuals having experience in playing them and an understanding of their fundamental elements, such as rules, participants, strategies, risks, rewards, and consequences. In the field of training and development, the integration of gaming theory and its practical application has become essential for designing learning experiences that are highly engaging, motivating, and effective.

The Amasian Way calls for professionals to learn the game, have a plan, and play to improve.

DEFINE SUCCESS

Have you ever heard a sportscaster praise a high-performing athlete for being a *student of the game*? Talent alone is never enough. You must understand the rules, the scoring system, and what it actually takes to win. Without that understanding, you risk becoming the proverbial hamster running endlessly on a wheel that expends tremendous energy while going nowhere.

The same principle applies to careers.

Many people assume that success in a consulting firm, for example, is driven primarily by technical expertise. Technical expertise matters but it is only one component of success. A consulting practice ultimately succeeds when its professionals are billable, client demand continues to grow, and the business sustains profitability over time. As a result, many technically brilliant subject matter experts struggle as practice leaders because they have never learned how to manage and grow a professional services business.

The same dynamic plays out across roles and industries. Many high-performing individual contributors believe they should be promoted simply because they are the best at what they do. However, the next level of responsibility often demands skills that were optional or entirely unnecessary at the previous level. A star athlete, for example, may lack the ability to coach, motivate, or develop others, making them ill-suited for a coaching role after retirement. I have seen countless high performers become stuck on this rung of the corporate ladder. They assume that excellence in their current role automatically signals readiness for the next one, especially if they have been rewarded and recognized along the way.

A true student of the game would have known what *promotion readiness* actually looks like and would have begun demonstrating those next-level skills and results well before ever asking for the promotion.

Complicating matters further, many organizations lack the maturity to recognize this gap. They promote technical experts, such as IT developers, physicians, lawyers, and engineers, into management or business leadership roles without giving them the opportunity to learn, practice, and demonstrate managerial and leadership skills required for success at that level. More mature organizations mitigate this risk through clearly defined career paths, competency models, and promotion or hiring readiness criteria. Some organizations go further by identifying high-potential talent using tools such as the 9-Box Model and investing in executive development rotation programs that deliberately build the skills and experiences required for advancement.

Still, not every rule of the game is written down.

You can read the rulebook to understand how success is formally defined, but you must engage other players to learn how the game is actually played. Culture, norms, and unwritten expectations often matter just as much as, if not more, than documented criteria.

Favoritism and unconscious bias may influence decisions regarding employee development and promotions within organizations. Professionals who are attuned to the cultural dynamics of their workplace tend to achieve greater consistency in their success. Conversely, individuals who are less aware of these dynamics may encounter challenges such as limited advancement, ambiguous career paths, and overlooked opportunities, often without a clear understanding of the underlying causes.

JOURNAL ACTIVITY: WHAT GAME ARE YOU PLAYING?

To plan your journey, you must first understand the game you are actually playing—not the one you assume you are playing.

1. Research your organization's internal and external sources to identify how success is explicitly defined. Document what you find across the following areas:
   - Mission
   - Purpose
   - Customer Experience
   - Financial and business goals (as articulated in leadership communications, such as the CEO or Chairman's letter, annual reports, strategy decks, or internal strategy documents)
2. Next, assess your current role and performance:
   - Map what you do well today to these definitions of success.
   - Identify where your efforts clearly contribute to organizational success—and where they do not.

Reflection Questions

- What definitions of success confirmed what you already believed?
- What surprised you?

- How much of your work can be directly tied to organizational success?
- Where are you expending energy that is difficult to connect to meaningful impact?

VOICE OF EXPERIENCE

The following examples from my experience illustrate why understanding the game and playing it intentionally are critical to career progression.

Example 1. Confusing Popularity with Performance

A close friend was interviewing for a supervisory role. When I asked what his priority would be for improving team performance, he confidently said he would bring back pizza night. He believed it would boost morale and be well-received. I asked how that aligned with the organization's performance priorities. Advocating for crowd-pleasing ideas rather than business imperatives highlighted a readiness gap for the next level. Leaders are expected to prioritize outcomes, not popularity.

Example 2. "My Work Should Speak for Itself"

A female employee expressed her disappointment after not being selected for a promotion, despite being the highest-performing member of her team. She believed the outcome was influenced by favoritism, as the successful candidate frequently dined with the manager. After further discussion of the requirements for the next position, she recognized that strong relationship-building skills would be essential. The individual who received the promotion had already displayed these skills in an informal yet noticeable manner. As such, cultivating professional relationships proved to be a critical component, whether explicitly outlined or not.

Example 3. Speaking the Language of Power

During a roundtable discussion, a woman expressed that she felt excluded from leadership conversations because others used language she did not understand. When pressed for examples, she cited business performance terms such as "above or below the line," "EBITDA," and "CAGR." These were not exclusionary tactics. They were the language of executive accountability and incentive structures. Fluency in performance metrics is table stakes at senior levels.

Example 4. Elevating the Narrative

A middle manager struggled for years to break into the executive ranks. He believed he was being held back because he was Asian. When I asked him to articulate his professional brand, he described himself as a fixer. He has a reputation for being sent into accounts to solve problems. When asked to quantify the scope of those problems, he reframed his story to, "He had repeatedly saved high–net-worth accounts by resolving multimillion-dollar issues." Once his narrative matched the scale of executive accountability, his advancement followed.

Example 5. My Own Wake-Up Call

In my early consulting career, I had an epiphany: success in a professional services firm requires far more than technical excellence. Early career consultants must build their craft. As they advance, they must also lead engagements, manage client relationships, sell their services, and build their practices. Because firms generate revenue through billable hours, technical brilliance alone will only take you so far.

Taken together, these experiences underscore several critical truths:

- You must understand the rules of success for both your current and next roles.
- Performance goals must align first with organizational business imperatives.
- Leaders are expected to measure, monitor, manage, and communicate metrics that matter.
- Your narrative of results and impact must scale with the level of accountability you seek.

Knowing the game does not mean abandoning your values. It means positioning your strengths where they matter most.

STUDY THE GAME

"What helped you be successful now will not get you to the next level." This is a phrase I often hear during promotion readiness discussions.

It is critical to understand what it takes to be successful in your *current role*. If you want to move to the *next role*, you must also understand what success looks like there—*before* you are promoted into it. I have sat through countless performance review discussions where high performers were held back because they had not yet demonstrated the "right to play" at the next level. Winning the game is not the same as being a popular player.

Recall that the first step of the Amasian Way was getting clear on what matters to you. Now, you must get equally clear on what matters to your organization. Becoming a true *student of the game* early in your career is one of the highest-return investments you can make. Building a habit of actively studying how success is defined will help you focus your energy, deliver meaningful impact, and drive results.

A word of caution: do not leave this to your supervisor. Some managers are excellent teachers; others assume you will figure it out on your own. Either way, ownership of your growth belongs to you.

KNOW WHERE TO LOOK

There are three primary categories of resources that will help you understand how the game is played. You need all three to see the full picture.

1. **Internal Resources.** These reveal how success is *officially* defined.
   - Company intranet and internal portals
   - Core values and leadership principles
   - Performance management systems and rubrics

- Career paths and job descriptions
- Strategy documents and operating plans

2. **External Resources.** These reveal how success is projected to the outside world.
   - Mission and purpose statements
   - Annual reports and shareholder letters
   - Press releases and media coverage
   - Industry benchmarks, awards, and reports
   - Conferences, trade publications, and newsletters
   - Job boards and employee reviews (e.g., Glassdoor)
   - Search engines, news feeds, and generative AI summaries
   - Company social media channels
3. **Network Resources.** These reveal how success is actually experienced.
   - Your manager and skip-level leaders
   - High performers and respected peers
   - Mentors and sponsors
   - HR partners
   - Customers and prospects
   - Alumni, professional associations, and affinity groups
   - Employee Resource Groups and volunteer organizations
   - Family and friends with adjacent industry insight

Each category tells a different part of the story. Together, they reveal the real rules of the game.

I recommend dedicating substantial time to reviewing both your organization's internal and external websites to become proficient in the terminology and standards your company uses for success. For instance, during performance review periods, I would intentionally align my self-assessment descriptions with the company's core values and key performance indicators.

The Game Changes as You Level Up

While organizational goals remain the north star, the game changes as you move through career stages. What would be a mistake is assuming that success is defined the same way at every level.

At some point in your career, you should no longer expect your boss to perform your job better than you can. This realization used to frustrate me early on. I often boasted that I could do my job better than people at the next level. What I did not yet understand was that we did not have the same job. We had different accountabilities and were measured by different outcomes.

I now coach experienced managers to expect this shift. At that stage, your manager is no longer there to tell you *what* to do. You are expected to present a point of view, a recommendation, and your reasoning.

Supervisors use the Socratic Method to challenge your thinking. This is not because they lack answers, but because they are developing your judgment. If you have ever thought, "Why won't my boss just tell me what to do?" you are likely being coached, not ignored.

How Success Scales by Role

Role	Game to Know	Why It Matters
Early Career/ Individual Contributor	Metrics that define a high performer	Improve personal performance
Supervisory	Team metrics and supervisory effectiveness	Improve team performance
Management	Group-level metrics (practice, region, function)	Improve group performance
Leadership	Organization-wide metrics and strategic outcomes	Improve organizational performance

As your responsibilities expand, so too does the breadth of accountability and the importance of effectively articulating your impact. A senior leader once advised me, "If you are irreplaceable, you may become unpromotable." This perspective highlights that career advancement depends on demonstrating readiness for future roles rather than simply excelling in your current position. Employers have little incentive to promote individuals who excel only in their current role without demonstrating readiness for greater responsibility.

The Long Game

I was recently introduced to the concept of the "Infinite Game," articulated by Simon Sinek. He challenges ideas like "winning" or "being number one" as short-sighted in environments where the game never truly ends. Even if you lose this season, there is another season, and another after that.

This idea was a game-changer for me. I still use terms like "win themes" and "award-winning" (old habits die hard), but I now think more in terms of continuous improvement, leveling up, and sustainability.

Progress still deserves celebration. If you do not acknowledge growth, effort, and advancement, you risk either celebrating poor performance or not celebrating at all. Neither builds momentum. The goal is not to win a single round.

The Amasian Way calls us to stay in the game, improve over time, and play with intention.

JOURNAL ACTIVITY: WRITE YOUR PERFORMANCE REVIEW

One of the most effective ways to understand the game is to practice playing it the way decisions are actually made. Writing your own performance review—*before* it is required—forces you to evaluate yourself using the same lenses others use to assess readiness, potential, and impact.

Step 1. Research the Rules

- Research the success criteria and performance indicators for your current role.
- Research the success criteria and performance indicators for your next desired role.
- Research leadership qualities and competencies as defined by your organization.

Step 2. Self-Assess Honestly

Give yourself a grade (high, medium, or low) for:

- Your current abilities and performance in your current role (current performance).
- Whether you consistently demonstrate success criteria for the next role (promotion readiness).
- Your demonstration of leadership qualities (future potential).

Step 3. Validate Your Perspective

- Review your assessment with your supervisor, trusted peers, or mentors.
- Encourage candid feedback, and look for patterns rather than one-off opinions.

Reflection Questions

- What are the things you do particularly well?
- How does your success align with your organization's definition of success?
- How does your success align with your customer's or client's definition of success?
- What will you need to improve to get to the next level?
- What must you demonstrate more consistently to be seen as high potential?
- What did you learn from other people's feedback on your review?

VOICE OF EXPERIENCE

In one of my previous roles, I did not receive a high-performer rating during a period when my personal life was in a rough spot. I had also put minimal effort into writing my performance review. In doing so, I forgot one of the most valuable lessons a previous manager had taught me. Although my success was notable and I would have been considered a high performer, my failure to advocate for my performance led to my first mediocre rating at the firm.

My previous manager always asked me to write a performance review that advocated for my success. She did not ask me to write my performance review because she was lazy, nor because she was unaware of my impact. She taught me to articulate my performance and results in a way that helped me grow as a manager and leader. Her coaching helped me frame my work using the same rubric the review board used to evaluate readiness and advancement. That skill, not the rating itself, was the real gift.

Since then, I have participated in many performance review panels. Being on the panel reinforced how powerful this lesson was. Strong performers are often overlooked, not because they lack impact, but because they fail to *translate* that impact into a narrative that aligns with organizational priorities.

So, the next time you are asked to write a performance review, do not treat it as an administrative task. Treat it as a *leadership exercise*. Pay close attention to the feedback you receive from your manager and from the process itself. It will tell you exactly how you are perceived, what you must improve, and how you need to raise your game to prepare for the next level. And if you are in a position to manage and coach others, provide feedback using the success language of your company and business so your direct reports can learn from it.

DEFINE LEADERSHIP

Much has been written about the qualities and competencies of effective leaders. If you want to plan your journey intentionally, you must understand how *leadership is defined and practiced at your workplace.*

Start with your organization. Research its documented leadership framework, and solicit feedback to evaluate yourself against it. Then broaden your perspective by studying external leadership frameworks to understand how leadership is defined and rewarded in the broader market.

Leadership frameworks typically cluster expectations into three domains: *leading yourself, leading others, and leading the organization.*

Lead Self

These qualities describe how you show up as an individual contributor, decision-maker, and owner of outcomes.

- Boldness: Ability to take on big, difficult, or ambiguous challenges
- Resilience: Ability to endure setbacks and recover from failure
- Passion: Intense commitment to purpose and outcomes
- Innovative: Ability to reimagine problems and generate new solutions
- Agile: Ability to adapt and adjust quickly to changing circumstances
- Accountable: Willingness to own both success and failure
- Results-Oriented: Focus on delivering measurable impact and value
- Bias for Action: Tendency to act rather than wait for perfect information
- Domain Expertise: Proficiency and performance in your field

Lead Others

These qualities reflect your ability to influence, develop, and mobilize people.

- Communicate with Impact: Inspire others to change behavior and take action

- Empathetic: Understand and leverage emotional intelligence
- Charismatic: Inspire confidence and devotion from others
- Trustworthy: Act in ways that earn and sustain trust
- Authentic: Show up genuinely, sincerely, and true to self
- Change Management: Solve problems and lead others through change

Lead the Organization

These qualities describe how leaders operate at scale and with enterprise-level accountability.

- Ethics, Trust, and Transparency: Do the right thing, always and visibly.
- Business Acumen: Drive financial and operational performance.
- Strategic Thinking: Evaluate critically, and focus on what matters most.
- Politically Savvy: Network, navigate, and persuade to achieve objectives.
- Sponsorship: Prioritize people and initiatives by allocating resources.
- Transformational: Lead organizations through disruption and change.
- Customer Focus: Prioritize solutions that create value for customers.

This list is not exhaustive or ranked. There is probably a leadership development bingo card somewhere with these and many more buzzwords printed on it. The point is not to memorize labels, but to understand *what behaviors and outcomes are rewarded* in your environment.

To become a manager, you need to study *management frameworks*. If you want to become a leader, you must study *leadership frameworks*. There are countless books and articles on each of these qualities. The more fluent you become in the language of leadership, the better equipped you will be to develop these capabilities intentionally throughout your career.

Reflecting on our recent introspection exercise, certain leadership skills and qualities may come more intuitively to you due to your multicultural background. For this reason, it is essential that AAPI professionals engage thoughtfully and proactively in their leadership development. This topic will be examined in greater detail throughout the subsequent chapters of this book.

JOURNAL ACTIVITY: ARE YOU A LEADER?

Step 1. Research

- Research your organization's documented leadership framework.
- Research two external leadership frameworks from companies or brands you admire or aspire to work for.

Step 2. Synthesize

- Build a combined leadership framework using elements from all three sources.

Step 3. Assess

Evaluate your proficiency against the combined framework.

- Identify gaps.
- Brainstorm opportunities to develop.

Sample Assessment Table

Leadership Quality	My Proficiency	My Gaps	Opportunities to Develop
Transformational Leadership	Low	Limited knowledge and experience	Internal training; volunteer for Project X

Reflection Questions

- Which leadership qualities stood out to you, and why?
- Which qualities are your strongest, and how did you develop them?
- Which gaps interest you the most?
- What is one concrete step you could take to begin developing those gaps?

CREATE A LEADERSHIP DEVELOPMENT PLAN

A famous quote associated with one of the greatest American ice hockey players, Wayne Gretzky, is: "Skate where the puck is going, not where it is." The point is straightforward: leaders do not wait for the future to arrive. They move toward it deliberately.

After investing time in introspection and learning the leadership game, it is time to determine *where you want to go and how you will get there, from where you are to where you want to be.* Where you want to go begins with *ambition.*

Why do you want to lead?

The answer must inspire *you* to do the work and *others* to follow you. Your ambition often lives somewhere between two poles:

1. **The Impossible Dream**, which fuels aspiration and courage, and
2. **The Art of the Possible**, which turns aspiration into progress.

The Amasian Way calls us to visualize a goal and plan our journey.

The Impossible Dream

We dare to dream the impossible dream because it gives us motivation to push through tremendous adversity. Dreams help us visualize where we want to go, especially when the path forward feels uncertain or overwhelming. Sometimes, we read a biography or watch a story where the main character holds onto an impossible dream long enough to overcome insurmountable challenges. Those stories resonate with us because they remind us of what is possible when belief precedes action.

The most charismatic leaders often inspire others through transformational change rooted in such dreams. Dr. Martin Luther King Jr.'s renowned "I Have a Dream" speech, delivered in 1963, continues to inspire movements for social justice today. Bruce Lee inspired many by example. He achieved what once seemed impossible through discipline, mastery, and self-belief, and challenged others to do the same. These individuals were not merely dreamers. They were doers. They rolled up their sleeves and did the work required to make their dreams real.

Steve Jobs articulated the difference between dreamers and doers in an interview with the Santa Clara Valley Historical Association: "Most people never pick up the phone. Most people never call and ask. And that's what separates sometimes the people who do things from those who dream about them."

A good friend of mine who helped me start my journey of giving back to the AAPI professional community, Lisa Ong, created a consulting firm based on the premise of "Wishing Out Loud." It is a deceptively simple idea that most of us never practice. We dream. We wish. But we rarely say our ambitions out loud, where they can be challenged, shaped, or supported.

I once served as a director in a learning and development organization. In my first meeting with the company's chief learning officer, he asked me what I wanted from my career with the organization. I replied, "I would like to be the chief learning officer someday. What's the path?" He looked surprised and said, "You are the first person who has asked me that question. I don't know that I know the answer right now, but I think we need to find that out." My boss later joked that, thanks to me, he and his peers were now tasked with defining a career path that had not previously existed. That moment reinforced something important for me: asking for what you want out loud can possibly change the conversation.

I envy those who can pursue and achieve their impossible dreams. Dreams are difficult to visualize and easy to abandon when obstacles appear. Personally, I need a future that feels more grounded. I need to see the steps that lead forward. That said, I still romanticize the impossible dream from time to time, not as a plan, but as a way to challenge myself to think further and reach higher.

Art of the Possible

I gravitate toward grounded visualizations because they let me plot a roadmap and celebrate progress along the way. The phrase "Art of the Possible" is often used to prompt pragmatic discussions that lead to achievable outcomes. While it lacks the freedom of blue-sky thinking, it enables leaders to translate ambition into action by defining a path from where they are to where they want to be.

I do not doubt that my Eastern upbringing influences this preference. For me, the appeal of the Art of the Possible is motivation. Growing up, the word "bothersome"—麻煩—was the most common excuse for why something should not be attempted. The more impossible a dream seemed, the more bothersome it was perceived to be. That mindset can quickly spiral into limiting beliefs such as hopelessness, powerlessness, or the idea that effort is useless. Unsurprisingly, those ideas are usually abandoned before they ever have a chance to take root.

You can be both a dreamer and a pragmatist. You can begin with blue-sky ideation and then translate those ideas into achievable goals and plans. Many ideation frameworks exist to help dreamers, planners, and doers work together to make the impossible possible. *The Imagineering Way*, published by Disney Book Group, documents how Disney Imagineers transform imaginative ideas into real-world experiences through structured creativity and disciplined execution.

VOICE OF EXPERIENCE

Both the Impossible Dream and the Art of the Possible answer the same question: *How can we achieve something?* I have found that many dreams die before they ever take root—not because they are impossible, but because we default too quickly to "why not" reasoning before giving space to the "why yes" list.

This may be influenced by where I grew up in the northeastern United States. Boston is one of the winningest sports cities in the country, yet it also carries a deep expectation of disappointment. From the 1986 World Series loss to the Super Bowl XLII upset that ended a perfect season, New Englanders have learned to brace for loss. Some call it the "Curse of the Bambino." I think it has more to do with tough winters and hardened expectations.

When you lead a team or a project, you must be the champion of what is possible. The moment you waver, others will too, and doubt becomes a self-fulfilling prophecy. Leaders must consistently anchor teams on the "why yes" list. I recently had to do this as a project owner when a team hesitated to commit to a launch date due to interdependencies and risk. The work could not move forward without commitment. By applying Art of the Possible thinking, I helped the team align on a path forward.

As a leader, you will inevitably be asked to drive change. Whether you are charismatic or reserved, inspirational or pragmatic, your role is to align stakeholders around a believable picture of success. The Impossible Dream paints the vision. The Art of the Possible makes that vision attainable.

This also applies to your leadership development plan. You need to focus on what is possible and move towards your ambition with conviction and commitment. For now, your career and leadership ambition are the dream. You need to believe in your own success. The project is turning your ambition into a journey map of milestones, actions, and progress.

So, where do you want to take your career?

JOURNAL ACTIVITY: WHAT IS YOUR DREAM?

At this stage of the journey, the goal is less about being precise and more about giving yourself permission and space to imagine without immediately filtering for practicality, feasibility, or risk. You may choose one, two, or all three of the activities below.

Option 1: Award-Winning. Imagine that, sometime in the future, you are recognized for an achievement.

- What did you do to earn this award?

- Who is issuing it?
- Why do you believe this is something you could realistically achieve in the future?

This exercise helps you reverse-engineer excellence by starting with recognition and tracing it back to action.

Option 2: Dream Role. Imagine being hired for your dream role sometime in the near future.

- What is the title of the role?
- Why does this role appeal to you?
- What impact does this role have—and for whom?
- What knowledge, skills, and attitudes make you effective in this role?

This exercise clarifies fit, not just aspiration.

Option 3: Art of the Possible. Imagine yourself one year from now.

- What will you be doing?
- What would you like to be different?
- What would you like to remain the same?
- What excites you about this version of your life and work?

This exercise grounds ambition in a time horizon that feels attainable and motivating.

Reflection Questions

- Did this exercise help you visualize your ambition more clearly?
- Where do you still feel uncertainty or ambiguity?
- What would you be willing to invest—time, effort, discomfort, or resources—to make this ambition real?
- How would realizing this ambition benefit you, others, your organization, its customers, or society?

VOICE OF EXPERIENCE

I have found that my personal career and leadership ambitions have shifted as I matured.

Early on, I knew one thing clearly: I never wanted to be my own boss. I did not aspire to sit at the very top of an organization. What I *did* know was that I wanted to lead and be accountable for something substantive and impactful.

As an early-career professional, I was impatient. I could not wait to be promoted. I have met many bright-eyed and ambitious professionals who threw themselves into their careers with similar intensity. My trajectory was steep at first: assistant vice president in a financial services firm before I turned 30, followed by a vice president role near the top of a start-up. The titles impressed my parents, but they still did not fully satisfy my ambition.

The next phase of my career was long and humbling. I shifted into consulting, a major professional reset. My advancement slowed, but this period proved the most critical in my development. I was no longer simply ambitious; I became acutely aware of how much I still needed to learn, develop, and unlearn. Advancement did not come easily, and that reality forced growth.

The truth is simple and uncomfortable. There are fewer people at the top of any organization because it is hard to advance into the middle and even harder to reach the pinnacle. There is no guaranteed upward trajectory. There is no entitlement based solely on tenure.

Looking back, I believe I have achieved my personal ambition, even if it doesn't look like what I once imagined. I have served as a director at top consulting firms, led multi-million-dollar initiatives for Fortune 100 companies, presided over a local nonprofit chapter, owned a line of business with full P&L accountability, and delivered keynotes around the world. I may not be an influencer, but I have built meaningful followership in my career, my community, and my life.

A pivotal moment occurred when I became a father, leading to a significant change in my priorities. I was no longer willing to sacrifice every night and weekend solely for career advancement. I wanted to be present and witness my children's growth. This isn't a critique of anyone else's decisions; it's simply an honest account of my own. I know remarkable leaders who are also excellent fathers. However, I understand myself well enough to realize that I can't fully commit to both a demanding executive role and spending quality time with my family at the same time. I recognized that I couldn't excel at both responsibilities simultaneously.

So, I chose differently. I chose to be the best leader I could be in the roles that came my way, rather than constantly chasing the next title.

Most importantly, I am happy. I have found harmony between my professional ambition and my life. I continue to grow at work, at home, and in my community. Maturity reshaped how I evaluate success, and introspection helped me understand *why*.

I am often reminded of Alexander Hamilton's arc in *Hamilton*: relentlessly ambitious, never satisfied. That was until a life-altering moment forced him to pause, look around, and recognize that what he had might finally be enough.

SMART CAREER GOALS

When you are ready to bring your ambitions to life, the next step is to articulate them into *career goals*. Goals are desired outcomes. They move from conceptual to possible when you refine them with enough specificity to guide action and decision-making.

SMART is a framework that helps you to turn ambition into something you can plan, monitor, and manage.

SMART goals are:

- Specific
- Measurable
- Achievable
- Realistic
- Time-bound

When you write goals in these terms, you give yourself clarity. You create a way to track progress, assess trade-offs, and course-correct without abandoning the goal altogether.

Consider the following examples.

Example 1. "I would like to be a billionaire."

This goal is specific and measurable, but it lacks clarity on achievability, realism, and timing. Without those elements, it is difficult to translate this ambition into meaningful action.

Example 2. "I have $1 million saved for retirement. I want to retire in 10 years with a nest egg of $5 million by investing in the stock market."

This goal is specific, measurable, achievable, realistic, and time-bound. It creates a clear planning horizon and invites concrete next steps.

Many organizations require annual performance and professional development goals to be written in SMART format. When paired with the *Art of the Possible*, SMART goals help you articulate what success looks like aspirationally *and* operationally.

Increasingly, organizations also use *Objectives and Key Results* (OKRs) alongside or instead of SMART goals. The two frameworks are complementary. SMART goals emphasize clarity and feasibility, while OKRs place additional emphasis on outcomes and measurable impact.

Bottom line: Knowing your organization's framework and success criteria helps you align your goals with how your performance is measured.

VOICE OF EXPERIENCE

Aligning your personal career vision, purpose, objectives, and plans with the organization's vision, mission, and strategic direction is critical to long-term success and fulfillment.

When your aspirations and values align with the organization's, you gain clarity and momentum. Your efforts compound rather than compete. This alignment fosters engagement, improves performance, and increases the likelihood that your contributions will be recognized and rewarded.

Misalignment, on the other hand, creates friction. At best, it slows your progress and makes growth feel forced or stagnant. At worst, it can derail your trajectory entirely, leading to disengagement, dissatisfaction, or an abrupt career pivot.

I have witnessed organizations where entire departments were misaligned with strategic priorities. This did not go well for those who were misaligned. Leaders and teams were removed because their direction no longer served the organization's goals.

As a leader, you must regularly reflect on whether both you *and* your organization benefit from a shared vision. Alignment should maximize impact and satisfaction on both sides. If aligning with your organization requires you to compromise your purpose or core beliefs, it will be difficult, if not impossible, to sustain joy, growth, or integrity in your work. You always have a choice. You need to see it and make that choice before someone else does.

DRAW A ROADMAP

I describe consulting in simple terms. You always have to:

1. Assess your current state.
2. Define your desired future state.
3. Analyze the gap between your current and future states.
4. Draw a roadmap that will get you from point A to point B.

Once you have visualized your leadership ambition (the desired future state), it is time to draw a *roadmap* to guide you toward it. Roadmaps can take many forms. Some people create high-level timelines with milestones and achievements. Others prefer detailed action plans with specific tasks and deadlines. There is no single "right" format. What matters most is that *your roadmap is simple enough to follow and meaningful enough to keep you committed.*

As you build your roadmap, consider the following questions:

- **Is everything on your roadmap strategically helping you achieve your goal?**
  Real life already provides more than enough distractions. Your roadmap should be intentionally selective. If an activity does not move you closer to your goal, it does not belong on the plan.
- **Does the roadmap call you to take action?**
  A good roadmap does not just describe intent. It compels behavior. Each step should drive action that produces observable progress or results.
- **Does the roadmap give you space to celebrate wins and learn from setbacks?**

You must periodically pause to take stock of what you have gained, what you have learned, and what needs adjustment. A roadmap should not be a rigid contract. It is a living document that should evolve as you do.

Sample Roadmap Activities for Specific Goals

Below are examples of how a roadmap might translate ambition into action.

Goal	Action	Timing
Promotion to the next level within one year	Research the next role through informational interviews	Q1
	Assess personal promotion readiness	Q1
	Socialize intent and solicit feedback	Q2
	Act on feedback and confirm readiness	Q2–Q3
	Apply for the new role	Q4
Improve public speaking skills and deliver presentations by year-end	Watch instructional videos	Q1
	Practice independently	Q1
	Identify and participate in a public speaking class	Q2
	Identify opportunities to speak publicly	Q2
	Practice in front of audiences and solicit feedback	Q3–Q4
Create five new network contacts at the XX	Identify and participate in a networking class	Conference minus 3 weeks
	Define networking goals	Conference minus 2 weeks
	Review the conference agenda and attendee list; identify target contacts	Conference minus 1 week
	Engage and establish rapport during the conference	At Conference
	Develop and execute a follow-up plan to build ongoing relationships	Conference plus 1 week

Bottom line: A roadmap transforms aspiration into execution. It helps you stay focused, intentional, and accountable, while giving you permission to adjust as you learn. Without a roadmap, even the clearest ambition risks becoming wishful thinking.

MATURITY MODEL

One consulting tool that can support your leadership roadmap is a *maturity model.* A maturity model breaks down success factors and describes how they look at different stages of development. It helps make growth visible, assessable, and actionable.

For example, let's define success factors for an Information Technology (IT) function as:

- Strategy
- Organizational Structure
- Talent
- Processes
- Technology

Now assume three levels of maturity for that function:

- Lagging
- Established
- Leading

A simplified maturity model might look something like this conceptually:

Factor	Lagging	Established	Leading
Strategy			
Org Structure			
Talent			
Processes			
Technology	Analog	Digital	AI-enabled

Each intersecting cell describes *observable characteristics* of that factor at a given level of maturity. For example, technology maturity might progress from analog tools to digital platforms to AI-enabled systems.

From here, you would conduct a *current-state assessment* by plotting your current position for each factor. Then, you would define a *desired future state* at a point in time. The gap between those two states becomes the basis for your roadmap. The roadmap answers a simple but powerful question: *What must I do to move from here to there?*

Example: A High-Level Career Maturity Model

You can apply the same concept to your own career. Below is a simplified illustration of how maturity might look across different career stages.

Dimension	Early Career/ Individual Contributor	Manager	Director	Executive
Soft Skills	Basic communication	Effective communication	Operational communication	Strategic communication
Business Acumen	Cursory knowledge across projects	Working knowledge across function and team	Intermediate knowledge across division	Advanced knowledge across the business
Technology Savviness	Familiar with available tools	Applying tools to improve productivity	Leveraging emerging technologies for operational excellence	Foresight to apply digital transformation and disruptive technology
Management	Manage self and projects	Manage team and project portfolio	Manage operations	Manage organizations
Leadership	Lead self and projects	Lead teams	Lead operations	Lead organizations

Many other dimensions and characteristics can be added. The point is not to create a perfect model. It is to *visualize gaps* between where you are and where you want to go next.

Behind every effective maturity model should be a *roadmap of concrete actions*—specific experiences, behaviors, and capabilities required to move from one level to the next. This is where the model becomes practical.

Try it this week: You may find it useful to experiment with generative AI to help draft a maturity model tailored to your career or industry. One prompt can help you generate the structure of the model, and a follow-up prompt can help you identify development activities that move someone from one level to the next.

VOICE OF EXPERIENCE

Many professional and leadership development programs end with a plan-of-action exercise. The intent is to help you build the habit of applying what you have learned, not just consuming information. But a plan is only as effective as your willingness to act on it.

Each plan should include specific objectives that align with your personal purpose and goals. You must believe that those objectives matter enough to follow through. Otherwise, like most training materials, the plan will end up forgotten in a junk pile.

Plans and roadmaps must strike a balance: *substantive enough to motivate action, yet flexible enough to adapt.* For some people with highly disciplined personalities, a plan becomes the primary engine for forward movement. For others, myself included, it serves more like guideposts or trail blazes that help us find our way back when we drift.

When I feel overwhelmed by competing priorities at work and in life, I find comfort in returning to a plan. It helps me regroup, refocus, and remember what matters most. Looking back on an old plan is also a powerful retrospective exercise. It shows how far you've come, not just where you still need to go.

Plans also matter most when things go wrong. Life will throw curveballs. No plan anticipates everything. But when you are knocked off course, a roadmap gives you something to recalibrate against. Imagine an executive with a multi-year business plan suddenly disrupted by industry upheaval. Careers face similar disruptions. A personal roadmap allows you to reassess, realign, and move forward with intention rather than panic.

Curb Your Enthusiasm

A Chinese proverb reads, "Eyes wide, stomach narrow." When you are in the career-planning stage, it is easy to become overwhelmed by the possibilities. Sometimes, we spend more time browsing and adding movies and shows to "My List" than actually watching them. The same thing happens when we evaluate skill gaps and research learning and development opportunities.

The solution is simple: *keep your appetite small.*

Create roadmaps designed to help you do a few things well at a time. Focus beats frenzy. You should target *no more than three or four performance improvement objectives per year.* This constraint forces prioritization, increases follow-through, and reduces the likelihood that your plan collapses under its own weight.

Not Everything Costs Money

Only some forms of development require financial investment. Many of the most effective growth opportunities are already available to you. They are often hiding in plain sight.

Here are several ways to improve your performance without breaking the bank.

Learning and Development Classes

Most organizations offer internal training programs. Early-career professionals are often enrolled in structured curricula, but many companies also provide elective courses. Take full advantage of these opportunities. They not only to build skills, but also to expand your internal network.

On-the-Job Training/Apprenticeship

Whether you work in the trades or not, treat every role as an apprenticeship. Partner with your supervisor to identify skills you need to learn and demonstrate. Keep a journal of on-the-job learning activities. This approach accelerates development and makes your growth visible to others.

Mentors, Coaches, and a Personal Board of Advisors

You should always have people to turn to for advice and feedback. Include those who will support you, and at least one person who will tell you the truth, even when it is uncomfortable. Diversity of perspective matters. The goal is not agreement. It is to gain insight through different perspectives.

External Resources

As you progress in your career, you will rely less on formal instruction and more on self-directed learning. There is an abundance of free or low-cost resources available to help you stay curious and relevant:

- Generative AI prompts: Research has evolved rapidly. I find that combining personal experience, traditional research, and generative AI responses significantly expands my understanding of complex topics.
- Generative AI summaries: Tools such as Google's NotebookLM and Microsoft's Co-Pilot can synthesize multiple sources into summaries or audio content, allowing you to cross-reference ideas efficiently.
- Trade magazines and newsletters: Most industries offer free digital publications. A simple search by role or industry can uncover high-quality thought leadership.
- TED Talks: A powerful way to absorb ideas, frameworks, and inspiration from diverse voices.
- YouTube videos: An excellent resource for interview preparation, skill-building, and just-in-time learning.
- Work-relevant books: While books may not always be free, summaries, reviews, and talks often are. Use those to decide where deeper investment is worthwhile.

Pay for Higher Stakes

Think of money spent on development as an *investment in future impact*, not a cost. This becomes especially important beyond middle management, where the stakes and consequences of underperformance are significantly higher.

The return on investment may show up as increased earning power, broader influence, or greater organizational and societal impact. I refer to these as *high-stakes learning and development opportunities.* They are investments that can materially change your trajectory.

Here are a few ways I have invested in my own performance:

- **Postgraduate Degrees.** Early in my career, I found the MBA to be increasingly commoditized—much as a bachelor's degree had been a decade earlier. While some companies emphasize hiring for raw talent over credentials, I still believe advanced degrees matter for long-term career progression in many fields.
- **Certifications.** Industry-recognized certifications are an effective way to close experience gaps. They signal competence and credibility through shared standards and reputation.
- **Executive Development Programs.** At senior levels, I believe there is a strong case for returning to high-touch, structured executive development. These programs often include role-playing, real-world problem solving, long-term mentoring, and peer collaboration—experiences that are difficult to replicate through self-study alone.
- **Executive Coaching.** Executive coaching has been tremendously valuable for me. A good coach does not tell you what to do; they provide perspective, challenge blind spots, and help you work through issues you may be avoiding or deflecting.
- **Paid Digital Learning.** I have also benefited from structured online learning, including MOOCs. For disciplined learners, these programs offer flexibility with rigor. You may even find skill-building content in unexpected places. Yes, even on streaming platforms. I am currently taking online courses to learn AI.

JOURNAL ACTIVITY: THE ROAD TO SUCCESS

Conduct focused research to ground your ambition in execution. This activity is designed to move you from aspiration to action.

Step 1. Build Your Foundation

- ☐ Conduct internet research to learn more about:
  - SMART Goals
  - Objectives and Key Results (OKR)
  - Strategic roadmapping

Step 2. Articulate Your Goal

- ☐ Write a clear career goal.
- ☐ Evaluate and adjust your goal to ensure it meets the SMART criteria:
  - Specific
  - Measurable
  - Achievable
  - Realistic
  - Time-bound

Step 3. Create Your Roadmap

- ☐ Write a high-level roadmap that will lead you to your goal.
- ☐ Identify milestones, actions, and checkpoints that will keep you moving forward.

Reflection Questions

- ☐ How does your career goal align with your company's and team's OKRs?
- ☐ Who could you share this goal and roadmap with to solicit candid feedback?
- ☐ What is the very first action you can take to begin executing this plan?

PLAN THE WORK, WORK THE PLAN

What happens to most people's New Year's resolutions? They are abandoned shortly into the new year. The same thing happens with career roadmaps. One effective way to avoid abandoning your plan too early is to apply *project management discipline* to your career development.

Project management represents a critical competency across all professional roles. Fundamentally, it entails formulating a plan to meet specified objectives and systematically overseeing its implementation until the desired outcomes are delivered. Whether project management is explicitly stated in one's job title or description, this ability remains vital to advancing in any career. Moreover, these skills are broadly applicable beyond the workplace; activities such as organizing a vacation, coordinating a home renovation, or planning a wedding all draw upon the same foundational principles.

Turn Your Career into a Project

Translate your career vision and roadmap into a project plan.

- Author a *project charter* that captures:
    - Your vision translated into SMART goals
    - Scope
    - Key milestones and timeline
    - Roles (including who supports or sponsors you)
    - Required investments and risks
    - How and how often you will monitor and manage progress
- List roadmap activities and identify a *critical path.*
- Develop a project plan that sequences all activities and produces a *Gantt chart.*
- Create a *project dashboard* to monitor progress against milestones and objectives.

Reminder: if you are not fluent in project management concepts, add them to your leadership development roadmap.

Most projects appear to progress well during the initial stages. However, as competing priorities arise, certain elements may be overlooked, and the plan may ultimately be disregarded. Therefore, it is essential to recognize that executing the plan is equally as important as creating it.

Actively Manage Your Career Plan

Managing your career plan requires ongoing attention.

This includes:

- Regularly reviewing progress against target dates
- Monitoring and managing risks and issues
- Managing changes that affect scope, timing, or priorities

To help you stay the course:

- Celebrate milestones and achievements along the way
- Hold yourself accountable to someone, such as a supervisor, mentor, or career coach, who sponsors your plan
- Set a regular cadence to review progress and solicit feedback

Hacks to Make Your Leadership Development Plan Stick

- **Make the impact compelling.** Anchor your development goals to outcomes that matter. For leadership development, connect your progress to your company's and team's performance. The more compelling the impact, the less likely you are to abandon the effort.
- **Remind yourself why you care.** Create visible reminders of why this plan matters to you. I still remember a public service announcement where a man slipped a photo of his daughter into his cigarette pack to remind himself why he wanted to quit smoking. Each reminder reinforces commitment.
- **Use digital assistants.** Leverage calendar tools, task managers, and AI assistants to schedule work, track progress, and set reminders. You could even use a passphrase when logging into your computer to prompt you to work on your plan.
- **Gamify your plan.** Break your Leadership Development Plan into smaller, achievable goals that build toward

your end state. Celebrate each win. Competition—whether with yourself or peers—can be a powerful motivator.

- **Socialize your plan.** Share your plan with others. Invite your personal board of advisors to critique it. Engage peers and team members to support you. Success is more sustainable when others are invested in it.
- **Digitize your experience.** Use apps, dashboards, and online communities to track progress and curate best practices. The more you automate, the less this feels like extra work.

BRING OTHERS ALONG

When you watch an award show, recipients often thank mentors, coaches, and advocates. Most of us can identify people who played a critical role in our personal and professional development: I can name individuals at every stage of my life who shaped, challenged, and advocated for me.

You will encounter three types of people who can help you on your career journey:

1. *Mentors* share wisdom to guide you through a particular stage
2. *Coaches* observe performance, provide feedback, and challenge you to improve
3. *Advocates* "pound the table" on your behalf for opportunities and advancement

Once, while delivering a program on mentoring and coaching at a college campus, a student asked, "How do I ask someone to be my mentor or advocate? I don't have anything to offer in return."

That belief is incorrect.

Students and early career professionals often have assigned teachers, counselors, onboarding buddies, supervisors, and HR partners. These connections are included in tuition or employment, and offer key opportunities to gain practical experience.

The more time you spend in mentoring relationships, the better you will become at:

- Recognizing when you need support
- Identifying who would be a good mentor or coach
- Asking for developmental relationships
- Understanding which mentoring styles work for you
- Maximizing the value of these relationships

You *do* have something to offer. Mentors, coaches, and advocates benefit from you as well:

- These roles are often part of their leadership expectations and performance criteria.
- You bring fresh perspectives that diversify their thinking.
- Over time, you can contribute directly to their priorities and passion projects.

That said, you cannot simply ask someone to be your mentor or advocate out of the blue, just as you would not ask someone to marry you upon first meeting. These relationships develop through exploration. A leader once described this process as starting with *mentoring moments*: conversations that feel right. They are followed by repeated interactions and, eventually, a formalized relationship.

Like any relationship, mentoring, coaching, and advocacy do not sustain themselves. You get out of them what you put in. I believe the person seeking the relationship should drive it. You should be setting meetings, defining agendas, and following through. Those behaviors signal commitment and motivate others to invest in you.

If you are unsure how to do this, ask directly: "How have successful mentoring relationships like this worked for you?"

How to Leverage Each Role

One person may play all three roles, or several people may play in each category. Diversity matters. You need supporters, truth-tellers, and challengers.

Mentor, coach, and advocate relationships can also have an end. When goals are achieved, it is healthy to close the chapter, express gratitude, and pay it forward. Ask for recommendations for your next developmental stage.

Role	Actions
Mentor	• Ask for recommendations on goals and activities. • Seek insight on success metric.s • Request perspective on critical success factors.
Coach	• Ask for feedback on performance. • Review goals and development plans. • Schedule coaching conversations to track progress.
Advocate	• Ask for opportunities to prove yourself. • Request support in advancing your goals.

Most mature organizations have a board of advisors. Successful leaders do the same. Your personal aoard of advisors should include people who encourage you *and* people who challenge you. As your career evolves, so should this board.

VOICE OF EXPERIENCE

You need to build a *deliberately diverse network.* Build a network that forces you to engage with people who do not always agree with you or see the world the way you do.

When I coached women early in my career, I often encouraged them to include other women as mentors because I am limited by my male perspective. I remember once telling someone that when I walk through an unsafe neighborhood, I smile and make eye contact with people. A woman immediately told me that this was the *worst* advice for women, because eye contact can invite unwanted attention or danger. That moment was a wake-up call. I realized I had never evaluated my advice through a woman's lived experience of a woman. From that point on, I became much more intentional about seeking perspectives different from my own, because every person's advice is shaped and limited by their experiences.

I have been fortunate to work with and be mentored by people from many different walks of life. I actively absorb their wisdom. When I became involved in affinity groups, such as Ascend

Global Leadership, I recognized something equally important: there is real value in learning from people who *look like you, sound like you, and may share similar experiences.* In my case, I learned from accomplished Asian American executives who had broken through the "bamboo ceiling." I also learned from leaders with very different journeys and identities. Together, those perspectives helped me see both common patterns and meaningful differences.

This diversity of input has made me a better thinker and a better leader. When I "workshop" ideas with people from different backgrounds, I receive a wider range of reactions and sharper feedback. Their diverse perspectives and feedback help me refine my thinking and improve my decisions.

There is comfort in numbers. But there is also strength in *allyship.* I have intentionally built a professional network across differences to expand the pool of advice, wisdom, and lived experience I can learn from and synthesize.

JOURNAL ACTIVITY: FIND YOUR YODA

> *"A single conversation with a wise person is worth a month's study of books."*

- Review your leadership development plan.
- Identify a person—or type of person—you may need as a *mentor, coach,* and *advocate* for each of your career goals.
- Set up informal "mentor moments" until a relationship naturally forms.
- Once a formal relationship is established, update your career roadmap to include mentoring, coaching, and advocacy activities.

Examples of How to Leverage Each Role

Goal	Mentor	Coach	Advocate
Promotion	Gain insight into promotion success criteria	Receive feedback on readiness, performance, and behaviors	Advocate for promotion opportunities
Improve public speaking	Suggest ways to improve	Provide feedback on delivery and presence	Help identify speaking opportunities
Increase network	Recommend people to connect with	Provide feedback on networking approach	Make introductions within their network

Reflection Questions

- Who did you choose and why?
- How will you approach this person and ask them to be your Yoda?
- Why do you think this person will keep you honest and help you progress through your development roadmap?

Bottom line: By bringing others along on your leadership and career journey, you gain access to their experience, benefit from their energy and feedback, and create accountability for yourself to follow through.

DRUCKER'S FIVE QUESTIONS

Peter Drucker, a seminal thinker in modern management, famously distilled his consulting advice into five deceptively simple questions:

- What is your mission?
- Who is your customer?
- What does your customer value?
- What results do you seek?
- What is your plan?

Up to this point, your Amasian journey has focused on *introspection* to understand who you are, what shapes you, and how you show up as a leader. This chapter begins to turn that introspection into *intentional action*. Drucker's five questions provide a powerful framework to bridge self-awareness and execution. The final question illustrates how important it is that your plan aligns with the responses to the questions that came before it.

These questions are not meant to be answered once and forgotten. Revisit them at the start of your journey and at key milestones along the way. They help you re-center your purpose, test your alignment, and ensure that your actions remain grounded in what truly matters.

An Amasian leader knows why they want to lead—and why others should choose to follow.

THE AAPI LENS

For many AAPI professionals, the idea of "planning your journey" can feel uncomfortable or even presumptuous. Cultural conditioning may emphasize humility, patience, deference to authority, and trust that hard work will eventually be recognized. This chapter challenges that assumption, not by rejecting those values, but by reframing how they are applied.

Planning is not arrogance. Advocacy is not selfishness. Visibility is not disrespect.

Understanding the game, defining success, articulating ambition, and building a roadmap are acts of responsibility not only to yourself, but to those who depend on your leadership. For AAPI professionals, this chapter invites a shift from *hoping the system will notice* to *intentionally navigating the system*. Do this while remaining grounded in discipline, collectivism, and long-term thinking.

The Amasian advantage is not abandoning Eastern values to succeed in Western systems, but *using clarity, preparation, and strategy to ensure those values translate into impact, influence, and opportunity*.

THE CAREER STAGE LENS

This chapter is intentionally comprehensive because the "game" is multi-layered. Do not try to master everything at once. Use your career stage to *skim with purpose*, pick *one priority*, and take *one first step*.

Early Career/Individual Contributor

- **Your priority:** Stop guessing what success looks like.
- **Skim these sections:** *Know the Game; Define Success; Know Where to Look; Find Your Yoda*
- **Do first (one move):** Complete *"What Game Are You Playing?"* and identify *one metric* your manager cares about this quarter.

Mid-Career/Manager or Senior Individual Contributor

- **Your priority:** Convert strong performance into promotion readiness.
- **Skim these sections:** *How Success Scales by Role; Write Your Performance Review; SMART Career Goals; Draw a Roadmap; Plan the Work, Work the Plan*
- **Do first (one move):** Write a *one-page draft performance review* mapped to *next-level criteria*, then validate it with a trusted peer/mentor.

Senior Leader/Executive

- **Your priority:** Stewardship—build clarity, alignment, and systems that help others win ethically.
- **Skim these sections:** *Define Leadership; The Long Game; Maturity Model; Bring Others Along; Drucker's Five Questions*
- **Do first (one move):** Answer Drucker's Five Questions for your team, and identify *one system* to strengthen (metrics, talent pipeline, process, or customer value).

Career Transitions (Plateaus, Pivots, Recalibration)

- **Your priority:** Restore agency with structure—one clear direction, one small win.
- **Skim these sections:** *Study the Game; Art of the Possible; SMART Career Goals; Curb Your Enthusiasm; Plan the Work, Work the Plan*
- **Do first (one move):** Choose *one 30-day action* that produces a visible signal of direction (project, credential, portfolio artifact, or targeted networking sequence).

Bottom line: You are not behind. You are building a system. Pick your box. Take one step. Repeat at a pace you can sustain.

CHAPTER SUMMARY

Know the game you are playing when trying to succeed in Western corporate culture. If this chapter feels dense, that is by design. Career strategy is multi-variable: the game, the metrics, the roadmap, the people, and the habits all matter. You are not expected to do everything at once. If you feel overwhelmed, use this simple sequence:

1. **Clarify the game.** Define how success is measured in your role.
2. **Identify one gap.** What the next level requires that you are not consistently demonstrating yet.
   Pick one move. One development action you can complete in the next 30 days.

   Then repeat. Small, consistent moves compound faster than occasional bursts of effort. Your pace should be sustainable, but your direction should be intentional.

Key takeaways:

- Research and understand how success is defined for your role.
- Research and understand how your potential is defined in your organization.
- Research and understand how leadership is defined in your organization.

- Research and understand how other organizations define leadership.
- Perform a gap analysis of your performance and leadership.
- Create an ambition for your leadership development plan.
- Draw a roadmap of activities to close your performance and leadership gaps.
- Identify others that can challenge, coach, and mentor you through this plan.

JOURNAL ACTIVITY: PUTTING IT ALL TOGETHER

- Revisit and refine your leadership purpose statement.
- Revisit and refine your goals and objectives to ensure. alignment with your purpose and your company's strategic goals.
- Revisit and refine your roadmap, and ensure you have milestones with actions and achievements.
- Socialize the above with your personal board of advisors, designated supervisors, and mentors—adjust as needed.

DISCOVER MORE

- Competency Models
- 9-Box Model for Performance Management
- Business terms: Above or below the line; EBITA; CAGR
- Internal resources about your company and talent management
- External resources about your company, industry, and role
- Network connections that can tell you more about your company and role
- The North Star Concept
- Socratic Method
- Success factors and metrics at different career levels
- *The Infinite Game* by Simon Sinek

- Performance reviews and promotion readiness
- Leadership frameworks
- WishingOutLoud.com
- Blue Sky Planning
- Art of the Possible
- *The Imagineer Way* by the Disney Book Group
- SMART Goals
- Objectives and Key Results (OKR)
- Current State versus Future Desired State Gap Analysis
- Strategic Roadmap
- Project Management
- Maturity Models
- Board of Advisors
- Drucker's Five Questions

SO WHAT

Knowing the game gives you guideposts. Planning gives you leverage.

Study your organization's performance and leadership frameworks. Define what success looks like now and in the future. Translate ambition into SMART goals. Build a roadmap you can execute. Surround yourself with people who will challenge, coach, and advocate for you.

Hope is not a strategy. Planning is.

LOOKING AHEAD

Planning clarifies direction, but learning is what builds momentum. For many AAPI professionals, growth has always been tied to mastery: earning competence before confidence, preparation before exposure. Once the destination is clear, the work becomes deeply personal: *how you develop the capabilities required to move forward without losing yourself.* The next chapter focuses on learning and development as a strategic, lifelong practice that compounds over time and turns ambition into earned credibility.

CHAPTER 3

Be Curious and Learn

In chapter 2, you clarified the destination: how success is defined, where your gaps are, and what your roadmap requires. This chapter is about building the engine that gets you there. Curiosity is a leadership discipline. When you stay curious, you learn faster, adapt sooner, and turn your plan into progress.

Curiosity is the starting point, but the "so what" is execution: what to learn, where to learn it, and how to convert learning into better performance and leadership judgment. Do not try to absorb everything in one sitting. Skim first, circle what is most relevant to your current career stage, then pick one idea and take one action. Momentum beats overload.

"To know nothing is to know everything."

—attributed to Socrates

Have you ever worked with someone, or had someone in your life, whom you could not tell anything they did not already "know?" Or worse, someone who shuts down the moment you offer a perspective that differs from theirs? In a politically polarized climate, you will meet many people who have dug in their heels and are not open to opposing arguments. One of my favorite funny (and truthful) memes captures this perfectly: "Your political social media posts changed my mind, said no one ever." When people are closed-minded and unwilling to learn, their perspectives become narrow and limited.

The biggest mistake any leader can make is to believe, out of ego, that they know everything there is to know. While it is difficult to imagine someone saying that outright, it is much easier to recognize the more common version: trusting your own judgment without seeking to learn from others. A workplace example is a product manager who spends more time deciding what customers need than actually asking them.

We all spent years learning in academia. That experience should have set us up to learn on the job. We were encouraged to be curious from a young age. Staying curious and choosing to learn early and often are vital habits to carry throughout your career.

Here's the map: we start with the mindset, then move into how learning works (competence and adult learning), and then get practical about where leaders learn and how to turn learning into a point of view.

CURIOSITY AS A MINDSET

You may have heard the phrase, "Curiosity killed the cat." You may also know the story of Adam and Eve, where they were tempted to eat the forbidden fruit to gain knowledge. I sometimes wonder if stories like these, subtle cautionary tales, are meant to keep people from asking too many questions.

I see this dynamic at home. My kids will question my directions with a simple "why?" and I will sometimes respond impatiently, "because I said so." It is not my best parenting moment, but it is an honest example of how authority can default to control when curiosity becomes inconvenient.

And yet, *the world advances because of curiosity.* Entire economies thrive because people ask, "What if...?" Innovation and disruption begin with a question and the willingness to follow it. Without curious people who were brave enough to test their ideas, many of the advancements we now take for granted would never have happened.

Curiosity can be complicated for those of us with an Eastern cultural upbringing. In many families, children may be raised to study hard, work hard, and respect authority. In *some* traditions, hierarchy is emphasized, and curiosity *can* be interpreted as a challenge to authority. Many communities also value harmony, so change *can* feel like it risks disharmony.

Curiosity is also a leadership skill, not just a personality trait. It is the choice to *pause before you default to what you already think you know.*

That matters because our brains love efficiency. When we run on autopilot, we rely on patterns, experience, and shortcuts. This maps to the *habit loop* idea: the brain rewards efficiency because it saves energy. If we answer questions using what we already know, we conserve mental bandwidth for other demands.

Curiosity asks you to do something different. It asks you to explore deeper before you fill in the answer. Curiosity *draws on cognitive flexibility*: the ability to break from assumptions, consider alternative frames, and generate new interpretations. The good news is that the brain also rewards learning. Curiosity creates its own form of momentum when you strengthen cognitive flexibility instead of living permanently in the habit loop.

Curiosity is also a deeply rooted human spirit. We think. We wonder. We imagine. We test boundaries. We rebel against norms. Every generation, in every culture, has advanced in part because someone challenged the established way of doing things and proved there was a better way.

So why isn't everyone curious? Why do people resist change?

Because curiosity has an enemy: *complacency***.** Complacency is the desire to keep things "good enough" because change feels disruptive, inconvenient, or risky. It is the voice that says, "Leave it alone," "Don't rock the boat," or "Why make this harder than it needs to be?" Complacency keeps people comfortable, but comfort rarely produces growth.

In my own upbringing, another obstacle showed up repeatedly: 麻烦 (*máfan*), the belief that something is too cumbersome to deal with. Asking questions can feel "cumbersome" on several levels:

- You might hear an answer you do not want to hear.
- You might uncover a problem you now have to fix.
- You might discover that the work is bigger than you hoped.

Ignorance avoids those emotions and responsibilities. But it also avoids progress. Over time, complacency and máfan thinking limit results, delay growth, and increase the cost of problems you could have addressed earlier.

Entitlement can compound the problem. People who have not had to earn what they have may lack the discipline or urgency to learn and improve. And modern convenience can quietly train entitlement into the rest of us: search engines, smart devices, and now AI can create an expectation that answers should be instant. Instant answers are useful, but they can also reduce the impulse to dig deeper, challenge assumptions, or learn past the surface.

Leaders who overcome complacency, máfan thinking, and entitlement are curious, motivated, and growth-oriented. Leaders do not settle for the as-is. They live in the *what if.* Curiosity is what a growth mindset looks like in action, and we will explore it further later. They get energized by the idea of a quest. The idea of discovering new knowledge, testing new approaches, and improving outcomes. They know the first step to becoming better is to build a curious mindset, and the next is to strengthen cognitive flexibility through continuous learning and development.

Before we can become movers and shakers, we must free our minds from complacency. Curiosity is already in you. Watch infants and toddlers for a while; you will see curiosity in its purest form. The goal is not to "become" curious. The goal is to unlock it again.

THE AMASIAN WAY calls for us to break free from complacency and stay curious about what we do not yet know.

Bottom line: Curiosity is a daily choice to challenge comfort, ask better questions, and stay teachable.

LIFELONG LEARNER

You often hear people say that they are *lifelong learners*, meaning they will learn throughout their entire lives. I believe this is true to the end. We are always learning and applying what we learn. We learn basic life skills to survive. We learn academics to progress through school. We learn to perform tasks to do a job. We learn to improve to accelerate. We learn to manage and lead others as we grow in our careers. We learn to be social and fall in love. We learn to live, and we learn how to help others live. Later in life, we learn to adjust as our bodies and minds age and change.

Human beings possess the capacity to learn and adapt. I have observed my parents, as they age, consistently making adjustments in response to changes in their physical and cognitive health. Similarly, as an individual in my fifties, I have also modified my activities to align with my current physical condition. For instance, I no longer breakdance at weddings, except perhaps doing "the robot."

There are many points where we have to learn to survive, such as how to cross the street safely. There are also many points in life when we discover the joy of learning something new. I always tell the story of how my dad brought us to the beach and threw us in so we would learn how to swim. Okay, I had those inflatable wings on my arms, so I was not in danger of drowning. I naturally figured out how to move my arms and legs to swim in the ocean. Eventually, I took formal swim lessons and learned structured techniques for swimming across a pool. When I swam on a team, I learned to correct my technique to improve my speed. There is a natural high for competitive people when they see their times improve and win races.

Exceptional people are always learning. They see a lesson in every experience. Some learn to improve immediately. Others later take what they have learned and apply it elsewhere. This is a good reminder that my kids (and smart devices) are always listening and picking up "lessons" from us. So, we should not be surprised if they use certain colorful phrases when we use them around them.

Just as we learned to be "cool" at school by mimicking the behaviors of the popular kids or pop idols, at work, we learn to mimic the behaviors of top performers to improve our performance and brand. Immigrating as a child meant that I was a sponge when it came to picking up the behaviors of other kids and quickly becoming Americanized. I think my ability to acclimate to a company's or a client's corporate culture comes from the same skills I used to adapt to Western culture as a kid.

Here is a simplified view of being a *lifelong learner*:

- As kids, we learn to survive—breathe, eat, drink, behave socially, etc.
- As adults, we learn to perform, manage, nurture, and lead.
- As retirees, we learn to live happily ever after.

Bottom line: Lifelong learning is about building capability through reps, reflection, and better questions.

VOICE OF EXPERIENCE

In business, there is a phrase: "Always be selling." Selling is the process of helping a buyer decide emotionally and rationally to buy something. A salesperson needs to connect the product or service to what the buyer values.

Transactional salespeople are essentially order takers. The buyer tells them what they want, and the salesperson processes the transaction. The salesperson is not curious, so the transaction stays limited to what was ordered.

A good-to-great salesperson asks questions to discover what the buyer values and then connects the offering to that value. Much has been written about the questions salespeople should ask to understand what motivates a purchase. A better understanding of the buyer's value proposition often results in a bigger sale or a loyal customer.

When I worked as a representative in a call center, we were trained to use *open-ended questions* to gain insights from callers. Open-ended questions cannot be answered with one word, such as "yes" or "no." They invite the responder to share more. We used open-ended questions until we understood the problem the caller was trying to solve, their motivation for solving it, and what they considered a good solution. From there, we tested a solution to see if it truly met their needs.

As a line-of-business owner, I have been impressed when customer support is genuinely curious. More importantly, I have been disappointed when a representative shows no curiosity and suggests an inappropriate solution.

Consider a scenario in which a customer requests menu recommendations from a restaurant server. If the server immediately suggests only the most popular or highest-priced dishes, the credibility of such recommendations may be questioned. In contrast, if the server begins by asking about dietary restrictions, preferences, taste profile, and the customer's objectives for the meal, and then provides one or two tailored suggestions that align with the information provided, patrons are generally more inclined to trust and value the recommendations.

The same applies to selling products or services as a business. Are you curious enough about your client's goals, time horizon, and preferences? Do you know whether other parts of the organization have similar needs? Do you know whether you are unseating an incumbent vendor or competing in an open bid? Do you know what your client considers alternatives?

My rule of thumb is simple: *ask at least five more questions* when someone places an order. You can learn a lot from five open-ended questions. As a line-of-business owner, I was always disappointed when the sales team could not articulate win themes or loss themes. It signals a lack of curiosity, and it often explains why we either left value on the table or lost a deal.

Now, reimagine yourself as a candidate in an interview. You are selling yourself to a hiring manager. What questions would you ask to demonstrate curiosity and align your responses to what matters most? Are you curious about the company culture or team dynamics? Are you curious about why the role is vacant? What success factors and metrics are applied to the role?

As an interviewer, I am always impressed with candidates who ask strong questions and then weave those insights back into why they are a good match. If you are an internal candidate, you should be even more curious: network with people who can give you insights that help you land the role and perform quickly once you have it.

Many experts have written about powerful questions for leaders, managers, sales professionals, and interviewers. Be curious and research questions that help you gain meaningful insights.

The Amasian Way calls for us to be curious and ask at least five questions to gain insights that matter.

Bottom line: If you want better outcomes, ask better questions because what you learn changes what you can sell, solve, and lead.

LEARNING AND DEVELOPMENT

Curiosity leads to learning. We learn to satiate our curiosity. As employees, we learn to perform as individual contributors. As managers, we learn to manage and elevate talent. As leaders, we learn to drive action and improve results.

We spend our entire lives learning. Our early childhood education is meant to cultivate curiosity and teach us how to learn. I said to my son and daughter in fourth grade, "You are unlikely to recall all these States and Capitals years from now. But your effort is critical because it teaches you how to learn through association, memorization, and repetition." As they began solving math word problems, they learned systems thinking by breaking problems down and translating them into equations. As they experimented with water droplets in the sun, they learned to approach problem-solving with the Scientific Method. Writing reports taught them to research and synthesize information into a point of view. As adults, we return to these same learning muscles repeatedly to solve problems at work.

There are fundamental principles of learning and development that can help you understand your habits and improve how you learn. *And before we talk about where leaders learn, we need a shared language for what learning feels like, especially when it feels awkward, slow, or uncomfortable.* If you can name what you're experiencing, you stop personalizing the discomfort. You realize instead of failing, you are learning.

UNCONSCIOUS INCOMPETENCE TO UNCONSCIOUS COMPETENCE

"To learn is to encounter one's ignorance."

—Chinese Proverb

You have likely forgotten how you learned to use a toothbrush. As a father, I remember watching my children attempt to brush their teeth with great interest. First, they knew nothing about brushing teeth. This is *unconscious incompetence*: "I don't know what I don't know." Then we told them about brushing their teeth. This is *conscious incompetence*: "I know I should do it, but I don't know how." With training and practice, they improved. This is *conscious competence*: "I know what I'm doing, and I can do it well." Eventually, they brush their teeth correctly without thinking about technique. This is *unconscious competence*: "I don't think about what I know; I just do it."

Feelings of anxiety often surface during stages of unconscious incompetence and conscious incompetence. You might worry about overlooking important details simply because you weren't aware they were significant, or suddenly realize you lack the necessary skills for a task. These experiences are common when starting a new job in an unfamiliar setting or when your team adopts a new technology.

You can take comfort in the fact that your life is filled with conscious incompetence, such as learning to ride a bike, drive a car, or play a game. Eventually, you moved those incompetencies toward conscious competence and unconscious competence. They say you never forget how to ride a bicycle, which feels like one of those traumatic learning experiences where you learned by failing painfully. I know for sure that after I received a deep cleaning from the dentist, I learned to take better care of my teeth.

Unconscious competence is the result of doing something so many times that it becomes second nature. In *Outliers*, Malcolm Gladwell discusses the "10,000-hour rule." Many challenge the literal number, but the gist is clear: if you invest enough time into something, you can become highly skilled at it. Taken figuratively, it means you need to practice something many, many times before you become good at it. We all understand this from lived experience. Whether it is singing, shooting a basketball, skating, or sketching, we had to spend time learning, practicing, and developing before becoming good.

This is a critical lesson as you learn to be better at your job or a better leader. You need to commit to learning, practicing, and developing. I strongly believe there is no such thing as a "natural-born leader." Leaders are groomed over a lifetime of learning and development. No one can attend a one-week intensive course, much less watch a few videos, and expect to become a great leader overnight. We all need to learn, practice, and improve leadership skills over time.

And here is the practical implication: *If leadership is learned, then leadership can be practiced.* Learning alone without development and practice will not grow your leadership skills.

Bottom line: When your leadership learning journey feels slow, awkward, and sometimes frustratingly painful, you are in the middle of forging your competence.

VOICE OF EXPERIENCE

Many people tell me they think I'm an excellent public speaker, but I'm just decent. I know others who are much more polished. Still, I frequently talk with people about oral communication. In nearly all these discussions, I see a pattern: those who wish they had good communication skills often don't try to improve. Their fear stops them from learning and developing this valuable ability.

I tell them I've been practicing for decades. I did stage acting from age 12 through college. I competed in dramatic readings. I gave speeches at school and emceed school events. I have served as a lector at Catholic Mass since high school and have read to my congregation for over thirty years. Early in my talent development career, I served as a stand-up instructor, and I remain a volunteer faculty member today. In my career and volunteer work, I have spoken on stages and webinars around the world to audiences of different career levels. All that is to say: I didn't just get up on a stage and "pull off" public speaking. I honed my skills through thousands of hours of speaking and reading to audiences.

Several points to take away:

- Whether it was public speaking or stage acting, I had to learn techniques to be effective. I still recall learning about stage presence from my high school drama coach. I still put into practice what I learned in corporate training about building and delivering presentations.
- No one is perfect the first time they try something. But you must take the first step and then keep taking steps.
- There are many ways to develop oral communication skills: corporate training, joining a Toastmasters club, reading to children at the library, reading at church, reading meeting minutes, or introducing a speaker. The more opportunities you take to speak publicly, the more you improve.
- If you want to be good at something, practice regularly. If you want to be great at something, practice obsessively.

In my experience, at a certain career level, your peers and everyone above you are polished presenters and communicators. It is one of the skills that earns you a seat at the leadership table. It is also a skill you do not want to practice for the first time when it really matters.

The lesson extends beyond speaking. If you want to be a great leader, someone capable of making decisions and influencing others, then you should actively make decisions in everyday life and persuade others to follow you. You cannot be the "whatever you want to do" person your whole life and then one day flip a switch and become a decisive leader.

THE AMASIAN WAY calls for us to learn leadership skills and practice regularly to improve them.

Now that we have a model for *how competence is built*, let's make learning easier and faster by understanding how adults learn, because adults do not learn the same way children do.

ADULT LEARNING DESIGN PRINCIPLES

Adults learn differently from children because they have a lifetime of experiences that shape how they absorb, interpret, and apply new information. Many of us naturally try to connect something new to something we already know.

When I taught customer service representatives at a financial services firm how to help customers understand stocks, bonds, and money market instruments, I used an analogy of a three-lane highway to illustrate risk and time horizons. Every adult in the room had been on a highway. Because the analogy was familiar, they could translate technical concepts into something they already understood.

When you understand how adults learn, you can design your own learning more effectively and help others learn faster, too. Below are a few practical adult learning design principles you can apply to your own development.

Adult Learning Design Principles

Principle	Method (How to Apply It)
Relevance (What's in it for me—WIIFM)	Why am I learning this? What will I gain if I improve? What happens if I do not improve?
Build on knowledge and experience	How does this take what I already know to the next level?
Engagement	How am I actively participating and applying what I am learning?
Structure	How does what I am learning connect to the big picture? To the previous topic? To the next topic?
Autonomy	How do I create space to discover, absorb, experiment, reflect, and apply on my own?
Feedback	How will I know whether I achieved learning and performance objectives? Who will give me feedback at each step?

As a learning and development professional, I can tell you firsthand that one of the best ways to force yourself to learn something is to stop and teach it. When you design training on a topic, you are forced to think in a structured, logical way that helps you and others absorb new concepts and change behavior.

In business, you are constantly trying to change behaviors. Adult learning design is ultimately about improving performance; just knowing something new is not enough. *Behavior change* is what drives improved business outcomes. Whether you are leading change, selling products or services, or requesting budget and resources for a project, you are asking someone to change what they do. The more you understand adult instructional design, especially motivation, practice, and feedback, the better you become at achieving business goals.

Bottom line: Design your learning like a leader. Start with WIIFM, practice in small reps, and demand feedback.

Adult learning principles explain *how* you learn best. But corporate environments add another layer: the organization also decides *what* matters and how capability will be defined and measured. That is where competency and skills models come in.

COMPETENCY-BASED AND SKILLS-BASED MODELS

Organizations have changed how they describe what people need to know and be able to do, shifting from *competency models* to *skills-based models*. While both approaches support workforce development, they differ in scope and application. Ultimately, these are talent management frameworks that help Human Resources and leaders recruit, hire, develop, manage, and promote talent.

- A *skills-based model* emphasizes specific, measurable abilities required to perform tasks, such as technical proficiencies (e.g., operating machinery, coding) and transferable skills (e.g., communication, teamwork). It is often task-oriented and commonly used for job-specific training and upskilling.
- A *competency-based model* is broader. It integrates skills with knowledge, behaviors, and attributes required for

success in a role or career path. Competencies describe not only what people can do, but how they apply their capabilities across contexts, demonstrating judgment, problem-solving, adaptability, and leadership behaviors.

Both models are useful. Skills-based approaches tend to support immediate job readiness and targeted upskilling. Competency-based approaches tend to support long-term development, leadership growth, and readiness for evolving responsibilities.

As you plan your learning and development for your current and next roles, pay attention to how your organization defines them. This will help you conduct a sharper self-diagnosis and target the most strategic areas for improvement. Be intentional: focus your efforts on the capabilities that matter most *now* and *in the future.*

Bottom line: Treat learning like operations at work. Define the inputs, set the cadence, and track the changes that result.

ALWAYS BE LEARNING

Now that you understand (1) how competence is built, (2) how adults learn, and (3) how organizations define capability, we can get practical about the real question: *Where do leaders learn, and how do they stay in motion without waiting for permission?*

In sales, there is a saying: "Always be selling" (ABS). I like to think that in life and at work, we should "*Always be learning*" (ABL). When you have a curious mindset, you naturally want to learn. The practical question becomes: Where will you go to learn? Today, there are more ways to learn than ever, whether you choose to go away to learn or learn on the go.

There are two modes of learning:

1. **Go away to learn:** deeper reps, more practice, and live feedback
2. **Learn on the go:** quick hits to close a gap fast, learning in the flow of work

Most companies have strong, and often underutilized, *structured learning* available to leaders, managers, and staff. Many also offer tuition assistance or reimbursement for learning provided by external vendors. "Go-away-to-learn" programs create focused space to learn, practice, and receive feedback. Instructor-led training also gives you the added benefit of learning from expert facilitators and classmates.

However, you may not always have the time to wait for a scheduled course or the capacity to step away from work for formal training. That is where *learn-on-the-go* options can help close a knowledge or skill gap in real time. These on-demand learning options are often light, fast, and practical, quick hits designed to help you solve a specific problem.

For example, I have a blind spot when it comes to remembering how to create pivot tables in Excel. A quick video tutorial is usually all I need to get back to work. That said, these resources have limitations. I can also attest that I once tried (unsuccessfully) to fix a faucet after watching several YouTube how-to videos. I ended up soaked after the water started spraying uncontrollably.

The internet has made it possible to learn through research, crowdsourcing, and expert guidance. Generative AI puts self-directed learning on turbo boost. You can now combine multiple thought leadership sources and generate summaries, study guides, and even podcasts. Familiarize yourself with these tools and use them intentionally to support your commitment to *always be learning.*

Where curious leaders learn (and keep learning):

- Learn from your role (your metrics, your rubrics, your gaps)
- Learn from your customers (needs, pain points, what they value)
- Learn from external perspectives (market signals, trends, competitors)
- Learn from others (mentors, peers, coaches, your board of advisors)
- Learn from experience (stretch work, gigs, volunteering, reps, and failure)
- Learn from reflection (turn learning into a performance objective and a "so what")

Bottom line: The main obstacle isn't a lack of learning opportunities. It's our tendency to avoid them. ABL is effective only if you consistently opt for the challenging practice loop.

VOICE OF EXPERIENCE

Early in my career, I applied for a project manager position at a contact center. The role sounded intriguing, and I was ready to move on from my work as a phone representative. During the interview, the VP asked me to define a "critical path." I could not. I tried to fake it, but it was obvious I did not know what it meant. I learned an invaluable lesson that day: I needed to be curious, research, and prepare for interviews. You can bet your bottom dollar that, thirty years later, I know what a critical path is, and I use it regularly.

Years later, I was asked to lead a project to implement a learning management system and eLearning for the company. This was in the infancy of the eLearning industry. There was not much available in eLearning format beyond management and desktop training. I knew little to nothing about it. I bought several books on eLearning (this was the early 1990s), took a week off, and immersed myself in learning the industry and its product offerings. That effort helped me pivot and reinvent myself as a knowledgeable eLearning professional, and I have been in the industry ever since.

More recently, I did a mock interview with someone preparing for an operational role supporting exchange-traded funds (ETFs). As an investor, I only had a definitional understanding of ETFs. Before the mock interview, I used generative AI to help me develop interview questions appropriate for ETF operations and a way to evaluate the interviewee's responses. It helped me show up as a more credible mock interviewer and gave the interviewee a better opportunity to demonstrate their technical understanding of a role I knew little about.

I have had countless meetings where I was invited into discussions that required preparation. I would research just enough to have a point of view and contribute meaningfully. Given today's generative AI capabilities, there should be no excuse for arriving at a meeting or discussion unprepared. You can use prompts to anticipate the applicability, potential needs, and wants of key stakeholders, and to prepare your own agenda for conversations on topics unfamiliar to you.

The lesson to take away is to use every resource available to satisfy your curiosity, learn, and improve your abilities. Use them to help you prepare for meetings, show up ready, research in the moment, and dig deeper after.

The Amasian Way calls for us to use resources at our disposal to go away to learn and to learn on the go.

JOURNAL ACTIVITY: Prepare for Your Next Role

Step 1. Identify the role.

- Identify a role you are interested in applying for (internally or externally).

Step 2. Study the role requirements.

- Review the job description, role responsibilities, and qualifications.

Step 3. Generate interview questions.

- Use generative AI to create a set of interview questions aligned to the role.

Step 4. Diagnose your gaps.

- Use generative AI to identify gaps in your responses and suggest areas to strengthen.

Reflection Questions

- What prompts did you use? How could you refine them to improve the quality of the questions and gap analysis?

- What gaps did you identify that you may need to close to become a stronger candidate?
- What other methods (besides generative AI) could you use to prepare in a similar way?

If ABL is your learning engine, the next sections are your learning inputs. Leaders do not just learn more, they learn better, from better sources, and they turn learning into action.

LEARNING TO DO NEW, DIFFERENT THINGS

Once we have achieved *unconscious competence*, we develop a natural preference for a steady state. We like doing what we already know how to do well. We often resist trying something different because it pulls us out of our comfort zone. There are neuroscience explanations for this: our brains crave efficiency and avoid overthinking. So, once we have learned to do something well, our instinct is to do it faster and more efficiently.

But the norm can keep us stagnant. Stagnation fuels complacency, and complacency is the enemy of innovation.

Most meaningful human advancement comes from someone breaking the norm and trying something different. That is why leaders must periodically move from *unconscious competence* back to *conscious incompetence*, essentially choosing to be a beginner again on purpose. You move past the dopamine of steady-state mastery and choose the reward of the unknown: the anticipation of discovery, the impact of better-than-expected results, and the novelty of learning something new. You learn to question the norm, reimagine the process, and stop defaulting to an approach simply because "we have always done it that way."

You may have heard the phrase, "You can't teach an old dog new tricks." The reality is that with age, we constantly adjust because our physical and mental capabilities change. When you were younger, you may have chosen activities that were more physically demanding or risky. As you get older, you adapt. You learn new limits and new realities. Even the norms you grew up with can change when you move to a new school, join a new community, or enter a new workplace culture.

Learning to be different is also a business imperative. Innovation and disruption are not about tinkering with the current state. They are about solving the same problem in a fundamentally different way. Traditional automobile manufacturers struggled to catch up to Tesla's early progress in producing electric vehicles profitably in part because they were unwilling to let go of legacy manufacturing and supply chain assumptions. Tesla did not treat traditional methods as sacred cows. In one annual meeting, an engineer shared that Toyota had complimented Tesla's manufacturing methods. While that was high praise, Tesla engineers were already focused on what to change next. They were already challenging their own norms and reinventing their methods.

If you study the top thirty companies in the Dow Jones Industrial Average (DJIA), you will see that the list has changed significantly over the past twenty-five years. Companies that fail to learn and reinvent get left behind by those that do. The principle is blunt: innovate or die. Learning to do something new or different is essential to survival.

You have to be clear about the "so what" that motivates you to learn something new and different, and that "so what" needs to translate into motivation for others to follow you. While survival constitutes a strong justification, it is necessary to provide additional well-founded reasons that resonate on both rational and emotional levels.

Bottom line: Reinvention requires you to volunteer to be a beginner again before disruption forces you to.

Holding Space for Test and Learn

Adopting a mindset focused on acquiring new skills and knowledge is essential for professional and leadership development. Fostering an environment that encourages experimentation and iterative improvement contributes to a dynamic workplace culture. Contemporary organizations increasingly prioritize adaptability, recognizing that waiting for perfected solutions can hinder progress.

Numerous studies have highlighted the role of ongoing learning in promoting individual and organizational growth. By nurturing curiosity and engaging in consistent skill development, professionals can navigate change effectively. Learning often involves implementing novel strategies and evaluating their outcomes, which requires accepting potential setbacks as valuable opportunities for improvement rather than perceiving them solely as failures.

Agile project management and design thinking both encourage an iterative *test-and-learn* mentality. "Perfect is the enemy of good when good is good enough" is a mantra often used to explain why software is launched in versions and improved over time. When working in these environments, leaders must hold space and create a sense of psychological safety for themselves and others to test, learn, and adjust.

For example, you can ensure every project ends with a retrospective where the team discusses lessons learned and commits to specific actions. Invite open discussion about what went well and what could have gone better. Encourage the team to stay open, receptive, and less judgmental, especially when the truth is uncomfortable.

There's an old dad joke: "Two guys walked into a bar. Which is stupid, because the second guy should've avoided it after seeing the first guy walk into it." The point is simple: when we learn from failures, we learn not to repeat our own mistakes or those of others.

For many AAPI professionals, this can be especially hard. Some of us grew up in environments where failure was frowned upon, and the pressure to be perfect was overwhelming. This is something we must balance. If you do not allow yourself to test, fail, and learn, you will either never start (because you fear failure) or you will move too slowly trying to be perfect. Allow yourself to fail if you are willing to learn, adjust, and improve. One way to help us overcome this challenge is to plan for failure as part of our risk management. This helps us to feel empowered to learn from failure.

Today's technology and business landscape has embraced iteration. Teams and projects are organized to be agile and to learn as they go. That transparency can cause traditionalists heartburn because they are accustomed to seeing only the final product, not the messy middle. It can feel like watching a game show where contestants are encouraged to think out loud. The leadership move is to set expectations clearly: if you are in test-and-learn mode, name it so others do not mistake iteration for incompetence. *Then make the "so what" explicit and take the next step because momentum is built by moving, not by waiting.*

Bottom line: Learning by experimenting, measuring the result, and committing to the next step.

LEARN FROM EXTERNAL PERSPECTIVES

There is nothing more frustrating than telling my parents something only to have them dismiss it, then hearing them accept the exact same point when it comes from someone outside the family. No matter what I have achieved in my life, education, or career, it simply lands differently when it comes from an external voice. If nothing else, this conditioned me to value external perspectives.

In business, it is common to improve your understanding of your position by looking at both internal and external forces. The *Strengths, Weaknesses, Opportunities, and Threats* (SWOT) analysis has long been a go-to tool for this purpose. By reviewing the forces that support you and the forces that work against you, you can learn what matters and plan actions to improve your position. There are many alternatives to SWOT that drive similar insight. The point is not the framework. It is about getting into the habit of studying external factors, such as competition, the market, and customers, to reveal insights that should shape your decisions.

A recent example from the AI market illustrates why external perspectives matter. In early 2025, many observers believed they understood the near-term direction of the AI industry and placed heavy confidence in specific winners. Then, new viable foreign entrants entered out of nowhere with new claims, quickly shifting assumptions. Whether or not you followed the details, the lesson is the same: the market changes fast, and certainty is fragile. The faster the world changes, especially with emerging technologies, the more important it is to widen your lens.

It is always better to disrupt than be disrupted.

I have found it useful to subscribe to trade magazines, join professional groups on social media, and occasionally join free webinars or attend trade conferences. These activities help me absorb external benchmarks, emerging trends, and leading practices without overcomplicating the effort.

As a leader, you cannot stay heads-down and assume your organization's internal perspective is the only one that matters. You need to stay current on market and industry trends. More importantly, you need to understand what your competition is doing or not doing. You also need to evolve your vernacular to include terms and concepts that are shaping the conversation. The alternative is becoming irrelevant or obsolete.

VOICE OF EXPERIENCE

I recently challenged my team to reimagine our online learning experiences to better align with today's digital learner expectations and preferences. As a twenty-five+ year eLearning professional who helped companies move training from classrooms to online self-study, I was accustomed to producing interactive, one-hour learning modules.

A few years ago, I attended a conference where a learning expert spoke about the challenge of designing for what she called the "TikTok generation." She cited a widely repeated claim that Gen Z attention spans are extremely short, on the order of seconds, and argued that if we do not capture attention almost immediately, we lose the learner. She also contrasted this with Millennials, often described as having slightly longer, but still shrinking, attention spans.

Whether you agree with the exact number of seconds, the "so what" staring me in the face was that my default design assumptions were outdated. I had been directing our team to produce the same one-hour module format that defined early eLearning. In that moment, I realized we needed to reimagine learning design through the eyes of the incoming workforce and their digital expectations.

We needed to keep asking ourselves whether we captured their attention quickly enough and to keep engaging them in rapid succession to maintain it while they learn. That required curiosity, humility, and a willingness to change, not defensiveness, nostalgia, or the claim that "this is how we've always done it." It required me to recruit a diversification of thinking from traditionalists who have never been exposed to short video formats such as TikTok, Facebook Reels, or YouTube Shorts.

The Amasian Way is about being curious, always learning from internal and external resources, and being willing to move and change.

Bottom line: External perspectives can unlock new ideas that fuel your momentum forward.

LEARN FROM YOUR CUSTOMERS

Trends tell you what's moving. Customers tell you what matters. You must be curious about your customers to meet them where they are and give them what they need. Most business leaders understand, at least conceptually, that customers matter. What is less common is the discipline to consistently learn *from* customers rather than merely learn *about* them.

A simple way to remember this is through the shift from the *Golden Rule* to what some call the *New Golden Rule*. The traditional Golden Rule says, "Treat others the way you want to be treated." In customer experience and leadership contexts, the New Golden Rule reframes this as: "Treat others the way they want to be treated." The "so what" is straightforward: customers do not value what you value; they value what they value. If you want loyalty, adoption, and impact, you must understand their motivations, expectations, and constraints, then learn what customers need and want.

I have been guilty of the most common customer mistake: assuming we know what customers need without asking them. We sit in fancy whiteboard-covered meeting rooms writing sticky notes after sticky notes about "the customer," instead of bringing the customer into the conversation. Another frequent violation is the hammer-and-nail problem: "When you have a hammer, everything looks like a nail." In other words, we use our solution and force-fit it to everyone's problems in general rather than taking the time to tailor it to our customers' specific needs.

Of course, customers do not always articulate their problems or potential solutions well. People who have only ridden in a horse-drawn buggy would not be able to describe an internal combustion engine. Apple's Newton (the original handheld device) failed, but its lessons informed what came later. The point is not to follow customer input blindly. It is to listen deeply and then apply good judgment. Strong teams combine customer insight with design thinking to solve the right problem, even if they deliver the solution differently from how customers initially described it.

Business history is full of cautionary tales in which organizations failed to learn from customers or the local context, resulting in avoidable failures. Whether the story is about language, living space constraints, or cultural norms, the lesson is the same: assumptions scale poorly.

This is also personal for me. In roles where I am not regularly customer-facing, I have to be intentional about staying connected to the customer voice. That means finding opportunities to join customer conversations, partnering with internal, external-facing teams, and positioning myself strategically and transactionally to observe and learn from both high-impact customers and everyday users.

As a leader, your responsibility is to build a customer-centric culture where curiosity is the norm. Instead of designing processes that are easiest for the company, challenge your teams to design processes that are easiest for the customer. Keep talking to clients. Keep collecting feedback. And keep asking whether the customer's needs have shifted, because they will.

Bottom line: Learning from your customers will help you deliver products and solutions that they will actually use and benefit from.

LEARN FROM OTHERS

Customers are one source of truth. Your network is another. There are many ways to learn from others. If you stay curious and do the work to engage them, then you will benefit from a diversity of thoughts and perspectives. Here are a few high-leverage channels.

- **Personal Board of Advisors.** Just as you can learn from customers, you can learn from mentors, coaches, advocates, and your personal board of advisors. When you socialize what you are learning with them, you gain perspective, pattern recognition, and practical advice for going deeper. You also signal something important, namely, you are someone who learns and processes. That is a brand they will add to your advocacy description.
- **Crowdsourcing.** In collaborative environments, teams get smarter when each person contributes to learning. Externally, communities (including online forums) can help you pressure-test ideas, compare experiences, and identify what you may not have considered. Crowd-sourcing does not replace expertise, but it can quickly expose blind spots.
- **Feedback and Coaching.** The hardest lessons often come through constructive feedback. It bruises the ego. It stings. But if you are not curious about your performance and not willing to learn from feedback, you will not improve. Seek feedback periodically from supervisors, peers, direct reports, and customers. Challenge yourself to receive it without defensiveness, translate it into action, and follow through.
- **Direct Reports, Coachees, and Mentees**. You can also learn "down and across," not just "up." I have

gained tremendous insights into the future workforce by paying close attention to the people I manage and mentor. Humans are social learners. Our ability to learn from one another is a privilege and one of the most underutilized advantages in any career.

Bottom line: Curiosity scales through people. Your network is how you borrow the experience you haven't lived yet.

LEARN FROM EXPERIENCES

Advice accelerates you. Reps transform you. I often advise early-career professionals to take full advantage of the learning available in their current jobs. When I was a call center representative right out of college, I could not wait to be promoted. Later, as a manager at a consulting firm, I felt the same impatience. What I did not fully appreciate at the time was how much those roles were shaping my skills and how those skills compounded into future opportunities.

As a call-center representative, I strengthened my oral communication skills by speaking with customers at an average of one hundred calls per day for three years. I learned empathy and needs-based sales techniques, how to listen for what a customer actually values, and guide them to the right solution.

As a consulting manager, I learned project management fundamentals that later prepared me to lead larger, more complex multi-million-dollar programs. I also learned how to build and pitch proposals. They became skills foundational in the business development roles I held.

One of my most treasured learning experiences was working at a start-up for four years. I learned the mechanics of running a business by rolling up my sleeves and doing what needed to be done. When you are clawing for every sale to keep the business alive, you develop conviction, urgency, and a commitment to continuous improvement. Start-up life forces learning because the margin for complacency is thin.

Another learning channel people often overlook is gigs, especially volunteering ones. In today's gig economy, there are countless opportunities to try something new, test yourself, and grow from it. You may bring your experience to a volunteer role, but you will also gain new skills that transfer directly to your work.

Here are a few skills you might build through volunteering:

- Working for a leader with a different style than yours
- Navigating ambiguity when direction is limited
- Being resourceful doing more with less
- Training others to do work you already know well
- Strengthening emotional intelligence by working with different types of people

VOICE OF EXPERIENCE

I am a strong advocate for leveraging volunteer opportunities to build work-relevant skills. Most people talk about volunteering as "giving back," but they do not highlight how often volunteering becomes a leadership laboratory.

I remember doing poorly in a consulting firm training where we role-played with C-suite executive actors. I believe my cultural upbringing played a role. I put executives on a pedestal and became starstruck in their presence. I was disappointed in my performance, and I knew it likely raised doubts about my ability to communicate and consult at the senior level.

Around the same time, I was serving as president of the New England Chapter of Ascend. That role forced me to practice executive presence, decision-making, networking, and relationship-building regularly. It gave me repeated opportunities to "face off" with senior executives and apply what I was learning in real time.

That experience also strengthened a core belief that shapes how I lead today: leadership is about making decisions and moving forward. Early-career professionals and middle managers often defer decisions to their superiors. Once you are a leader, your senior leaders or board are less likely to know how to do your job better than you do. Their role is not to tell you what to do. Their role is to support or challenge your decisions. You must make sound decisions using disciplined decision-making frameworks that you can clearly explain and defend.

Today, I channel what I gained from that volunteer experience to build executive relationships and lead my line of business at work.

I also continue volunteering in board roles to strengthen my senior leadership acumen. The governance and strategy exposure I gain there continues to compound and advance my leadership capabilities at work.

Lastly, and most importantly, do not miss the opportunity to learn from failure. The most talented people I have met are grateful for the failures that taught them how to win. Some failures are harder to recover from than others, but we have been getting back up our whole lives. The worst failures are not the ones that happen. The worst failures are when we give up, play the victim, or repeat the same mistake because we refused to learn. Failing in volunteering roles is often less damaging and more forgivable, but the lessons learned are still very impactful.

Bottom line: Experienced lessons are often the lessons that you retain forever. Seek experiences where you will learn and learn from every experience you gain.

COMING UP WITH A "SO WHAT?"

Learning that does not change performance is just consumption. Do you know anyone who loves to learn, is constantly taking classes, earning degrees, and collecting certificates, and yet never seems to *do* anything different because of what they learned? Curiosity is valuable, but in the workplace, curiosity has to lead somewhere. Learning that does not translate into performance is just consumption.

In *Performance Consulting*, Dana Gaines Robinson and colleagues emphasize that learning should result in a *performance objective*. In other words, what you learn at work should improve your, your team's, or your organization's performance.

Of course, you can learn purely for enjoyment or personal satisfaction, like picking up conversational Japanese for a trip to Tokyo. But when learning is tied to your career, you should be able to point to the measurable "after" picture. If you invest time in improving time management, you should see increased productivity and output. If you learn Photoshop, you should apply it to improve the quality, speed, or creativity of work products.

Here is the core principle: *Curiosity should produce a performance objective, and that objective should lead to measurable improvement.*

Examples: Turning Curiosity into Performance Objectives

Curiosity	Performance Objective
Performance metrics for my role	Meet or exceed performance metrics
SWOT analysis	Improve organizational performance
Business Model Canvas	Visualize and improve the business model
Competitive analysis	Improve competitive advantages
Emerging industry trends	Stay relevant; innovate
Customer insights	Improve customer impact
Total addressable market	Size the opportunity for a product or service
Urgency for change	Achieve change goals on time
System release notes	Leverage updates to improve work
Budget to actuals	Improve budgeting discipline or sales execution
360-degree feedback	Improve how others experience me
Win/loss themes	Improve win rate
Business case development	Inform investment decisions
Emotional intelligence	Improve relationships and loyalty

PERFORMANCE OBJECTIVE IS NOT ENOUGH: LEADERS NEED A POINT OF VIEW

Beyond performance objectives, leaders must also synthesize what they learn into a *point of view—the "so what."* People do not look to leaders for information alone. They look to leaders for interpretation and direction. Knowing is not the same as leading.

A leader's perspective provides a foundation for informed decision-making and strategic actions. For instance, leaders may examine how organizations within their sector leverage generative AI to obtain a competitive edge. Rather than merely gathering examples, effective leaders systematically assess available information, develop a well-founded point of view, identify opportunities and risks, formulate recommendations, and translate these insights into actionable business cases and implementation plans.

Bottom line: The "so what" is the bridge from learning to leadership. A well-formed point of view sets direction, drives action, and delivers key results.

THE AMASIAN WAY calls leaders to synthesize what they have learned into a point of view, the proverbial "so what."

THE AAPI LENS

For many AAPI professionals, curiosity can feel risky, especially when curiosity looks like questioning authority, challenging the norm, or "making things awkward." Cultural conditioning may emphasize harmony, humility, respect for hierarchy, and the belief that good work should speak for itself. In practice, that can train us to stay quiet, agreeable, and within the lines.

This chapter challenges that default by reframing how those values are applied.

Curiosity is not a sign of disrespect. Asking questions is not inherently confrontational. Learning out loud is not incompetence. Being curious about your role, your customers, your market, your blind spots, and your own development is an act of responsibility. It is how you prevent avoidable mistakes, break through complacency, and stay relevant as the world changes.

The Amasian advantage is not abandoning Eastern values to succeed in Western systems. It is using discipline, humility, and long-term thinking to fuel a stronger habit: *ask*, *learn*, *synthesize*, and *move*. You do not need to be loud to be curious. But you do need to be intentional.

THE CAREER STAGE LENS

Early Career/Individual Contributor

- **Your priority:** Stop guessing. Build your learning engine.
- **Skim these sections:** Unconscious Incompetence → Unconscious Competence; Adult Learning Design Principles; Always Be Learning; Learn from Your Role (metrics/rubrics/gaps).
- **Do first (one move):** Ask your manager *five questions* to clarify what "great" looks like this quarter (metrics, behaviors, examples), then choose *one skill* to practice for thirty days.

Mid-Career/Manager or Senior Individual Contributor

- **Your priority:** Turn competence into versatility and versatility into readiness.
- **Skim these sections:** Adult Learning Design Principles; Competency-Based vs. Skills-Based Models; Learning to Be Different; Holding Space for Test and Learn; Feedback and Coaching; Coming Up with a "So What?"
- **Do first (one move):** Pick one capability you need for "next level," design a *four-week test-and-learn plan* (practice + feedback + reflection), and write a one-paragraph *point of view* on what's working and what you'll change.

Senior Leader/Executive

- **Your priority:** Stewardship: stay relevant and build a learning culture that keeps others relevant.
- **Skim these sections:** Learn from External Perspectives; Learn from Your Customers; Holding Space for Test and Learn; Performance Objective → Point of View ("So What?")
- **Do first (one move):** Create a simple leadership cadence: *one external signal, one customer insight, and one internal learning* you review monthly then translate it into one decision, one adjustment, or one experiment.

Career Transitions (Plateaus, Pivots, Recalibration)

- **Your priority:** Restore agency with structure: learn what you need, prove it fast, show evidence.
- **Skim these sections:** Always Be Learning; Prepare for Your Next Role (Journal Activity); Learn from Experiences; Coming Up with a "So What?"
- **Do first (one move):** Run a *two-week learning sprint* for your target role: gather role requirements, generate interview questions, diagnose gaps, and produce *one visible artifact* (a short POV post, a project plan, a portfolio sample, or a case write-up).

CHAPTER SUMMARY

As a learning and development professional, I have often described the journey of a *lifelong learner* as a series of "aha moments" that string together into growth and capability. The point of curiosity is not to become an information collector. The point is to become a better performer and a better leader.

This chapter is intentionally dense because learning is multilayered: how you learn, where you learn, who you learn from, and how you turn learning into results. Do not try to absorb everything at once. *Skim with purpose, choose one priority, and take one first step.* Then march forward at a pace you can sustain.

Your aha moments are not souvenirs. They are fuel. Take what you learn, turn it into a point of view, and use that point of view to drive action.

Key Takeaways

- **Develop a curious mindset to overcome complacency.** Do not settle for the norm or surface-level answers from instant-gratification learning.
- **Ask five more open-ended questions** to get to what matters (needs, motivations, constraints, and opportunities).
- When you realize what you do not know but need to know, **learn progressively and develop continuously**.
- **Understanding *how adults learn*** helps you learn faster and apply what you learn more effectively.
- **Hold space for test-and-learn.** Progress requires iteration, feedback, and adjustment.
- **Always be learning** from resources around you: your role, your customers, your network, external perspectives, and lived experience (including failure).
- **Synthesize what you learn into a point of view— "so what,"** and then translate it into a decision, a behavior change, and measurable improvement.

JOURNAL ACTIVITY: PUT IT ALL TOGETHER—BUILD YOUR LEARNING SYSTEM

This exercise is designed to turn curiosity into a repeatable learning engine—one you can use throughout your career.

Step 1. Map your learning resources.

- List the go-to channels you can use to learn (internal training, mentors, customers, industry sources, communities, books, podcasts, AI tools, stretch assignments, etc.).

Step 2. Scan the external environment.

- Search the internet or use generative AI to identify top trends affecting your industry.

Step 3. Pick one trend that matters to your role.

- Choose one trend that is most relevant to your current job or your next role.
- Identify five ways you can learn more about it (people to talk to, sources to follow, forums, courses, internal experts, etc.).

Step 4. Make it real: schedule the work.

- Set time aside in your calendar over the next five weeks to use those five resources to learn (one resource per week).

Step 5. Form your point of view and ship it.

- Write a short article or post to summarize your learning and your point of view.
- Publish it on a professional platform (e.g., LinkedIn) or share it with a trusted internal audience.

Reflection Questions

- Which resource felt most natural for you—and why?
- What would it take to make that resource easier to use again (subscribe, bookmark, join, schedule, build a habit)?
- What did you learn from the comments or feedback on your point of view?
- What is your "so what"—and what is the one action you will take next because of what you learned?

DISCOVER MORE

- Habit Loop vs. Cognitive Flexibility
- Asking powerful questions
- Conscious competence model
- *Outliers* (Malcolm Gladwell)
- Adult learning design principles
- Agile project management
- *The Only Thing That Matters* (Karl Albrecht)
- Human-centered design thinking principles
- *Performance Consulting* (Dana Gaines Robinson, James C. Robinson, Jack J. Phillips, Patricia Pulliam Phillips, Dick Handshaw)

SO WHAT

As a leader, you need to be curious and build knowledge, skills, and insight from internal and external sources. The more you learn, the better you can lead with a point of view and the more credible your decisions become.

Those who do not invest the time and effort to remain relevant and competitive will be disrupted and become obsolete. In an age of abundance, your competition (people who want your job or the job you want) has access to the same information and tools you do. The advantage goes to the ones who *do the work*: ask, learn, synthesize, and move.

Do not sleep on curiosity. *Curiosity without action is trivia.* Build your learning system, clarify the "so what," and take the next step.

LOOKING AHEAD

Curiosity is the spark. Learning is the fuel. But none of it matters if it stays in your head. The next chapter is where we turn insight into momentum. You do not need a perfect plan. You need the next step. *Show up. Make the call. Take the meeting. Do the rep. Ship the draft. Move.*

CHAPTER 4

Show Up and Move

As a parent, I constantly check myself on a simple standard: Am I showing up for what matters? We all make sacrifices, and there is always one more thing competing for attention.

I remember the night before a conference I was running. I was under heavy pressure, managing last-minute details and stepping in as a late replacement for a closing keynote. That same night, my kids wanted to go to our local church fair. I was tempted to say no. Then I looked at their faces, and I knew what the right decision was. I put the work down, took them out, and chose presence over productivity.

That moment is not unique. Parenting forces the same decision again and again. So does leadership. Showing up is not an intention. It is a choice you make when it is inconvenient, and it becomes your brand when you make it consistently.

This chapter is built around one idea: *Showing up is the entry point, but moving is the differentiator.* We will cover:

- *How to show up* in a way that builds a reputation for reliability (in-person and remote).
- *How to show up again* demonstrating follow-through and consistency, so you are associated with results.
- *How to move*: take action on the big rocks, solve problems, make decisions, and navigate ambiguity.
- *How your brand is experienced* (your "Personal NPS") and why perception becomes opportunity.

Bottom line: showing up gets you seen. Moving gets you trusted.

SHOWING UP

Showing up is the entry point to building your brand. If you are a no-show, you cannot contribute and will not be seen as reliable.

Being available, present, and ready to go are all attributes that shape how others experience your dependability.

If you're not present, it's hard for others to view you as a leader or valuable resource. I recall working at a consulting firm years ago, where it was customary to leave work just "ten minutes after the boss." There was a clear order of departure: partner first, followed by director, manager, senior associate, and finally associate. Today, workplace norms are more flexible. Some people may step out early to exercise or volunteer and then log in again later. Still, the key lesson remains: when a partner needs someone to take notes at an important meeting, the person who is available often gets the chance to participate, learn, and handle follow-up tasks. This *increased visibility can lead to more opportunities* to excel. Simply being present ensures you don't miss out.

Remote work has made this easier and harder. There are now digital signals that tell people whether you are "there" when needed. A "Do Not Disturb" status clearly signals you are not available. An "Away" status can signal that you are not immediately reachable. In a virtual meeting, being off camera and on mute can also read as not fully present, even if your intent is simply to listen. I have also seen people who use the chat well in large virtual meetings stand out and get recognized, which increases visibility. The point is to *be aware of the signals you send and intentional about them.*

Showing up is important, but being present while you are there counts just as much. When we go out to dinner, I get disappointed when my kids choose devices over engagement with the family. When I look around, I see adults doing the same thing.

People can usually tell when you are in a meeting, in person or virtual, and you are not paying attention. It creates friction and wastes time because someone has to repeat what has already been covered. A long time ago, someone told me to close my laptop and set aside my BlackBerry so I could be fully present for an important conversation. I learned then how distracting devices can be. Today, I often take notes on a laptop or device, but I make it clear to everyone that I am taking notes, not multitasking. If you are not present, then showing up and being there is still does not measure up. *Being present shows that you care and allows you to be effective in the moment.*

There is a phrase: "Showing up on time is being late." I do my best to be early and ready to go. I want people to know their time matters to me, and I want to give myself space to be mentally and physically ready. People who develop a brand of always being late often drift toward being seen as unreliable. *Timeliness can also be a signal that you are ready to contribute.*

Edward Thorndike described the "Law of Readiness," which states that a person will not learn unless they are physically, mentally, and emotionally ready to learn. *When someone is ready, they are more open to learning.* Similarly, when you are ready, you are more effective in delivering impact and growing from the experience. Mindfulness meditation is one way to prepare. Actors take quiet time to get into character before they perform. Being early and ready to go is part of the brand you want to build in your career.

How you show up also matters. Your outward appearance, your attitude, and your body language contribute to the story people tell themselves about you. I am not arguing that you must conform to every norm, but you should dress for the occasion. I just had a fun night with friends, swapping stories about trying to get our sons to help shovel snow. We traded examples of them pretending not to know we were outside shoveling, showing up with zero enthusiasm, and whining about the effort, while the "old folks" did most of the work. The lesson is simple: *If you plan to show up, then show up enthusiastically.* If you are going to show up and complain the entire time, do yourself a favor and do not show up at all.

Finally, examine why you show up. I admire people who show up because they want to, not because they need validation. I know that when I was little, much of what I did for church, whether serving as an altar boy or becoming a lector, was mostly driven by wanting to make my parents proud. Many AAPI professionals grew up similarly, doing what they did to make their parents proud. I found a deeper commitment the day I decided what I was doing was for God, for me, and for the parish community. If you show up primarily to chase approval, you can end up on a lonely road. Find a greater purpose for showing up than adoration. *Find ways to strengthen yourself and others by showing up.*

Bottom line: *Showing up is the price of admission.* If you want a brand of reliability, you have to be available, present, and ready to contribute when it counts.

VOICE OF EXPERIENCE

Showing up is often tied to confidence. I would be lying if I said I show up confidently to every event or interaction. I am highly aware of how my upbringing has influenced my self-image. My parents were often critical and seldom encouraging. This was the way they were raised, and it was how they raised me. Their intention was to push me to be better than I was. However, the resulting effect was that I never felt good enough.

So, how do I show up and appear confident? It turns out that the trick to appearing confident for me is to remind myself that I did not need confidence to show up. I just needed to show up and be in the moment. The need to feel confident was tied to my imposter syndrome. I needed to feel like I belonged at the table when I was already invited to the table, and I just needed to bring what I do well rather than compare myself with everyone else around the table.

I discovered that my need to feel confident was hindering me from opportunities because I either did not show up to events or showed up but did not stand out. Here are a few things I tell myself as affirmations when I start to feel a lack of confidence.

1. **Trust in yourself.** Reframe confidence to being comfortable in your own skin and trusting that you belong. Get comfortable with the fact that you are not perfect, you do not know everything, and you are not good at everything. Acknowledge that you were good enough to be invited, which means you belong in that situation.
2. **Don't overthink it.** I know there is a fear of embarrassment for doing something wrong in a public setting. You can learn the event's norms and navigate accordingly.

The best advice I got from my friend when he invited me backstage at a concert to hang out with the band was, "Act like you have scored a touchdown before." Clearly, he could tell I was overthinking it. But then he also gave me great tips about not asking for selfies and what to expect.

3. **I am not alone.** Others in the room are also unsure and trying to find their way. In my experience, even those who appear very confident have reasons to feel unsure.
4. **Be humble and curious.** Confidence could actually be detrimental because it can close your mind to learning from others. I have found it better to accept that I am unsure and seek to learn when I show up.
5. **Authenticity supersedes façade.** People would rather engage in authentic interactions than feel that they had a superficial one. It is more important to focus on being myself than on impressing others with my confidence.

For example, I recently met a CEO of an AI company. I knew that I had a gap in foundational understanding of AI. However, when he invited me to go out for drinks, I did not let my lack of confidence in being able to hold a conversation about what he did to hold me back from accepting his invitation. I showed up with the humility of not knowing, curiosity to learn more, and trust in my ability and experiences to contribute to our conversation. And I did not let his CEO title intimidate me. This was big because I used to be very starstruck by senior executives. He invited me. I belonged in the moment.

Confidence does have its place when advocating for points of view or in public speaking. However, it should not prevent me from showing up when opportunity knocks.

SHOW UP AGAIN

I remember being a last-minute invite to a wedding. I had been on the "B or C list." The couple were acquaintances I knew through a friend. When the groom reached out, he told me there was a last-minute cancellation on the A list and that he wanted to offer me the spot. I said I was honored and would love to go, but I asked if he was sure there wasn't someone else higher on the alternate list.

He told me he was surprised when I showed up at his bachelor party, especially since I hadn't been invited to the wedding at the time. Then he said he realized he shouldn't have been surprised at all, because even though we didn't know each other well, I consistently showed up for his friends' gatherings and always helped make them a good time.

That is the point: *Show up when it matters and make your presence count.* You need to show up when expected and when you are not. You need to show up prepared and ready to contribute. Your presence should be felt. Just showing up will not make you memorable; you have to stand out when you show up.

That can be difficult if you grew up in a household that coached you not to make waves or draw attention to yourself. You will have to find the right balance: visible enough to be remembered, grounded enough to stay authentic. *The pinnacle of showing up is being associated with a positive impact.* One company I worked for described top performance this way: "Someone who can be associated with the success of a project." In other words, when people think of that project's success, your name comes up immediately.

There are also the in-between times when you need to show up. I have sat through awkward meetings where important international delegates show up year after year, and every year the agenda feels the same because no progress has been made between meetings. If you want a reputation for leadership, *you must follow through after you show up*, so people experience you as someone who drives progress, not just someone who attends.

Consistency is one of the key factors that differentiates performance. Someone who consistently exceeds expectations is more likely to be rated higher and promoted than someone who exceeds expectations occasionally. Do not show up in a big way once and then disappear. You have to show up again for the next thing.

At the same time, avoid being overly selective about when you show up. Yes, you should *show up when it matters most.* But you do not want a reputation as someone who "only shows up for the high holidays," as my uncle used to call people who came to church only for Christmas and Easter.

THE AMASIAN WAY calls us to be visible leaders who show up again and again and consistently make a difference.

JOURNAL ACTIVITY: SHOWTIME

Think about a recent event where it was important for you to show up, such as a key team or client meeting, or a work or networking event.

- Why did you show up?
- What was your goal while you were there?
- How might you have been memorable?

Reflection Questions

- Was it easy or difficult for you to show up? Why?
- What follow-up do you need to complete because you showed up?
- How would you like to show up for the next event?

Bottom line: The leaders who get trusted and promoted are the ones who show up repeatedly, follow through between moments, and become associated with results.

BRAND AND PERSONAL NPS

If "showing up" is how you become visible, your *brand* is what people remember once you leave. Showing up gets you in the room. Your brand decides whether people want you back in the room and whether they move you into bigger rooms over time.

Personal brand is one of the most critical parts of your career. In many ways, your personal brand is how people perceive your decisions, actions, and results. Your *Personal Net Promoter Score* (NPS) is how people experience you. Net Promoter Score is a customer satisfaction metric that measures how likely someone is to recommend a product or service to someone else. Your personal NPS translates that same concept to you: *How likely is someone to recommend you for a role, a task, or a leadership opportunity?*

In marketing, brand is almost sacred. It communicates what customers should expect when they buy a product or service. There is a brand promise, whether stated explicitly or implied. A brand can convey status. People wear premium brands like Louis Vuitton or Gucci to signal taste, identity, or purchasing power. A brand can also provide peace of mind. Many people feel more confident in an audit opinion from PwC, Deloitte, EY, or KPMG because those names signal rigor. Some people associate Volvo with safety for similar reasons.

Brand damage can be costly, but not always permanent. Wells Fargo's fake accounts scandal created skepticism and customer loss, and the company has had to invest heavily to rebuild trust. More recently, brands like Bud Light have been scrutinized for taking positions that land in polarized cultural debates. Whether you agree with a company's stance or not, the lesson is clear: when brand trust is shaken, it affects consumption and loyalty.

Your professional brand works the same way. It is not just what you say your brand is. It is what people have experienced, what they believe they can count on, and what they repeat when you are not present.

For AAPI professionals, the brand challenge can be even more complicated because stereotypes often show up before we do. Many of us have been placed in the "model minority" box at work. We are often viewed as hardworking, reliable, technically strong, and not disruptive. Those assumptions can create opportunity, but they can also be career-limiting, especially when they feed the "bamboo ceiling," the perception that AAPI talent is strong at execution but not suited for leadership visibility, influence, or decision-making roles.

There have been many trailblazers who broke the mold, and many who did so by building a brand that could not be ignored. Some people became household names through mastery and presence. Others changed the game through entrepreneurship, visibility, and taking outsized risks. The point is not celebrity.

The point is agency. If you do not actively shape your brand, you may be placed into a narrative that feels "safe" to others, but small to you. In Lisa Sun's *Gravitas: The 8 Strengths That Redefine Confidence*, she talks about the importance of manifesting the way you see yourself so others can see it too.

Your personal career brand becomes the narrative about you when you are not in the room. *It shows up before you do.* Here is what that looks like in real workplaces:

- **Staffing decisions:** "Who should we put on this project or client?"
- **Stretch opportunities:** "Who can handle this with minimal supervision?"
- **Promotion calibration:** "Is this person ready for the next level?"
- **Trust moments:** "Who do I want in the room for this conversation?"
- **Visibility and sponsorship:** "Who should be invited, backed, or put forward?"

When your brand is strong, people are drawn to your promise and consider you for opportunities before you even ask. If your brand is weak, you may be passed over. Those outcomes are obvious. The less obvious risk is when you have no clear brand at all. When you are not memorable, one of two things usually happens. Either people make up a generic brand for you, such as "solid worker, dependable, keeps their head down," or you are not part of the conversation in the first place.

This is why you need to be intentional about how you show up, what people remember about you, and what they associate with you. You need to help shape your brand's narrative by advocating for your impact. I call it: *Bring your own brand, or someone else will.* I recently met a retired teacher who, as she tells me, focuses her time on telling the right stories. She emphasized the importance of owning the narrative down to the words used. She described in a documentary, *Love, Chinatown*, how the word "slum" was used to describe her neighborhood, which made it easier for the city to approve knocking it down and displacing its residents to make way for the Massachusetts Turnpike. Had the word been "neighborhood," rather than "slum," perhaps the city planners would have realized there were families thriving in those buildings they tore down.

How people experience you when you show up matters just as much as what you deliver. If the experience reinforces a strong brand, you build what marketers call brand equity. That is the premium that opens doors. Over time, you can also build brand loyalty, the desire for people to come back to you again and again for future work. Your personal NPS answers a blunt question: *Would the person who experienced you recommend you to someone else?* When your NPS is positive and your leadership brand is strong, you will be offered more opportunities. When it is negative, you may quietly disappear from high-potential conversations.

PRACTICAL WAYS TO MANAGE YOUR BRAND

- **Be authentic.** People can quickly spot fake brands and knockoffs. Your brand should be true to who you are and the impact you deliver. People who embellish often become branded for the wrong reason. I remember interviewing someone who kept using "we" in his responses. I kept asking what he personally contributed, but he could not answer. After several rounds, I began to label him as someone who borrowed credit and could not take ownership of the results.
- **Get in character.** Before entering a room, joining a meeting, or stepping on stage, I often remind myself who I want to be in that moment. This is not about being artificial. It is about being intentional. If your brand is "calm, prepared, and decisive," you should not walk into a high-stakes meeting scattered and reactive. How you show up should match the story you want people to talk about you.
- **Test and learn.** Ask for feedback. Check with your customers, peers, manager, direct reports, and mentors. Compare their perception with your ambition. The NPS

concept is a simple way to take the temperature. Ask: "If a role opened tomorrow, would you recommend me for it?" Then listen carefully to why.

- **Own your brand.** Decide how you want to be known, and advocate for the evidence. None of us performs perfectly all the time. If you falter, do damage control and take responsibility quickly. How you handle failure becomes part of your brand, too. It can be an opportunity to build a reputation for agility, humility, and resilience.
- **Evolve.** As you grow, your brand should evolve with your scope and accountability. An individual contributor brand will not fully serve you as a manager. A manager brand may not fully serve you as a senior leader. The environment also changes. For example, "collaboration" in a hybrid environment may require different habits than collaboration in a fully in-person culture. Keep your closest advocates updated on how your brand is evolving so they can sponsor the right version of you.

One caution: I am not advocating an addiction to validation or "likes and subscriptions." Social media made it easier than ever to become your own brand ambassador, and I have seen how constant feedback can become unhealthy, especially for teenagers and young adults who are still building confidence and emotional regulation. This is not about obsession. It is about ownership. Do not ignore the power of your brand, and do not let your brand consume you.

THE AMASIAN WAY calls us to actively manage the narrative of our career brand promise.

Harvey J. Coleman introduced the *Performance, Image, Exposure* (PIE) model as a career development framework in his 1996 book, *Empower Yourself: The Organizational Game Revealed.* It proposes that promotion success relies on 10 percent performance, 30 percent image, and 60 percent exposure. His concept emphasizes that visibility often matters more than hard work alone. *If 30 percent of your success truly depends on image, how strong is your brand image?*

Bottom line: Bring your own brand, or someone else will tell your story, and it may not be the way you would have wanted it told.

BUST A MOVE

Being present ensures you are included in important discussions. Proactively managing your professional brand influences how others perceive you after the conversation ends. The distinction between top performers and effective leaders lies in this principle: *Your brand promise is only as valuable as your commitment to take action.* Mere visibility without substantive contributions amounts to background noise, and a reputation unsupported by tangible achievements remains vulnerable. To leverage your brand effectively, demonstrate its value through thoughtful decisions, consistent execution, and measurable results.

One of the most common leadership qualities used to evaluate leaders and high-potential candidates is a *penchant for action*. We have all worked with people who have a reputation for getting things done. Ultimately, your career trajectory is shaped by what you deliver. You cannot achieve meaningful outcomes if you do not execute. And you cannot execute if you are unwilling to make a move.

In my experience, leaders who move stand out because their actions create impact. They are not reckless. They are decisive. They do not overthink everything. They evaluate, commit, and execute. There is an old saying: "When the going gets tough, the tough get going." The point is not toughness for its own sake. The point is that in tough moments, action separates the people who shape outcomes from those who watch outcomes unfold.

Before we go further, here are the most common occasions when leaders need to move.

- **Move on the big rocks** when priorities compete and time is limited.
- **Move to solve problems** when obstacles block the way to business objectives.

- **Move to make decisions** when indecision becomes a cost.
- **Move when things are unclear** and ambiguity tempts you to wait.
- **Move in a crisis** when urgency requires fast action and calm leadership.
- **Move to get back up** when failure or setbacks knock you down.
- **Move to transition** when your job has been eliminated.

These moments are where leadership is earned. Anyone can talk about action. Leaders build a reputation by moving when it matters, especially when it is uncomfortable.

The Amasian Way calls us to move when others may stand still.

VOICE OF EXPERIENCE

A good analogy for the need to move is the 1980s arcade game Frogger. The premise is simple: get the frog from the bottom of the screen to the top by hopping onto objects that move across the screen. Two clear lessons:

1. **Make the right move.** You have to study patterns, identify what is safe, avoid what will hurt you, and time your hops. If you move randomly, you fail quickly.
2. **Consequence of inaction.** If you do not move forward or backward, the object you are standing on eventually moves off-screen, and you lose a life. In other words, you can take too long contemplating your next move.

As you advance to harder levels, the game gives you fewer safe openings. You must spot opportunities faster and move. Sometimes, you must make multiple moves in succession without pausing.

Work is not that different. There are consequences to moving without assessing risks and next steps. There are also consequences to doing nothing. As you grow in your career, your decisions need to become more timely and more intentional. You need to anticipate the next few moves, not just the next task.

And this lesson shows up in real life. Watching an elderly parent move less is difficult. When people move infrequently, their muscles weaken. Then, when they finally try to move again, it is harder and more painful. The same is true professionally. If you repeatedly avoid action at work, you can build habits of hesitation that make leadership harder later.

Move On Things That Matter Most

Dr. Stephen Covey, famous for authoring *The 7 Habits of Highly Effective People*, uses the metaphor of *big rocks* to explain priorities. At work and in life, some priorities matter more than others. When you focus on the highest priorities, your impact is larger than if you spend your energy on dozens of small tasks.

The classic demonstration is a jar filled with big rocks, pebbles, sand, and water. If you put the big rocks in first, you can still fit pebbles, sand, and water around them. If you start with sand and water, you cannot fit the rocks later. The point is straightforward: *If you do not act on the big rocks first, you will not have room for them at all.*

I have seen this pattern throughout my career. People burn themselves out "putting out fires," then feel productive because they checked off many small items. But when you look at the results, the high-value priorities did not move.

When you learn to prioritize and execute on the work that yields the highest value, everything else becomes true "above and beyond." If you complete many low-priority tasks but miss the high-value outcomes, you may be at risk of failing to meet expectations. Leaders are strategically focused. They move the big rocks first.

Move to Solve Problems

Problems are the obstacles that keep you, your team, or your organization from achieving business objectives. They do not disappear because you notice them. They require action.

When I was growing up, the *G.I. Joe* cartoon ended with a public service announcement, and the catchphrase was, "Knowing is half the battle." That phrase stuck with me because I always wondered, "What is the other half?"

As I matured, I answered my own question: *the other half is doing something about it.* In my career, I have seen a clear divide between problem observers and problem solvers. Problem observers can be entertaining. Jerry Seinfeld built a legendary career as a comedian observing problems. In business, though, the people who become leaders are the ones who solve problems.

Problem solvers use discipline. They apply frameworks such as the scientific method or hypothesis-based problem-solving to define the problem, test potential causes, evaluate options, and implement solutions. They do not just point or assign blame. They move.

Move to Make a Decision

Leaders cannot live in indecision. They can and should take time to think, pressure-test, and consult. But they cannot become stuck. Also, a decision not to take action is still a decision, and it often becomes the most expensive one.

Growing up in a risk-averse culture and being a naturally carefree, go-with-the-flow person, I had to practice to become more decisive. What helped me most was serving in positions where I had to make decisions. Volunteer leadership roles in higher education, the church, and professional associations forced me to decide, communicate, and own outcomes. Real-world pressure is an effective teacher.

Sometimes, you are asked to decide on something you do not fully understand yet. In those moments, ask questions that quickly clarify the essentials:

- What is the problem statement?
- What are the consequences of inaction?
- What benefits do we get from acting?
- What is the strategic alignment?
- What are the risks and tradeoffs?
- What investment is required?

Decision script: "Given the goal, the cost of inaction is X. The lowest-risk next step is Y. Success looks like Z by (time)."

If you cannot make a sound decision on the spot, ask for a reasonable amount of time. Moving to make a decision does not mean deciding instantly every time. It means not hiding behind indecision. Use the time to research, gather perspectives, and come back with a recommendation.

I also believe in the wisdom behind the old Chinese idea of "think thrice" before deciding. We can move quickly and still be thoughtful. Speed without judgment becomes recklessness.

A few common "bad mottos" to watch for:

- **"Act now, apologize later."** This can create speed, but it can also create avoidable harm if you ignore safety, policy, ethics, or downstream consequences.
- **"Someone else will figure it out."** Assuming others will catch what you missed is risky. Communication and collaboration exist for a reason. Do not wait and criticize when you should be contributing up front.
- **"The end justifies the means."** This is a villain's mindset for a reason. How you get results becomes part of your reputation and your brand.

Move When Things Are Unclear

Another leadership attribute employers value is the ability to navigate ambiguity. This is the ability to show up and work when direction is incomplete, priorities are shifting, or outcomes are not fully defined. Many people stall when the path is unclear. Leaders find ways to move using their curiosity and experience.

Workplaces change constantly due to innovation and disruption. In some environments, priorities also swing with leadership changes, budgets, and external forces. When that happens, "wait and see" becomes a common default. The people who stand out are those who can make progress amid uncertainty while still managing risk.

Sometimes, uncertainty is personal. People stress about the long-term future so much that they freeze on the next step. A common example is choosing a first job. Many graduates burn enormous energy trying to find the “perfect” first move, as if the first job is the destination. It is not. Entry-level roles are the beginning. They are designed to build skills, confidence, and options. You can make the first move meaningful, learn from it, and then make the next move. Your first move is not forever.

There also comes a point in your career when you become more competent in your role than your immediate supervisor. That can be frustrating until you recognize what it means: you can no longer delegate your decisions to someone above you. Your supervisor’s job becomes coaching and challenging, not doing your work for you. A major leadership inflection point is recognizing you are at that stage, soliciting counsel, and then owning the next step.

VOICE OF EXPERIENCE

Each of us has faced big, scary moments and survived. As an immigrant, one of the most traumatic changes I experienced was leaving everything I knew and moving to a new country and culture. Then there was moving out of my parents’ home. Then marriage. Then kids. Each of those turned life upside down. Like anyone else, I moved forward regardless of whether I felt comfortable knowing what to do.

Because I spent time in the theater as a teenager, I learned to draw from past experiences to “get in character” for something new. Most of us do this in our own way. We remind ourselves, “I’ve done hard things before. I’ll be okay.”

For small things, I laugh at how obsessive I can get about a giant pimple on my face, then realize I completely forget about it once it’s gone. For bigger things, I draw from moments where I took real risks, like joining professional wrestling school at 28 and learning to dive from the top rope, or jumping from the Stratosphere in Las Vegas on a 108-story cable-assisted descent.

I have also drawn on personal, painful experiences. Being able to say, “I’ve faced the same or worse before,” gives me confidence to move through most challenges.

Move When There Is a Crisis

Moving in a crisis sounds obvious until you are in one. In moments of urgency, many people freeze. Some get emotionally flooded. Some default to denial, hoping someone else will take charge. That is why a crisis reveals leadership so clearly. When the stakes rise, the room looks for someone who can stay calm, assess the situation, and act.

I have experienced this in real time. Twice, I noticed a fire starting in a meeting space and jumped into action to help put it out. Both times, I was surprised by how many people stood in fear or ran away. Those moments taught me something about myself: I am the type of person who takes action in crisis situations.

A common metaphor used in business during times of crisis is the "burning platform." This originates from an incident involving a blazing oil rig in the North Sea, where workers had to choose between leaping into icy waters from a dangerous height or remaining and risking death by fire. Such crises require us to carefully weigh the outcomes of taking action versus doing nothing, then decide and act quickly.

In a workplace crisis, you may not have perfect information. You still need to move. The leadership discipline is to get oriented quickly, name the risk, make a decision, and coordinate the next steps. This is where your ability to communicate becomes part of your leadership brand. People need to hear calm direction, not panic. They need priorities, not noise.

Robert J. Thomas explores these high-stakes moments as "crucibles," arguing that leaders are often forged through adversity rather than comfort. The lesson is that when a crisis arrives, leadership is not a title. It is behavior.

Even pop culture gets this right. If you have watched *Squid Game*, you may recall that the protagonist survives not because he is the strongest, but because he learns to observe quickly, decide, and move under pressure.

Bottom line: In a crisis, leadership is movement with composure. Those who can assess reality and take action become anchors when others feel unsteady.

VOICE OF EXPERIENCE

In 2020, the world paused because of the COVID-19 pandemic. In-person gatherings shut down for months. At the time, I was a line-of-business owner running a training company. More than half of our revenue came from in-person instructor-led classes. The shutdown was devastating.

At first, we were optimistic that things would reopen quickly. As the months dragged on, it became clear that "waiting it out" was not a strategy. Meanwhile, the workforce had more time than ever to invest in learning because commutes disappeared and travel stopped.

That is when I began leading an effort to move our instructor-led training onto live virtual platforms. At the time, we did not offer live virtual training. Like many organizations, we had just rolled out Microsoft Teams to help employees stay productive while working from home. Zoom also became a dominant platform for training and webinars. I knew our competitors would adapt quickly, and if we stayed still, we would bleed revenue and relevance.

Inside the organization, I encountered significant pushback. Some people wanted to slow down until everything was perfectly designed and "buttoned up." Others were simply hesitant to move into an offering we had never delivered before. The resistance was understandable. The risk felt real. But the risk of inaction was bigger.

My team and I pulled others along because we had a burning platform. Millions of dollars in revenue were at stake. More importantly, our mission was at stake. We did not let the shutdown stop us from fulfilling our purpose to train professionals to be safer.

We moved quickly, learned in real time, and stood up live virtual training. That decision saved millions in revenue that would have been lost if we had offered nothing during the shutdown.

The Amasian Way calls us to bring others along who cannot move.

Bottom line: Crisis rewards leaders who can name reality, commit to a direction, and mobilize others to move.

Crises are the moments where you must move fast to protect people, performance, and purpose. But leadership is not only proven in urgent moments. It is also proven once the moment has passed. The next test is quieter and more personal: what do you do when you fall, fail, or get hit with a setback you did not plan for?

Move to Get Back Up When We Fall

In *Batman Begins* (2005), Thomas Wayne asks his son, "Why do we fall?" and answers, "So we can learn to pick ourselves up." It is a simple line, and it lands because it is true. Leadership requires resilience. You will get knocked down by failure, disappointment, loss, rejection, or a decision that did not work. The question is not whether you will fall. The question is whether you will learn and get back up.

Getting back up is not easy. Resilience is not denial. It is the ability to take the hit, process it, extract the lesson, and keep moving.

I once heard an entrepreneur accept an award and use the stage to talk about failure, not success. He described setbacks that cost him millions of dollars and the emotional strain of staying in the fight. It was obvious he had plenty of reasons to quit. He kept going anyway. His persistence and support from others carried him forward.

We all have "fall down" moments. In my lifetime, I lived through September 11 and the COVID-19 pandemic. Both events did not just affect Americans emotionally. They disrupted the work I was doing at the time. In careers, we fail to meet expectations, lose opportunities, and get caught in restructurings. In life, we face illness, divorce, and death. In those moments, despair can feel like gravity. There is a global phenomenon of people giving up hope amid challenging job markets and unforgiving work cultures. They chose to stay home and do nothing rather than grind and move ahead.

The leadership move is not pretending you are fine. The leadership move is choosing to continue. Learn the lesson. Regain your footing. Take the next step.

Bottom line: Resilience is movement after impact. You do not earn the brand of leadership by never falling. You earn it by learning and getting back up.

VOICE OF EXPERIENCE

It is easier to talk about getting back up than it is to live it. I know because I have moved and gotten burned in my career.

When that happens, I take responsibility for what was within my control. Most lessons come back to stakeholder management:

- Did I fully vet my intention with the right stakeholders?
- Did I involve the right people early enough?
- Did I consider downstream consequences for others?
- Did I map risks and mitigation, or did I assume things would work out?

Then there are the things outside my control. Unforeseeable risks. Hidden agendas. Decisions made above or around you that change the game. Lack of positive exposure.

It would be easier to pull back after getting burned. But I strongly believe I have grown each time by learning from what I could control and adjusting to what I could not.

I do not have the personality to take the easy way out. There was a trend in parts of China called *tang ping* (Chinese: 躺平; lit. "lying flat"). It is a movement of young professionals giving up on the pressures of work and society. Instead of looking for work or working, they are choosing to "lie flat" at home and indulge in gaming. Western culture has a similar trend called "quiet quitting," in which employees give up the hustle and do the bare minimum. I do not have that in my work ethic. I personally cannot give in and give up.

I believe adversity, pressure, and failure are part of growth. If I quit the first time I fell off my bike and scraped my knee, I never would have known the freedom of riding. If I stopped driving after my first accident as a teenager, I would have limited my independence for decades. Yes, moving can lead to pain. But not moving guarantees stagnation.

It also helps to reframe setbacks as part of forward progress. John C. Maxwell's *Failing Forward* captures this well. Michael Jordan famously described his missed shots and lost games as part of what led to his success. Thomas Edison reframed his repeated failed attempts as a process of finding many ways that did not work.

I refused to waste time romanticizing failure or letting it define me.

MOVE TO TRANSITION

Setbacks happen at work. But being laid off or terminated can be one of the hardest falls in a career. For most of my career, I did not experience it. I watched close friends and family go through it, and I carried a false sense of security that it would never happen to me. Then it happened to me, twice.

The first time, I felt vulnerable, ashamed, and afraid. The weight of adult responsibilities hit hard. I was triggered easily. I was full of resentment and self-doubt. I kept thinking of the Chinese saying about having "no face to see people." I also felt pressure to hide what I was going through. I was the sole breadwinner at the time. We had toddlers. I felt like I had no room to fall apart.

Like many people, I carried impostor syndrome throughout my career. I worried that someone would discover I was not as good as my brand promised. When I hit a rough patch, I told myself the other shoe had finally dropped. I isolated and spiraled. Each rejection during my job search reinforced the fear and increased the anxiety. On the outside, I tried to keep it together. On the inside, I was struggling.

My friends and colleagues helped me stand back up. A few of them reminded me relentlessly who I was and why I was valuable. One of them said something that finally pierced through the fog: at some point, I needed to believe what the people who knew me best were telling me. Their support and the evidence they brought forward helped me regain perspective and self-trust.

I also needed strength to overcome the inaction that can come with despair. I found that strength in the serenity prayer: *accepting what I could not change, committing to change what I could, and having the wisdom to know the difference.* That "difference" mattered. It kept me from giving up on everything. It also kept me from playing the victim.

From there, I returned to the fundamentals that usually help me move forward: *reconnecting with purpose, drawing strength from previous setbacks, leaning into my strengths, and activating my network.* Over time, I loosened the grip impostor syndrome had on me. I moved on. I rebuilt.

In my next role, I found real sanctuary. I was proud of the work, proud of the legacy, and deeply connected to my team and stakeholders. And then suddenly, I found myself in transition again.

This time was different. I had matured. Because I had lived through this before, I faced it with more dignity and more faith in a positive outcome. I had less desperation and less panic. I could analyze what was happening and focus on what I needed to do next. My mom shared a Chinese proverb that loosely translates to, "A good horse does not eat the grass behind it." The message landed. Do not live in reverse.

I will share three thoughts for anyone who experiences a setback like being laid off or let go:

1. **Let yourself feel what you feel.** Do not bottle it up. Unprocessed pain leaks out sideways. If you need support, seek it. Therapy, trusted relationships, and community can help you heal and stabilize.
2. **Do not lie down and become a victim.** Own what you can own. Learn what you can learn. Then move forward with dignity. Do not let hurt feelings turn into permanent stagnation.
3. **Focus on what is ahead, not what is behind.** Deprogramming from the intensity of a role takes time. But the only way forward is forward. Standing still and looking back will not help you rebuild.

I would not wish these experiences on anyone. But if you find yourself there, you can get through it. Listen to those who believe in you. Silence the endless "could have, would have" loops. Recommit to your purpose and plan. Learn, grow, and make your next move.

Bottom line: Career transitions are not failures. They are opportunities for learning and moving forward.

JOURNAL ACTIVITY: ARE YOU A MOVER AND SHAKER?

Think about a time at work when there was a crisis situation.

- What did you do to help the team get through it?
- What decision(s) did you make, influence, or accelerate?
- What drove you to action in that moment?

Reflection Questions

- Would you consider yourself a mover (someone who takes action) and a shaker (someone who creates measurable impact)? Why or why not?
- If you asked others, would they describe you the same way? What evidence would they point to?
- If your answer is "not yet," what is one small way you could practice taking action this month (one decision, one problem solved, one uncomfortable conversation, one visible deliverable)?

Your brand may open the door, but movement is what earns trust, creates results, and changes your trajectory. Move when it matters: on the big rocks, on real problems, on decisions, in ambiguity, in crisis, and when you need to get back up. *Prioritize. Solve. Decide. Navigate. Respond. Recover.* That is when leaders move, and that is why.

As AAPI professionals, we don't just inherit cultural strengths. We also inherit cultural reflexes, like staying humble, not taking up too much space, and waiting to be invited in. Those instincts can keep us grounded, but they can also keep us unseen in workplaces that reward visibility and initiative. If your brand is the story people tell about you when you are not in the room, then the next question is simple: What story are your actions writing? Let's shift from concept to execution with practical ways to show up brilliantly and move with purpose.

WAYS TO SHOW UP AND MOVE

As AAPI professionals, many of us carry hang-ups about showing up visibly and moving boldly. We were often raised to be respectful, not disruptive, and not "make waves." Those instincts can keep us safe in some contexts, but they can also keep us invisible in Western work cultures that reward visibility, initiative, and decisive action.

And here is the inconvenient truth. Whether Diversity, Equity, and Inclusion is gaining momentum or losing ground in your organization, the expectation to prove your impact does not go away. If anything, it increases. When the environment is supportive, you have more room to be seen. When the environment is skeptical, the cost of being overlooked rises. Either way, if everyone needs to show up and move forward, many of us will need to do so more intentionally and consistently to avoid being pushed back into the "model minority" box.

I saw a version of this dynamic recently as a parent. I held my daughter through tears after she felt she was not selected for a role in her school play because of perceived favoritism. Whether that perception was accurate or not, the experience was real to her. She felt unseen. She felt dismissed. That is what invisibility feels like. In the workplace, the emotions may be quieter, but the impact is similar. If you want to be considered, trusted, and promoted, you cannot rely on "they'll notice eventually." You must show up in a way that is visible, and you have to move in a way that is undeniable.

What follows are practical tools to do both.

10 WAYS TO KEEP SHOWING UP BRILLIANTLY

By "showing up," I mean more than attending meetings or events. Showing up also means being present, engaged, and consistently connected to the people and work that matter.

1. **Give yourself a reason.** Purpose drives presence. I will never forget a public service announcement where a man taped a picture of his daughter to a cigarette pack to remind himself why he was quitting. When your reason

has conviction, showing up becomes less optional. Align your reason for showing up with your broader purpose.

2. **Plan your entrance.** Decide how you want to arrive, not just where you want to be. Who needs to know you showed up? What is the first impression you want to create? Your entrance is often the first "data point" people use to form an impression of your brand.
3. **Plan your stay.** Once you are there, what is your role? What will you contribute? What impact do you want to deliver? Preparation reduces anxiety and increases confidence. I do this even with restaurants. I look up the menu and reviews ahead of time, so I show up ready.
4. **Plan your exit.** Define what "good" looks like. How will you know you achieved your goal for showing up? Who needs to know what you contributed before you leave? One firm I worked for used the phrase "leave a place better because you were there." That is a useful test. What legacy do you leave behind?
5. **Be curious about impact.** If you are unsure what matters most, ask. You will be more valuable when you focus on high-priority tasks. I often open a meeting with: "What would be the best use of our next XX minutes, and how can I contribute to those outcomes?" It signals respect for time and commitment to impact.
6. **Be brilliant.** Executive presence is difficult to teach, and many of us have spent years training ourselves to blend in. Leaders do not blend in. They become visible in a way that is grounded and credible. Practice presence by taking opportunities to lead a discussion, present, or facilitate. I learned something about this in professional wrestling school. My trainer said many people were bigger, taller, or more athletic than me, but I had showmanship and presence. When I entered the ring, people paused. Presence creates attention. Use it.
7. **Be valuable.** Presence without value is performance. Value without visibility is often ignored. Make sure your impact is measured and communicated. Also, remember emotional value. Maya Angelou is often quoted as saying,

"People may forget what you said or did, but they will remember how you made them feel." I once had a client with family ties to the Adams family. Living in Quincy, I had access to souvenirs from the Adams estate. I brought her a small souvenir at the end of our engagement. Years later, we are still connected. People remember thoughtful value.

8. **Schedule it.** Consistency is rarely accidental. The most reliable way I have found to show up again and again is to put it on the calendar. Book time to prepare, time to show up, and time to follow up. Sometimes, "showing up" is a check-in message to someone in your network. Scheduling protects what you say matters.
9. **Find a ride-or-die.** If showing up feels intimidating, do not do it alone. Bring someone who will help you walk through the door, stay grounded, and debrief afterwards. In Chinese culture, there is a concept of having someone who serves as your reflection and looks out for you. Showing up with a partner increases follow-through.
10. **Plan to show up again.** Visibility compounds through repetition. After you show up, pause and assess. What worked? What did not? Who do you need to follow up with? What would you do differently next time? This reflection will reveal the purpose and agenda for your next visit.

Bottom line: Showing up once can create visibility. Showing up again and again creates a brand.

10 WAYS TO HELP YOU MOVE

Showing up earns you a seat. Moving earns your credibility. It is not easy to stay motivated and decisive. I think about this often in the context of exercise and dieting. Knowing what to do is not the same as doing it.

Many AAPI professionals were raised with a risk-averse mindset. Bold moves can feel unsafe. This is even more complicated for professionals who rely on employment to maintain a work visa. Taking action can feel like gambling with stability. The goal here is not reckless risk. The goal is calculated movement.

Here are ten ways to move with intention. The goal is to achieve *calculated momentum.*

1. **Use strategic thinking.** Move on to what matters most. Focus on the "big rocks" that drive organizational outcomes and your performance. You cannot do everything. Ask: What will create the most impact? Is this aligned to strategy, or is it a distraction?
2. **Use critical thinking.** As a manager, I value people who can articulate their reasoning. At some point, managers may not be as closely involved in the technical aspects of the work as their direct reports. Their job becomes coaching and challenging. Critical thinking begins with good questions: what, why, how, when, and where. It also helps you anticipate risks and design mitigation.
3. **Move with purpose.** Conviction fuels action. Belief often moves people faster than logic. Purpose can become a stabilizer when confidence is shaky. Confidence is not arrogance. It is steadiness. People follow steadiness.
4. **One bite at a time.** "How do you eat an elephant?" One bite at a time. When a task feels overwhelming or the next step is unclear, break it down into the smallest meaningful move. In change management, we build momentum through "low-hanging fruit." In New England snowstorms, when you are staring at a driveway buried in snow, you do not win by thinking about the whole driveway. You win one shovel at a time.
5. **Work smarter.** Movement does not have to mean grinding alone. Bring others along. Find better tools. Use automation. Use AI where it genuinely accelerates and improves quality. The goal is not activity. The goal is progress.
6. **Focus on solving the problem.** Identify the problem clearly, then keep your moves anchored to solving it. Tangents kill momentum. Stay close to the outcomes. Use regular touchpoints to evaluate progress and adjust.

7. **Build a business case.** Bold moves become safer when they are backed by rigor. A business case clarifies the problem, consequences of inaction, options, recommendations, risks, investment, and expected outcomes. That structure turns emotion into decision-ready logic.
8. **Gamify it.** Motivation often needs a system. In learning, gamification uses incentives and progress markers to keep people engaged. Adults are not immune. Compete against your personal baseline. Reward progress. Create milestones that make momentum visible.
9. **Stronger together.** There is truth in the proverb: If you want to go fast, go alone; if you want to go far, go together. Consult your personal board of advisers. Build a hype team that pulls you forward. Use accountability partners, including a gym buddy if that is what keeps you moving.
10. **Go/No-Go.** Decisive does not mean reckless. Define criteria for when to move and when to pause. Design an "undo button" when possible so you can unwind a false move. Move, but move intelligently.

Bonus: Take a break. Sometimes, the most strategic move is rest. Earlier in my career, someone described me as someone who worked hard, played hard, and prayed hard. I later realized I was burning the candle at both ends. I stopped pulling all-nighters and started sleeping through the night, then waking up early. Those few hours of sleep increased my productivity and decision quality.

Bottom line: Movement is not about speed. It is about building momentum and making progress. When you move with purpose, rigor, and support, you increase both your impact and your odds of success.

5 NO-NO PITFALLS TO AVOID

You will stand out when you show up and move. You can also stand out for the wrong reasons. These pitfalls create reputations that are hard to recover from. These are brand-killers because they repeat. Catch them early.

1. **No-show.** If you repeatedly fail to show up, people stop expecting you. Then they stop inviting you. Then they stop remembering you. Consistently being late is also a poor showing. It is tough to rely on people who are no-shows or constantly late.
2. **Slow-go or no-go.** If you consistently hold others back because you are unwilling to take reasonable risks, you eventually become the constraint. People will route around you.
3. **Poor attitude.** Leaders notice chronic negativity. No one wants to slow down for someone who whines and complains. Energy is contagious. So is drag.
4. **No follow-through.** A damaging brand is someone who promises and does not deliver. Reliability is not what you say you will do. It is what people have seen you actually do.
5. **No blame.** Playing the victim becomes an excuse for stagnation. It is especially toxic after failure. Learn, remediate, and move. Do not default to blame and refusal.

Bottom line: Your brand is built by what you repeatedly do. Protect it by showing up, following through, and moving with discipline.

VOICE OF EXPERIENCE

Early in my career, we used to have nicknames for people whose reputations worked against them. One that still sticks with me decades later was "Crisis Dave."

Dave was highly sensitive to problems at work. He would spend the day moving from cube to cube, updating everyone on the problems he noticed. He was passionate and convincing. In Dave's world, everything was urgent. Everything was a crisis.

The problem was not that Dave saw issues. The problem was that he did not solve them. He rarely proposed a path forward. Worse, he became less productive because he was frozen by the problems he observed. And because he needed others to talk him down, he also took up their time. Eventually, it got so bad that people started avoiding him, not because they disliked him, but because they did not want to absorb his anxiety.

Watching Dave helped me build a rule I still rely on today:

- Prioritize problems so not everything becomes a crisis.
- Move beyond observation into options and recommendations.
- Take action instead of becoming the broadcast channel for worry.

At the end of the day, people remembered Dave for the wrong reasons. I wanted to be remembered as someone who gets things done.

There's an age-old debate: does success come from luck or hard work? The truth is usually both. But I tend to believe that what people call "luck" is often the byproduct of reputation and repetition. Your brand earns you opportunities that look accidental from the outside.

You are less likely to be "in the right place at the right time" if you don't show up. An advocate is less likely to pull you into a conversation if your brand is inconsistent, passive, or unreliable. But *when you show up, deliver value, and follow through, more doors open.* Not because the world suddenly became fair, but because you built a track record people can trust.

So when opportunity knocks, here is the real question: will you show up, and will you move?

THE AAPI LENS

For many AAPI professionals, "showing up" is not the hard part. We were raised to be dependable, to work hard, and to avoid embarrassing mistakes. The career risk is that we show up quietly, deliver consistently, and still remain indistinct in rooms where visibility and advocacy determine who gets tapped for the next opportunity.

Western workplace cultures often reward people who are *seen*, *associated with outcomes*, and *known for movement under pressure*. That can clash with cultural conditioning, such as saving face, not making waves, and waiting for direction. Chapter 4 is a reminder that the bamboo ceiling is not only about capability. It is also about *visibility*, *narrative control*, and *action*. If you want your leadership to be recognized, you must show up in ways people can feel and recall, then move when others stall.

THE CAREER STAGE LENS

Early Career (Entry–Individual Contributor)

- Build a "reliability brand" fast: show up prepared, be present, follow through.
- Seek visible reps: projects, meetings, and moments where leaders notice who contributes.
- Start managing your narrative early, so others do not define it for you.

Mid-Career (Senior IC–Manager)

- Shift from "helpful" to "associated with outcomes." Own a problem, a workstream, a result.
- Strengthen your personal NPS by making it easy for others to recommend you.
- Practice decisive movement: prioritize big rocks, solve problems, and manage ambiguity.

Senior/Executive (Leader of Leaders)

- Model the pace and posture of action. Your movement becomes permission for others to move.
- Create clarity in ambiguity and momentum in crisis.
- Bring others along, especially those who freeze or hesitate, without letting the organization stall.

CHAPTER SUMMARY

As an Amasian Leader, you need to show up consistently, especially when it matters. You also need a *penchant for action*: the willingness to move when others hesitate, while staying thoughtful, strategic, and grounded.

Key takeaways:

- Show up again and again, and make your presence matter.
- Own, manage, and advocate for your personal brand.
- Use a "Personal NPS" mindset: would others recommend you for the next opportunity?
- Move on the big rocks first, not just the small fires.
- Move to solve problems, make decisions, and create momentum.
- Navigate ambiguity by taking the next best step, then the next.
- Move decisively in a burning platform moment.
- Build resilience: learn, recover, and get back up when you fall.
- Bring others along when you move forward.
- Avoid pitfalls that damage your brand: no-show, slow-go, poor attitude, and no follow-through.

The Amasian Way calls us to make our own luck by showing up brilliantly and moving boldly.

JOURNAL ACTIVITY: PUTTING IT ALL TOGETHER—YOUR "SHOW UP AND MOVE" SCORECARD

Think honestly about how you show up at work and in life. Score each statement using: 1 = Never, 2 = Sometimes, 3 = Always.

_______ I show up when it matters.

_______ I show up consistently.

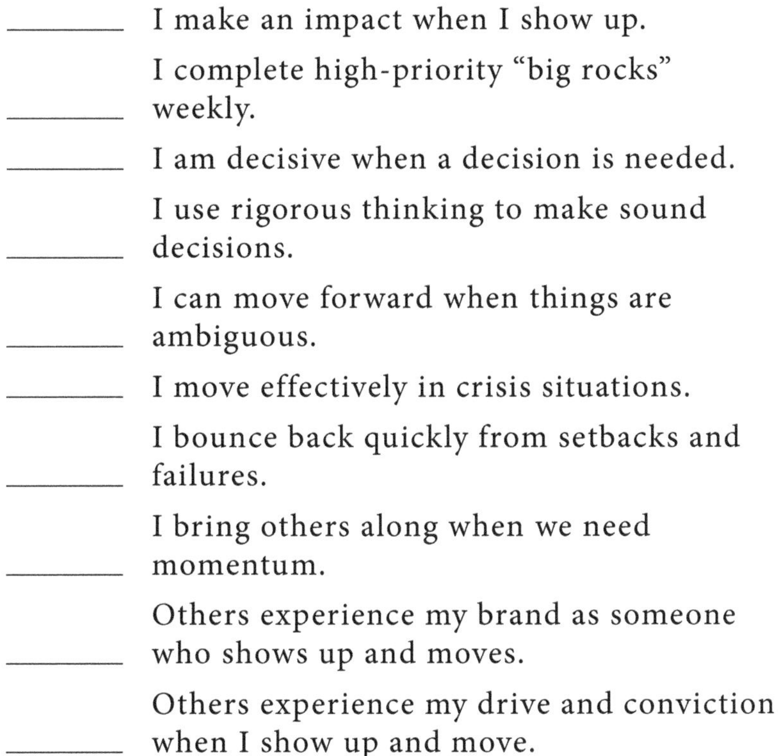

________	I make an impact when I show up.
________	I complete high-priority "big rocks" weekly.
________	I am decisive when a decision is needed.
________	I use rigorous thinking to make sound decisions.
________	I can move forward when things are ambiguous.
________	I move effectively in crisis situations.
________	I bounce back quickly from setbacks and failures.
________	I bring others along when we need momentum.
________	Others experience my brand as someone who shows up and moves.
________	Others experience my drive and conviction when I show up and move.

Reflection Questions

- How did you score, and what patterns do you notice (highs, lows, contradictions)?
- Which two items matter most for your next career move, and why?
- If you asked three to five trusted colleagues to score you, where do you expect the biggest gaps would be?
- Who should you ask for that feedback, and what is the simplest way to ask?
- What is one behavior you will start this week to improve your "show up" score, and one behavior you will start to improve your "move" score?

Discover More

- "Law of Readiness" (Edward Thorndike)
- Brand promise, brand equity, brand loyalty
- Net Promoter Score (NPS)
- Model Minority
- Bamboo Ceiling
- *Gravitas: The 8 Strengths That Redefine Confidence* (Lisa Sun)
- *Empowering Yourself: The Organizational Game Revealed* (Harvey J. Coleman) (The PIE framework)
- *7 Habits of Highly Effective People* (Stephen Covey)
- Scientific Method; Hypothesis-Based Problem Solving (HBPS)
- Burning Platform
- *Crucibles of Leadership* (Robert J. Thomas)
- *Failing Forward* (John C. Maxwell)
- "People will forget what you said… but they will never forget how you made them feel." (Maya Angelou)

SO WHAT

Leadership is not only what you can do. It is what people *experience* from you. When you show up consistently and move with purpose, you become visible, reliable, and associated with outcomes. That is how you build a leadership brand that travels ahead of you, opens doors, and brings others with you.

Show up in ways that are felt. Move in ways that create momentum. Repeat until your impact becomes undeniable.

Looking Ahead

When you consistently show up and move, your brand starts to travel ahead of you. In the next chapter, we shift to the skills that make that brand usable: communication and relationships. They are the tools that turn credibility into connection, and connection into influence.

CHAPTER 5

Communicate and Connect

In the previous chapter, we focused on showing up and moving. That is how you earn credibility. But credibility is not self-executing. You can deliver real results and still be overlooked if no one is willing to say your name when you are not in the room. That is why advocates matter. *Communication skills help you advocate for your results* without sounding like you are bragging. *Relationship skills help you earn champions* who will speak for you in performance discussions, staffing decisions, stretch opportunities, and promotion readiness debates.

"Soft skills" is the label we use for skills that are not tied to a technical domain or business acumen. The problem is that the word "soft" makes them sound optional. They are not. Communication and relationship skills are often as important as technical and business skills, and in many leadership moments, they are more important. An acquaintance once told me she believed many AAPI professionals enter tax or accounting because they can rely on technical skills and avoid communication gaps caused by language barriers. We both agreed that it is a misconception. No matter your domain, you will not advance far without the ability to communicate clearly and build relationships that create leverage.

To lead is to influence. Leaders align people on goals, change behavior, and drive action. They do this through communication that reaches the masses, small groups, and one-on-one moments. Great leaders know how to elicit both rational and emotional responses. They also depend on relationships to do more than they can on their own. Relationships are amplifiers. They help leaders learn faster, move farther, and influence more.

In this chapter, we will focus on practical ways to sharpen your communication and deepen your relationships, so your credibility becomes an opportunity. You will learn to:

- clarify purpose
- land the "so what"
- tailor your message to your audience
- advocate without apology
- build the network of allies and champions who help your leadership travel

THE AMASIAN WAY calls us to inspire others through impactful communication and relationship skills.

THE ART OF COMMUNICATION

My son is currently learning how to construct paragraphs and essays. While helping him, I was reminded of how much our school teachers tried to teach us to be good communicators from a very early age. The basic structure of a paragraph or an essay introduces a hypothesis, reinforces it with supporting details, and ends with a strong conclusion.

Effective communication should resonate with both rational and emotional audiences. *It must convey a clear and compelling message that motivates prompt action.* To achieve this, it is essential to structure your arguments thoughtfully, ensure they are relevant to the intended audience, and articulate a clear call to action.

VOICE OF EXPERIENCE

A sure way to stand out is to be a strong communicator. I tend to associate great leaders with the "gift of gab"—the ability to communicate well verbally. Great communicators can move people in large and small settings. They influence. They inspire. They get others to act.

Some people seem to be born with it. I do not buy that story. Like any other leadership skill, verbal communication is built through reps. You get better by doing it, getting feedback, and doing it again.

One of the best lessons I learned about public speaking came from training to become a lector at church.

As lectors, we are instructed that our primary role is to serve as vessels for delivering God's message to the congregation. The emphasis remains on the message rather than the individual lector. This training provided a valuable perspective, allowing me to understand that much of the anxiety associated with public speaking stems from an inward focus.

People are afraid of being embarrassed. Afraid of looking unprepared. Afraid of saying the wrong thing. Afraid of being judged. When the spotlight is on, most people's brains treat the moment as a threat.

The lector mindset flips that. When I present now, I focus on delivering the message in a way that serves the audience. My job is to carry the idea clearly, not to perform for approval. That shift does not eliminate nerves entirely, but it reduces stage fright by moving the center of gravity away from the ego and toward the purpose.

If you want to become a better verbal communicator, start now. Practice often. Put in the reps. But do not just practice words. Practice orientation. If church is not your cup of tea, try reading to children at a school as a volunteer, or join a Toastmasters club. There are many ways to get practice reps in for public speaking.

Make it about the message, not about you. When your message is clear and your purpose is real, your communication becomes more than talking. It becomes influential. Stop performing. Start delivering.

For What, To Do What, So What?

Have you ever walked out of a conversation and thought, "I'm not sure what that was about," and "I'm not sure what I'm supposed to do next"? Or listened to a speech that sounded impressive but left you wondering what its point was?

Now compare that with the opposite experience. A message that was clear. A point that landed. A call to action that made you move.

A recent manager of mine used to challenge us with a simple question: "For what, to do what?" In high school, when someone droned on, the guys would put their index fingers together in the shape of an inverted V, signaling get to the point. And one of my close friends and former colleagues used "So what?" as his go-to tool for strategic thinking.

When I craft communication, I use all three prompts as a quick discipline:

- **For what?** Why does this matter?
- **To do what?** What do I want the audience to do differently?
- **So what?** What changes if they do, and what happens if they do not?

If you cannot answer those three questions, you are not ready to communicate. You are ready to talk.

Here are a few ways to ensure your message is clear and lands with your audience:

The Parable of the Sower Test

Communication fails when it falls on deaf ears and results in nothing. If I can borrow from the Parable of the Sower, communication is like a seed sown by a farmer. The seed must land on fertile soil to grow and yield crops. If it lands on poor soil, it does not take root. You can have a brilliant message, and it can still fail if it is not received, understood, and acted on. Find a way to connect with the audience and make sure you land your messages with an audience that is ready, mindful, and listening.

Structure Is the Shortcut to Clarity

As mentioned, I was recently reminded of basic paragraph structure while helping my children with English homework. In school, we learned to write with:

- a *topic sentence* that conveys the main idea
- *supporting details* that explain and prove it
- a *conclusion* that lands the point and drives the next step

That structure works far beyond school. It works in meetings, in emails, in presentations, and in performance conversations. Whether you prepare your message or deliver it spontaneously, structure helps the audience follow your point.

For longer communication, the other basic tool we learned as children is an outline. For multimedia, an outline becomes a storyboard. It is funny how often experienced professionals skip this discipline and dive straight into building slides.

If you want to save time and improve flow, pause and outline first:

1. What is the point?
2. What are three to five supporting points?
3. What proof or examples do you need?
4. What do you want the audience to do next?

A solid structure keeps the audience focused, reduces confusion, and increases follow-through.

Always Land with a Call to Action (CTA)

Good communicators drive action. Yes, communication can introduce new information, elicit feelings, and drive behavior change. But in business, the payoff is usually the next step: Approval. Rejection. Purchase. Adoption. Commitment. A decision.

Marketers call this a *call to action* (CTA). Leaders need the same discipline. If the audience cannot describe what happens next, your message did not finish the job.

Amasian leaders communicate with purpose and drive action.

Tell them what you are telling them.

A practical reminder from training and speechwriting is:

- Tell them what you are going to tell them.
- Tell them what you are telling them.
- Tell them what you told them.

This is repetition with intent. It is not a filler; rather, it provides structure and repetition to help your audience recall your key point. It is how you increase retention and reduce misinterpretation.

Common Purposes for Communication

Use this as a quick planning grid. Before you speak or write, name your purpose, define the action, and choose a method that supports the outcome.

Purpose	Communication
Provide Direction	• **Call to action:** Audience follows direction • **Method:** Explain the goal and rationale, give clear instructions, show what success looks like, check understanding.
Advocate/Inspire	• **Call to action:** Alignment and action • **Method:** Make a compelling argument, support it with evidence, build the business case, invite reflection and agreement.
Sell	• **Call to action:** Purchase • **Method:** Ask discovery questions, tie value to needs, address objections, ask for the decision.
Give Feedback	• **Call to action:** Reinforce desired behavior or correct harmful behavior • **Method:** Describe the observed behavior, explain impact, reinforce positives, clarify consequences if behavior continues, check understanding and commitment.

Each category can be refined further. "Advocacy," for example, might mean asking for a budget, a raise, or a promotion.

The point is to build the muscle of thinking through:

- Purpose
- Desired action
- Method of delivery

Map the Conversation Before You Have It

As I am writing this chapter, I just put together a short map for a difficult conversation I need to have with a colleague. The exercise helped me clarify where I wanted the conversation to go and capture supporting points I did not want to forget in the moment. That map helped me stay on track and reduce emotion.

I also look ahead at my calendar by week, day, and half-day and block time to prepare for important communication. When I do, I show up calmer, clearer, and more effective. In one recent case, those notes helped me defuse a situation that could have become contentious.

You likely have resources available to help you prepare, too. Human Resources often provides templates for performance feedback, especially constructive feedback. There are interview resources that help you communicate value and impact. Find what works for you and build your toolkit.

And if a spontaneous conversation goes off the rails, it is okay to table it. Ask for time. Most "shooting from the hip" is less productive than stepping away from the heat and coming back with clarity and a better plan.

Bottom line: If your message does not land a clear "For what, to do what, so what," it is not effective communication. Structure your communication, repeat key points with intent, and drive a specific next action.

VOICE OF EXPERIENCE

You may have heard the term "Always Be Selling" (ABS). I have found that in most forms of communication, I am almost always advocating for something, even when it does not look like "sales."

- In *sales*, you advocate for your company, your products, and your services so the buyer chooses to purchase.

- In *interviews*, you advocate for your performance, value, and readiness to be hired or promoted.
- In *politics*, you advocate for a bill, so people vote for it.
- In *trial*, attorneys advocate so a jury reaches a verdict.
- In *coaching*, you advocate for improvement, so people commit and perform.

The common denominator is influence. To be effective at advocacy, it helps to understand the art and discipline behind *selling*, *teaching*, and *influencing*. They all aim at the same endpoint: changing someone's decision and behavior. In sales, you want someone to buy. In teaching, you want someone to improve. In influencing, you want someone to agree and act. I have been in all three arenas throughout my career, and one lesson keeps showing up: people do not resist information as much as they resist change.

That is why understanding basic motivation is not "nice to have." It is leverage.

- **Maslow's hierarchy of needs** reminds us that people are more willing to change when their basic needs are threatened or met. If someone is worried about security, stability, or belonging, they may not be emotionally available for your brilliant idea.
- **Knowles' andragogy** reminds us that adults need relevance. They want a clear value proposition, a practical reason to care, and a sense of involvement in the process.

Even with just these two concepts, your odds of successful advocacy improve. *Meet people where they are.* Tell them why acting is in their best interest. Give them a role in the outcome rather than forcing compliance.

In my experience, the most effective "sales" technique is not pushing. It is *helping someone reach the conclusion that they want to make a move*. That usually means drawing out needs and wants, surfacing pain points and wish lists, then presenting a case that fits what you admit out loud. That is also why powerful communicators know how to engage both rational and emotional drivers. A sermon that moves a congregation to shout

"Amen" aligns with its conviction and lands a call to action that people can feel.

If you want to become a stronger advocate, study human behavior. Learn how adults change. Learn what makes people resist. That knowledge becomes tools you can "bake into" your communication, so your message does not just land. It moves.

THE AMASIAN WAY calls us to plan our communication to drive rational and emotional responses.

JOURNAL ACTIVITY: MAP YOUR COMMUNICATION

Consider an upcoming communication you need to prepare (a difficult conversation, a presentation, an ask, or a feedback discussion).

Step 1. Create a one-page map

- **Purpose:** For what?
- **Desired action:** To do what?
- **Message:** So what?
- **Delivery plan:** How will you deliver it (story, data, examples, tone, medium)?
- **Objections:** What might they push back on, and how will you respond?

Step 2. Create a simple outline

- Opening (purpose + why now)
- 2–3 supporting points (evidence, examples, rationale)
- The ask (clear call to action)
- Close (confirm agreement, next steps, ownership)

Reflection Questions

- How did this feel compared to your usual preparation?
- What will you do differently going forward?
- How will you make those changes stick?

What Do You Stand For?

A common purpose for communication is *advocacy*. In Western work environments, you are constantly called upon to advocate for yourself, your team, your company, and your customers. For many AAPI professionals, that can be uncomfortable. Many AAPI professionals were raised to believe that advocacy is boasting and that humility is safer. The problem is that when you do not advocate for yourself, you often lose out to those who do.

VOICE OF EXPERIENCE

In my experience coaching AAPI professionals, one of the hardest pieces of advice to implement is self-advocacy. I used to deliver a presentation called *Bring Your Own Brand* (BYOB) with the subtitle, "or someone else will." The point was not ego. The point was agency.

Many AAPI professionals were raised to equate self-advocacy with bragging. We were taught to keep our heads down, work hard, and let the work speak for itself. The intention is honorable. The consequence can be costly. In many Western workplaces, advocacy is not optional. It is part of how performance is understood, remembered, and rewarded.

When you do not advocate for yourself and your results, others will do it on your behalf. Sometimes, they will do it well. Other times, they will under-represent you because they do not have the full picture, the right metrics, or the right story. That is when you hear painful statements like:

- "My manager should have known I was the best at my job."
- "They promoted someone else because that person knew how to sell themselves."

Here is the uncomfortable truth: many higher-level roles require proactivity, influence, and advocacy. You cannot demonstrate those skills if you assume your output is sufficient and remain silent about your impact.

As you advance, advocacy expands beyond you.

Type of Advocacy	What It Shows
Advocating for yourself	initiative and readiness
Advocating for others	leadership, generosity, and talent development
Advocating for your team	stewardship and focus on shared outcomes
Advocating for a project	business acumen and ownership
Advocating for your organization	loyalty and client orientation

I was promoted to director at a consulting firm because I built a brand for navigating ambiguity, spotting opportunity, and turning around difficult situations on complex projects and important clients. But I did not get promoted simply because I worked hard. I had to advocate for my case using metrics and outcomes that mattered.

In a matrix organization, you often work for different leaders throughout the year. No single person sees the full arc of your performance. That means you are the only one who can pull your impact into one coherent narrative. I worked closely with a coach and built a director case to demonstrate my readiness, value, and results. If I had waited for someone else to assemble that story without my input, I likely would not have gotten the promotion.

The road to partnership is even more demanding. You must articulate a partner case that resonates with the admissions committee and inspires advocates across the matrix organization.

Based on my experience, self-advocacy becomes increasingly important when pursuing promotions at higher executive leadership levels. Often, if you are not already under consideration for the position, it is necessary to demonstrate your ability to surpass hand-picked internal candidates or challenge the belief that external recruitment is required to secure the appropriate expertise.

Bottom line: If you don't write your story, someone else will edit it.

Know Your Audience

Have you ever heard the phrase "preaching to the choir?" It is typically used when someone is trying to convince an audience of an idea they already agree with.

I was in a meeting recently where a speaker kept complaining about being "old," and most of the audience was older than she was. Someone muttered under their breath, "She really needs to learn to read the room." That is the point. If you do not know your audience, even a good message can land poorly.

One of the most effective ways to communicate and influence is by doing your homework ahead of time, so your message resonates with the people in the room. In many situations, you can learn your audience's context before you walk in. For example, I have found it valuable to have an inside coach before a pitch—someone who understands the decision-makers' preferences, communication styles, and hot buttons.

If the communication is more spontaneous, you can still do real-time discovery by asking open-ended questions that surface what matters:

- "How are things going with ____ right now?"
- "What do you like most about ____?"
- "What concerns you about ____?"
- "If you could change one thing, what would you wish for?"
- "What is keeping you from making a decision today?"

In today's world, it also matters how you communicate. You want to be thoughtful and precise, so you do not alienate or offend your audience. Avoid language that can be heard as degrading or dismissive. Planning helps. When I prepare, I can catch references that might be misunderstood or unnecessarily polarizing. This becomes even more important across cultures and in global business, where a careless misstep can cost trust, relationships, and sometimes real dollars.

Demographics

It is useful to consider your audience's demographic makeup. Knowing the average age group, for example, can keep you from relying on dated references or overusing contemporary slang. Other factors may also matter depending on context: role, industry, education level, geography, and cultural background.

If you do not know these things in advance, you can always poll the room and adjust in the moment. I have seen comedians, musicians, and even professional wrestlers warm up a crowd by quickly surveying them:

- "Anyone here from ____?"
- "Anyone a fan of ____?"
- "Anyone had this happen recently?"
- "Show of hands, how many of you ____?"

One caution: do not lean too hard on stereotypes to connect with people. Demographics do not explain the whole person. We all have invisible diversity layered on top of what you can see. If you use a demographic reference to build rapport, do it lightly, and acknowledge it will not apply to everyone. My kids boo me out of the room when I start waving my hands and saying, "Six, seven!" Even though many other kids would respond enthusiastically, my kids are among the minority who cannot stand mainstream trends. In this case, they are not wrong.

VOICE OF EXPERIENCE

I have watched instructors struggle when they failed to anticipate cultural differences and adjust their style. I once led a global training rollout to train regional sales teams on compliance with the U.S. Foreign Corrupt Practices Act. The training was designed to be engaging and interactive.

When the class was delivered in China, the audience sat quietly, nodded, and rarely spoke. In Greece and Italy, the audience challenged the content so actively that after an hour, the instructor was still on the first slide. The lesson was immediate: the same "good training" can have very different outcomes depending on cultural norms. If you want your message to work, you must understand how your audience participates, what they consider respectful, and what "engagement" looks like in that context.

Bottom line: Knowing your audience is how you avoid misfires, earn trust faster, and deliver a message that actually lands.

Personality

Have you ever been in a conversation where someone keeps cutting you short and pushing you to move faster? Or the opposite: someone who wants to tell long stories and turn a five-minute check-in into a 45-minute detour. Most of us have dominant communication preferences, and those preferences show up quickly.

In more intimate settings, such as one-on-one conversations and small meetings, knowing your audience's personality can be a force multiplier. You will not always know it formally, but you can learn it through reputation, observation, and pattern recognition. *The better you understand someone's style, the more effectively you can deliver your message and still protect the relationship.*

One common framework for this is the Dominance, Influence, Steadiness, and Conscientiousness (DISC) model. You do not need to become a DISC expert to benefit from it. You only need to recognize what your audience values, then flex accordingly.

Personality Type (DISC shorthand)	What They Often Value	Effective Communication Approach
Direct ("bossy")	speed, clarity, outcomes	Lead with the point. Be concise. Make the ask explicit.
Warm, friendly, relationship-focused	rapport, tone, trust	Start human. Ask about them. Then connect the topic to shared goals.
Methodical, analytical	logic, precision, risk control	Send pre-reading. Use data. Show reasoning. Do not rush the decision.
Wanderer, distracted	structure, simplicity, momentum	Use a clear agenda. Repeat key points. Confirm understanding and next steps.

The point is, you cannot communicate only in your preferred style and expect it to resonate with everyone. Preparation and structure help, but flexibility is what makes your message land.

Bottom line: If you want to influence outcomes, learn to match your message to how your audience processes information.

VOICE OF EXPERIENCE

When I took the DISC assessment, I hit the bullseye in the middle. My responses suggested I was comfortable flexing across all styles without one being dominant. The upside is agility. I can adapt quickly, fit into many groups, and communicate effectively with people of different personalities. The downside is that if I am not intentional, I can blend in. Flexibility can make you effective, but it can also make you less memorable.

When I look back, that result makes sense. My dad was highly extroverted. My mom was deeply introverted. My immigration experience also shaped me. I grew up in a mostly white community and wanted to assimilate. Then I took up acting, the profession of becoming someone else. All of that trained me to read the room and adjust.

At work, I have had managers with very different styles. One was detail-oriented. One was direct and fast. One was relationship-driven. Learning to flex my communication was the key to managing up with each of them. It was not only what I said, but it was also how I packaged it:

- For **direct leaders**: executive summary first, then options, then a clear recommendation.
- For **analytical leaders**: the detailed logic, assumptions, risks, and the appendix.
- For **relationship-focused leaders**: quick context, human connection, and then the ask.

I also learned that you sometimes have to communicate beyond your boss. Your boss's peers and your boss's boss may have different preferences, and your message must travel well.

Even small habits matter. I often open with a quick "I hope you're doing well" to create warmth when it matters. If I have time, I ask one personal question and acknowledge the answer. People remember how you make them feel. With more direct or methodical personalities, I go slower and earn the right to be more personal. I have worked with clients who had a reputation for being "tough." The reason they extended me or asked for me again was not only my output. It was that I found a way to connect with them human to human.

Given we all have different defaults, communication is about balance. Flex when it matters. Keep your core voice intact. Use the right style at the right time for the right purpose.

The Amasian Way calls us to flex our communication style to resonate better with our audiences.

Agendas

It is important to surface your audience's agenda before you communicate. When you know what someone wants and needs, you can meet it head-on instead of guessing. You can ask ahead of time or at the beginning of the meeting.

I often start one-on-one conversations with a simple question: *What would make this conversation a win for you?*"

In training, instructors will ask learners to share their desired outcomes and capture them on a flip chart. Then, throughout the session, they return to that list and check off what has been addressed. You can apply the same discipline in meetings. Ask. Document. Return to it. Your audience will feel heard, and you will stay anchored to what matters.

Understanding agendas also helps you avoid being blindsided by objections. I remember being grateful for a sales representative who warned me that one person in the room was dug in and wanted to stay with the incumbent provider. That intelligence helped me tailor my approach. The opposite is also true. When you know who is an ally, you can invite them to help move the room.

Finally, pay attention to roles. Different roles come with different concerns. If an attorney is in the room, anticipate legal risk and compliance questions. If HR is in the room, address employee impact, fairness, and adoption. If Finance is in the room, be prepared to discuss costs, ROI, and trade-offs. If IT is in the room, expect questions on feasibility, timeline, and security.

When you know what people want, what they fear, and what they are responsible for, your communication becomes more compelling, inclusive, and resilient.

Bottom line: Do not walk into a conversation without knowing what "success" looks like for the people you need to influence.

Make the Interaction Matter

Communication works best when it changes something. It shifts thinking. It creates a feeling. It moves behavior. That is easier in a one-on-one conversation than it is on a stage, in an email, or in a recorded video. But the same rule applies: *impact requires intention.*

If you want your communication to land, focus on the audience. Care about what they need and what they are experiencing. When communicators overlook their audience and focus only on delivering their message, the message may be heard but not felt. When it is not felt, it is rarely acted on.

In one-on-one settings, be fully present. Modern distractions are relentless: phones, smartwatches, laptops, and notifications. If you want to connect, remove the distractions and give the other person your full attention.

In large-group settings, you can create a sense of intimacy by the way you speak. Use language that feels personal, as if you are talking to one person at a time. Make eye contact with each section of the room long enough to be felt, not just flashed.

In written messages or videos, you can still create tone. There may be "no tone" on a screen, but there is always a felt experience. Use clear, human language. Avoid cold distance. Write like you are speaking to a person, not broadcasting to a crowd.

Think about a time you were moved by a conversation or presentation. Now think about a time you left feeling empty because the speaker did not seem to care about the audience. Those experiences land differently. Make your communication matter. Be present. Care about the reaction. People will remember how you made them feel more than they will remember your exact words. And when they feel a real connection, they are more likely to act.

VOICE OF EXPERIENCE

When I was in college, I decided that my "purpose" (before purpose was a trend) was to touch the lives of everyone I met. Even back then, I cared deeply about relationships and connection. Today, I am not the best at remembering every name or face, and I can feel time catching up to me. But I can still see the impact of that early decision because people from different eras of my life still reach out. Whether they bump into me in public, see me at an event, or message me on social media, they often share a moment when I made them feel seen, encouraged, or understood.

I also benefited from leaders who communicated with presence. My journey is filled with bosses and mentors who inspired me in the moment. They were not only articulate. They were attentive. They made their words feel personal. They pushed me to learn, develop, move, and grow.

Being in the moment matters. Giving someone your full attention matters, whether you are the communicator or the audience. Wonderful things happen when you make a deep connection on purpose.

Be an Influencer

Be an Amasian influencer, not an Asian influenza! Apologies for the "dad joke," but I love them so. You are not trying to spread noise. You are trying to spread movement. Influence is the skill of getting people to align, decide, and act. If your words do not change anything, you did not influence. You just talked.

As a leader, you will be called upon to inspire others to action. That could be one-on-one, in a small group, or in a room full of people. Many assume influence requires charisma and charm. Those can help, but they are not the only path. Sometimes, the topic itself is compelling. Your job is to *communicate it in a way that lands.*

There are different ways people influence others. Some are constructive. Some are manipulative. Knowing the difference matters because influence without integrity becomes control.

Bottom line: Influence is a skill. Your job is to learn the styles, recognize them in the wild, and choose the ones that move people with credibility.

Here are some personas leaders adopt to influence others.

- **The Visionary.** Visionaries attract people to a clear picture of success. They use "the art of the possible" to describe where we are going and why it matters. Dr. Martin Luther King Jr.'s "I Have a Dream" speech (March on Washington for Jobs and Freedom, August 28, 1963) remains a widely cited example of vision-based influence. A visionary sets a bold direction, grounds it in shared values, and invites others to build it together.
- **The Fear Monger.** Fear mongers influence by triggering anxiety and threat. Authoritarians and dictators use fear to force compliance. Some leaders use fear to motivate performance by painting a catastrophic picture of what happens if people do not follow. Fear can spur action, but it often erodes trust and yields short-term obedience rather than long-term commitment.
- **The Guilt-Tripper.** Guilt-trippers influence by leaning on obligation and reciprocity. They know many people are loyal and conscientious, and they use that loyalty to secure agreement. It is a form of pressure that can look like "responsibility," but it is often manipulation in disguise.
- **The FOMO Influencer.** Social media popularized "fear of missing out." FOMO creates urgency by making people feel behind, late, or excluded unless they follow. In business, this can show up as "limited time" offers or implied status signals. Used carefully, it can create momentum. Overused, it creates cynicism.
- **The Philosopher.** Philosophers influence rational audiences. They use logic, evidence, and structured argument to help people arrive at a conclusion that feels like their own. They anticipate objections, address

tradeoffs, and build a case step by step. This is especially effective with analytical decision-makers.

- **The Catalyst of Feels.** On the other end of the spectrum are influencers who lead with emotion. They evoke hope, belonging, pride, anger, or courage, triggering a visceral response. Think of an uplifting sermon that moves a room to say "Amen," or a concert where the crowd becomes one voice. Used with integrity, emotional influence creates unity. Used irresponsibly, it becomes manipulation.
- **The Negotiator.** Negotiation is influence with constraints. Styles vary between cultures, and negotiation is not the same as bartering. In graduate school, my negotiation class emphasized transparency of agenda, clarity on what you can offer, and discipline about what you will not give up. Over time, I have found that strong negotiators synthesize multiple influence styles. They build rapport, ask for transparency, and push toward mutual benefit. They also know when to fold and when to walk away.

Ask yourself: Am I moving people through clarity and credibility, or through pressure and anxiety? Am I being authentic to my ultimate self in how I influence others?

The Amasian Way calls us to learn multiple influencing styles, then synthesize them into our own with integrity.

VOICE OF EXPERIENCE

After two years of attending professional wrestling school part-time, my coach offered me the chance to wrestle in front of a live audience. He told me I had an "it factor" that he could not teach. He liked that every time I stepped into the ring during class, people stopped to see what I was going to do. I have heard something similar in professional settings, too, especially in meetings. People have told me that I know how to "own a room."

Presence is something I have practiced for years. Theater since I was eleven. Reading at church since I was a teenager. Early in my career, I became a corporate training instructor. Over the past fifteen years, I have taken opportunities to serve as a keynote speaker, presenter, and panelist whenever available.

I am not claiming I am a natural. I never had a leading role in a show. I never wrestled in front of a live audience. I have not spoken to crowds of thousands. I have not been trained to speak with a teleprompter or to the media. But the reps did something. Practice, feedback, and repetition conditioned my body to know what to do when the spotlight hits.

Here is the part that surprises people. I do not love being the center of attention. I feel the weight of being watched. I am often exhausted after being on stage or at networking events. People assume that means I must be an extrovert who loves the limelight. The truth is more complicated. I feel like an introvert wearing an extrovert skin, and that skin was earned, not gifted.

My conclusion is that presence can be trained. With enough practice, your body learns to show up with calm, clarity, and control, even when you feel nervous underneath it. You do not need to become someone else. You need to become more practiced at being yourself under pressure.

Presence and charisma amplify your ability to influence. The more comfortable you become with attention, the more you can turn that attention into movement.

CREATE YOUR INFLUENCE STYLE

Knowing different methods of influence can help you lead others. These are not personality traits. They are practiced skills. The goal is not to copy someone else's style. The goal is to develop a style that is *authentic to you*, credible to others, and effective in the moment.

Your Authentic Style

You must show up as yourself. It is absolutely okay to be a little quirky and different if that is who you are and who others know you to be. Do not copy and paste someone else's style as your own.

I learned that the hard way. As a kid, I tried channeling the Fonz from *Happy Days*. Later, I tried Andrew Dice Clay and his rebellious comedian energy. (Yes, I am dating myself.) People could tell I was impersonating someone else. They did not take me seriously because it did not feel real.

Lean into who you genuinely are. Authenticity is how people decide whether to trust you. It took a long time for me to move from assimilation, where I tried to erase my authentic self and my Chinese cultural influences, to acculturation, where I learned to embrace both Eastern and Western influences as a Chinese American.

Believable in Your Conviction

We have talked about purpose throughout the Amasian Way. If you want to inspire others to act, you need a serious purpose and conviction. If you cannot take the topic seriously, no one else will either.

You need to understand the urgency for change. Your drive to improve needs to be infectious. If you waffle, others will lose commitment. Talk the talk and walk the walk consistently. As Mahatma Gandhi said, "Be the change you want to see in the world." People need to believe you mean it.

FIND YOUR OWN VOICE

Have you ever been in a conversation where someone constantly quotes someone else to get you to comply? "You should do this because the big boss will like it." "So-and-so would be disappointed if you don't do it." That person quickly becomes a messenger rather than an influencer.

You need to be clear and transparent about your role as the person leading and influencing. Use your own words. You can absolutely align with a larger vision, but do so in your own language.

Instead of:

"Our CEO expects us to do X."

Try:

"By doing X, we'll align to our company's vision and deliver impact against its goals."

That shift moves you from messenger to leader.

Craft Your Message

The substance of your message is the key to success. You need to know why people should care, rationally and emotionally. You need to know how it connects to their goals and values. You need to be able to describe success and the consequences of doing nothing. You also need a point of view. A message with no point of view rarely moves anyone.

Here's a note about generative AI: use it thoughtfully. Overreliance on AI when writing can dilute your personal voice. While AI is useful for refining structure, clarity, and grammar, it shouldn't replace the unique perspective that makes your influence authentic. Lately, I've noticed more people pointing out obvious signs that content was written by generative AI instead of a real author. Many feel disconnected from messages that seem exaggerated or lack a human touch.

TEN PRACTICAL METHODS TO CRAFT YOUR COMMUNICATION

1. **Q&A Tree.** In a business writing class, I learned to organize communication through a series of questions and answers. Start by writing what you want to communicate at the top of the page. Then create a two-column table: questions on the left, answers on the right.

   Step into your audience's shoes. After reading your main point, what is the first question that comes to mind? Write it down. Answer it. Then ask the next question. Repeat until you have exhausted the likely questions and objections.

Include the basics: who, what, where, when, why, and how. A question tree forces your message to earn agreement.

2. **Thud Factor.** A great way to grab attention is to start with something provocative. In public speaking, this is sometimes called a "thud factor" because a speaker might literally drop a heavy object on a table to create a loud bang.

   Many James Bond films do this with an action sequence before the opening credits. In safety training, we used this by opening with a real incident to help learners feel the gravity of the protocols. Your "thud" can be a story, a question, a surprising contrast, or a consequence. The point is to create immediate attention and curiosity.
3. **Big Picture with Guideposts.** Adult learners like to see the forest for the trees. They want the big picture and to know where they fit within it. For complex messages, give your audience structure: pillars, phases, steps, or a map. Guideposts reduce cognitive load and increase follow-through.
4. **Tell Them What You Are Telling Them.** Because retention is never 100 percent, build purposeful repetition into your communication, especially for the main point. In training, we said: "Tell them what you will tell them, tell them what you are telling them, and tell them what you told them."

   In court, this looks like opening arguments, evidence, and testimony, and then closing arguments. The repetition is not filler. It is reinforcement.
5. **Tell a Story.** Storytelling is as old as human history. A personal story makes the message memorable. Sometimes, a true, non-personal story can work too, as long as it is provocative and clearly tied to the point. Stories help people connect to a concept that would otherwise feel abstract.
6. **Catch Phrase and Sing-Song.** Yes, I am a big fan of professional wrestling. You know a wrestler is popular

when thousands of people repeat their catchphrases. They are even more popular when the catchphrase becomes a call-and-response.

One of my managers called me "the phrase guy." He noticed my phrases made my presentations stick. I use @now, @next, and @future to describe current state, near-term state, and future state. I've also used "Moving from MOUs to MSAs" to drive home the difference between intent and paid commitment. The right phrase makes your idea simple, memorable, and repeatable. I know I have had a positive effect when I begin to see my catchphrases used by other leaders to make the similar points.

7. **Get Them to Say Yes.** The art of influencing is not forcing agreement. It is guiding people to conclude, out loud, that they want to act. Build participation into your communication. Ask questions that invite ownership.

   Be careful with verbal habits like "right?" and "correct?" If overused, they feel like coercion. Open-ended questions and strategic pauses work better.
8. **Logic.** Rational decision-makers need a logical path. If you skip steps and force the conclusion, you lose them. Build the case. Let them arrive at the conclusion with you.
9. **Rhetoric.** People are emotional creatures. Strong emotions can override logic. Emotionally appealing communication can reinforce rational agreement and, at times, overcome rational objections. Use this carefully and ethically.
10. **Call to Action.** Be explicit about what you want someone to do differently as a result of your message. Make the next step easy. "Buy now" is crude, but the concept is correct: remove friction. If your audience must guess what happens next, you did not finish the job.

Bottom line: Influence works when your style is authentic, your conviction is believable, and your message is engineered for action.

ORGANIZE, SOCIALIZE, PRACTICE

The most foolish thing any of us does in life and at work is make *preventable* mistakes. We forgo the disciplines ingrained in us throughout our development and are surprised when the outcome is not what we want. We are taught to pay attention when we walk in the street, and yet so many of us have walked into something because we were looking at our phones instead of our surroundings. If we do not apply what we have learned about communication, we should not be surprised if we miss our intended outcomes.

You have been taught your whole life how to author and organize communication to be more effective. You organize your message to give it structure. You socialize it with the right people so you can pressure-test it. Then you adjust and practice until your delivery matches your intent.

Distractions such as disorganized messaging, contradictory supporting points, or plot holes in your story can keep people from agreeing—or worse, they reinforce their reasons to oppose your idea.

Ten Practical Tips for Delivering Communication

1. **Practice, practice, practice.** Rehearse your communication many times before delivery. I have read at my church for thirty years, and I still rehearse the readings ahead of Mass. Practice is your sandbox for testing emphasis, timing, and tone.

   Practical ways to practice:

   - Record a video of yourself and watch for what to keep and what to improve.
   - Practice in front of a mock audience, and ask for blunt feedback.
   - Test with sample stakeholders who understand the real audience and can predict objections.
   - If you are presenting, practice your commentary. Do not practice reading the slide.

When I worked in consulting, we practiced sales pitches for large engagements. Senior partners took rehearsal seriously. Other partners role-played the prospective client and gave direct feedback. That level of seriousness is one reason those teams win.

2. **Presence.** Presence helps your message land. Confidence shows you believe in your message. Humility shows respect for your audience. Authenticity builds trust. Charisma and likability attract attention. The opposite also holds: nervousness, pomposity, harshness, and pretentiousness can quickly lose the room.
3. **Pace yourself.** Most people speak too quickly when nervous or excited. In larger rooms, your voice needs time to travel, and your audience needs time to process. Slow down until it almost feels unnatural. Use pauses intentionally so people can absorb the point and have their "ah-ha" moments.
4. **Clap to change.** Even as an experienced speaker, there are moments when my voice shakes or my breathing quickens. Butterflies get worse if you do nothing.

   A trick I learned in a communication class is to reset your nervous system with a quick physical "shock." Clap once and feel the sting travel through your palms. Then reset your mind and body from that moment forward. Stomping your foot or snapping your fingers can do the same thing.
5. **Eye contact.** Eye contact connects with your audience, whether one-on-one or in a large room. This can be difficult for AAPI professionals raised in cultures that emphasize hierarchy and deference, but it is absolutely a skill you can practice.

   In a large audience, you cannot make eye contact with each person. Simulate it by holding your gaze in each section of the room for a five-count. Avoid scanning too fast from side to side, and avoid staring at one spot the entire time.

6. **Zone of silence.** There are positions where you should not speak, especially when your mouth is not facing the audience or is out of range of the microphone. The most common mistake is talking while looking back at the projected slide.

   If you are not wearing a mic, the audience will not hear you. Even with a mic, your clarity drops when you turn away. When you move across the room, consider pausing your talking until you are planted again. Do not let movement noise or volume fluctuations disrupt your message.
7. **Modulate.** One of the most powerful tools in your toolbox is modulation: pace, volume, and tone. Advanced communicators know how to lower their volume to draw people in, then raise it to emphasize. This is also why you should use a microphone in a larger room. Without amplification, you lose the ability to go low and still be heard.
8. **Imagine.** People often say, "Imagine the audience naked," to boost confidence. I have never found that helpful. I find it distracting.

   Two things I do instead:
   - I imagine I am having a smaller, intimate conversation, even in a large room. That keeps my tone conversational and helps the audience feel closer.
   - I imagine an invisible barrier between the crowd and me. That helps me stay grounded and reduces my need for external validation.
9. **Eliminate distractions.** Distractions pull your audience away from the moment and your message. Typos and formatting issues distract detail-oriented people. Controversial content can trigger resistance unrelated to your point. Fillers like "um," "like," and "you know" can irritate audiences who want polish. Weak body language can evoke pity rather than confidence.

Your job is to remove anything that competes with the message.

10. **Close strong.** Have you ever been disappointed by a series finale that did not deliver a satisfying conclusion after all the hours you invested? Ahem… *Lost.*

    To inspire action, you have to land the plane. Your close should be definitive and satisfying. Make statements, not questions. If you want something, ask for it. Resources. Approval. Promotion. A decision. Make your ask clear, and sound confident. Do not be coy and make your audience work to figure out what you want.

Public speaking is one of the most common phobias. At the same time, I have rarely met a leader who was not a polished presenter. I have benefited a lot from communication skills training at work. I also know people who gained confidence through groups such as Toastmasters. Senior leaders often have coaches and media training for high-stakes communication.

There are also newer tools: virtual reality (VR) training that simulates audiences for presentations and difficult conversations, and AI tools that can help you rehearse and get feedback. You have more outlets than ever for learning, developing, and practicing communication and influence. The real limitation is whether you will use them.

One more thought. If we use AI to provide feedback on our communication, instead of teaching it our style and strengthening our point of view, will we eventually lose our unique, authentic voices? Maybe the win is using AI to sharpen clarity and grammar while protecting what is most human: your point of view, your conviction, and your presence.

The Amasian Way calls us to find our voices and points of view and lead others with authenticity and conviction.

Bottom line: A message rarely fails because the idea is bad. It fails because the message is messy, untested, or unpracticed.

VOICE OF EXPERIENCE

One evening after a networking event, I spent time with a Korean American professional who shared an extraordinary story. He grew up in Korea, served in the Korean army, and immigrated to the United States as an adult, barely speaking English. His life was a case study in adversity, resilience, and reinvention.

And yet, inside our organization, he felt stuck.

He centered the challenge on his accent. He told me he feared speaking up in meetings because people had difficulty understanding him. The irony was painful. He had strong ideas and real substance, but the "delivery" was getting in the way of the "value."

At one point, he said, "B. Jae, I am too old to lose my accent. I am not sure I have what it takes."

I asked him to humor me in a quick experiment. I asked him to sing a verse of "Happy Birthday." He did. Then I asked him what he noticed.

His accent was dramatically less noticeable.

I have been fascinated by that phenomenon for a while. Across genres, many singers sound more "American" when they sing in English, regardless of where they are from. I have noticed it with Adele, the Spice Girls, Ed Sheeran, and BTS. I do not have a scientific explanation for it. But I do have a practical takeaway: if you can shape sounds differently in singing, you can train your mouth and ear differently in speaking, too. Not overnight. Not perfectly. But more than you think is possible.

Another time, I spoke to a group of international MBA students. Several voiced frustrations that American companies were not more accommodating of language barriers. They felt they should get a pass because they had strong grades and strong professional backgrounds.

I paused and asked a simple question: "What would you advise an American expatriate working in China to do in order to be successful?"

Their answer was immediate: "Learn the language and culture."

Then the irony landed. Some laughed. The room shifted.

So, I asked one more question: "What makes it difficult to learn the language and culture?"

We eventually arrived at a hard truth that applies to expatriates and international students alike: comfort can become a cage. If you spend time only with people who communicate like you, your growth rate slows. If you spend time with people who communicate the way you want to communicate, you start building new instincts. You learn faster because your environment is teaching you.

I saw the stakes even more clearly in performance reviews. I have been in discussions where an associate had the right capabilities, but teammates, managers, and clients struggled to communicate with her. She could not reliably capture meeting notes because she could not follow the discussion. The team recommended investing in her through language coaching and structured development. But I also saw how quickly some environments jump to the harsh conclusion: "Not ready. Not promotable." In high-pressure cultures, it is easy to celebrate the strongest communicator and quietly push out the person who needs development.

Language barriers and heavy accents matter because they can create friction in the most important leadership skill: communication. And communication becomes more critical, not less, as you move up.

The good news is you have options. Traditional classes. Coaching. Practice communities. Simulations. Newer tools, including virtual reality and AI-enabled practice, can create safe reps before you take it live. The path is "be willing." Be willing to get uncomfortable, learn, and practice.

And yes, if you want a low-pressure way to practice pronunciation and rhythm, karaoke might not be a bad start.

JOURNAL ACTIVITY: Practice. Practice. Practice.

Write a five-slide presentation that convinces someone to take action. Use only these slides:

1. Position
2. Supporting detail 1
3. Supporting detail 2
4. Supporting detail 3
5. Conclusion + Call to action

Then:

- Record a video of your delivery.
- Watch it once without judgment.
- Watch it again and take notes on what to change.
- Optional: Deliver it to a real audience, and ask for direct feedback.

Reflection Questions

- Did you clearly answer, "So what?"
- Would you be convinced to take action if you were the audience?
- What felt easiest for you?
- What felt most challenging?
- What is one change you will make in your next delivery?

CULTIVATING RELATIONSHIPS THROUGH CONNECTION

Up to this point, we have focused on how you communicate and influence. Now comes the multiplier. You can deliver a compelling message and still lose momentum if nobody repeats it when you are not in the room. Credibility is earned by showing up and moving, but credibility scales through advocates. Communication helps you articulate your value and your results. Relationship skills help you connect with the people who will champion your performance, opportunities, and promotions when decisions are made behind closed doors.

You will never truly work alone. You will also never accomplish anything purely on your own. Work relationships are inevitable. Great relationships can propel your career. Bad relationships can tank it. Relationships make you capable of doing more than you can alone. You will have many relationships throughout your career, and different types of relationships will help you in different ways.

Bottom line: Your performance creates credibility. Your relationships determine how far that credibility travels.

Relationship Type	Supports Your Career Through...
Peers	Teamwork, healthy competition
Managers	Performance management through observation and feedback
Mentors	Sharing knowledge and experiences
Coaches	Challenging you
Advocates	Championing you
Advisors	Providing guidance
Customers	Purchases and feedback

Career-oriented relationships, when cultivated and managed, can be very rewarding. I recall during a partner training I organized, the lead partner shared a simple but powerful insight about client focus. He pulled out a small piece of paper from his wallet. On the paper were three top priorities for his most important client. He said he regularly pulled it out and asked himself whether he and his team were working on one of those priorities. By keeping those priorities close, he stayed aligned with what mattered most to the relationship.

The Amasian Way calls us to prioritize building and managing meaningful relationships.

Sometimes, when I hear people describe networking, it sounds like they are trying to collect all the Pokémons. They want a diverse collection for different situations and opponents. They chase rare and legendary ones because those people have influence and status. But the most important part of the analogy is this: Ash and Pikachu are widely considered the most successful trainer-and-Pokémon pairing because they share a strong bond.

One of the things you learn as a consultant is to build deep relationships with your client counterparts. As they level up and evolve, so does their ability to help you reach your goals. Sometimes, that looks like access, sponsorship, or inside context. Other times, it becomes purchasing power and the ability to hire your firm or fund your work.

How to Start a Relationship

If there is one thing we were raised to be good at, it is starting relationships. We spent years in school learning social skills and finding allies to help us navigate those awkward years. My son values fewer relationships. My daughter seems to have an endless supply of "BFFs." That feeling of navigating life with a best friend can be as comforting as a toddler carrying around a safety blanket.

If we practiced meeting new people throughout our school years, it should be simpler as adults. But many of us become complacent in our cliques and besties and stop branching out. Then we join the workforce and realize that relationship-building is not optional. Sure, some people make it look easy, like sales professionals, fundraisers, and politicians. But the truth is, we all need networking and relationship skills to be successful.

Here are my tips for starting a conversation:

1. **Do not overthink it.** Sometimes, we cannot start a conversation because we treat it like an all-or-nothing outcome. We put so much pressure on the interaction that we freeze. A conversation starter is just that: a start. Focus on opening the door, not closing the deal.
2. **Find connections and fascinations.** You are already connected by context: a meeting, a conference, a location. Use that.

   "What brought you here?"

   "Who are you here representing?"

   After the opening, the rest of the conversation becomes a test: do we have a connection or a fascination worth continuing? Commonality feels comfortable. Fascination feels energizing. Both can be reasons to keep going.

3. **Be authentic and curious, but do not overshare.** Come as you are. Listen actively. Ask thoughtful questions. But respect boundaries early. Do not overprobe for sensitive information. Do not "one-up" the other person's story. Too much too soon can scare people off. Keep the pace respectful and mutual.
4. **Do not pitch.** Refrain from sales pitch language like, "I work for the world's largest…" Do not try to close a sale before you build trust. You would not ask someone to marry you right after meeting them. Pitching too early changes the intent from relationship-building to transaction. If they are not ready to buy in that moment, you may have lost a relationship that could have led to a larger opportunity later.
5. **Read the signs.** Body language matters. Fronting, eye contact, mirroring, and receptivity are signals that the person is engaged. If you are not seeing those signals, do not force it.
6. **Do not overstay.** Respect the person's time. Especially in networking settings, they may want to meet others. Look for a natural break. Acknowledge what clicked. Ask permission to continue the conversation another time.

VOICE OF EXPERIENCE

Late in my junior year, there was a new president that took over my college. I did some research and discovered we were both Boston College High School graduates. When I met him, I introduced myself as a fellow alum.

Over the next year, if I was present, he would include me in his introduction to the crowd, "And B. Jae and I graduated from the same high school...a few years apart." That helped him connect with the audience.

When I received my first interview before graduating, I thought it was odd because I had never applied for a job at that company. I discovered the president of the college had personally reached out to his friend to get me an interview.

I had unintentionally networked my way to my first job out of college. I found a way to connect with the new president, and he leveraged me to connect with the students. In the end, I had a job before graduation because he proactively advocated for me.

Whether you are in a crowded networking event or a one-on-one setting, take the interaction for what it is: a test to see if there is more. Both parties need to maintain the freedom to choose whether to engage and continue the dialogue. If the test did not yield a connection or fascination, and you do not have a reason to continue, it is perfectly fine to end with: "It was very nice to meet you. Good luck with ____. Hope to see you again."

Also, *relationships are built on moments that click*. Sometimes, it happens quickly. Sometimes, it takes multiple encounters. There are complications: personality, openness, trust, context, status, and titles. Two things not to do: (1) assume a relationship should happen quickly, and (2) assume that if you do not click right away, you never will.

Some relationship targets are not optional. If you need the relationship, be more intentional. Do your homework. Find a warm introduction. Put yourself in the right place at the right time.

I highly encourage you to research and learn how to network at live events. There is a science to engaging one-on-one, breaking into a group, active listening, communicating with authenticity, and managing intent. Your company may offer training, or you can find it externally. The more you learn and practice, the easier it becomes.

Bottom line: Your performance earns credibility. Your communication makes it legible. Your relationships make it travel, because advocates talk about you when you are not in the room.

Following Up and Following Through

Often, people do not follow up or follow through on those initial moments that click. Many networking conversations go nowhere because neither party follows up or follows through. I have had many engaging conversations where the other party failed to follow up afterward.

I believe the *initial follow-up is the first real test of whether the relationship will begin*. If you want to cultivate a meaningful relationship, you need to follow up quickly.

The worst thing I get from people is a follow-up that feels impersonal or overly automated. For example, I am suddenly added to marketing distribution emails, or I receive a generic note asking me to schedule time on a calendar app. No, thank you. If you found a connection or fascination that clicked, reference it in the follow-up. Make it human.

Following up and following through matters even more when you are the one who needs something, such as when you are looking for a mentor or cultivating a client relationship. In those situations, you should initiate and lead early interactions to show that the relationship is important to you.

Here are a few tips on maintaining and managing meaningful relationships:

- **Define the relationship.** Sometimes, things fall apart because they go unspoken. In business relationships, be clear about what the relationship is intended to be: mentoring, peer support, client, and so on. Relationships can evolve. Many business relationships become friendships. A well-defined relationship gives you permission to check in, continue, evolve, or pause as needed.
- **Manage the relationship at first.** To achieve your relationship goals, take the initiative to set up a meeting cadence and agenda. Once your goals are achieved, you can manage the relationship with less structure.
- **Ongoing touch points.** I love it when someone in my life I haven't connected with in a long time reenters it, and when we do, it feels like we were never apart. You know what I would love more? If we were never apart. So, it is important to stay consistent with touch points, even if they are brief.

- **Be kind and helpful without keeping score.** Look for ways to contribute and be valuable. It is how you made the other person feel that they will remember. Staying engaged, even if the relationship pauses for a season, helps maintain that positive impression. Stay in touch through social networks such as LinkedIn, and engage with the other person's posts.
- **Deepen trust and relationship when appropriate.** Some relationships benefit from growing beyond their original purpose. Know how to maintain meaningful relationships and know when to evolve them.

When relationships are well managed and maintained, both parties welcome continuity and requests for assistance.

Bottom line: Relationships do not grow from a great first conversation. They grow from consistent follow-up that proves you meant it.

BEING STRATEGIC WITH RELATIONSHIPS

Relationships are tricky, especially in the workplace. Some relationships are strategic in nature. They create alliances that help you get things done. Many people call this "office politics" and slap a negative connotation on it. But gaining alignment and support through relationships is a critical path to execution.

Literally, nothing gets done if people do not work together and gain alignment. Politics is what gets housing and roads built, schools funded, and laws passed. To dismiss politics as "dirty" is often to dismiss something critical simply because you do not understand it, you do not have the skills to engage in it, or you do not feel motivated to work on relationships to achieve an objective. It becomes dirty politics only when someone undermines others through unethical tactics, such as gossiping, manipulation, or blame-shifting.

Strategic relationships are an important multiplier inside the workplace. It is no different than at home. If you wanted something from your dad, you might get your mom and siblings on your side to help you advocate for it. Alliances are not "dirty." Relationships are how things get done.

The people you want to build intentional strategic relationships with are often those who have influence and decision-making power. They may or may not have the title, but they can affect outcomes. For example, sometimes it is more important to have a relationship with the executive assistant who controls the executive's schedule and meetings. Gatekeepers often decide whether you get the meeting at all.

Here are some of my tips on intentionally building strategic relationships

- **Know the players.** Map the stakeholders based on the role they play in influencing the outcome. Research and engage others to learn their personalities, tendencies, and agendas. Study the decision-making culture and process. Do not overlook anyone, especially the people close to the decision-maker.
- **Bring your brand.** Your reputation should precede you. You want to be a known quantity before the first real ask. Your value and impact should be respected and reinforced by others. People should want to invest time in a relationship with you.
- **Align on the "why" and the "so what."** Strategic relationships are built on shared objectives. Get on the same page about what success looks like, and use common language to describe it. That could be OKRs, Critical Success Factors (CSFs), and Key Performance Indicators (KPIs).
- **Add value, especially when it matters.** Show up again and again, especially when it matters most. Lean into your strengths, move, and deliver. Be memorable for impact. Be memorable for how you delivered it: trustworthy, reliable, committed, industrious, and resourceful.
- **Build the relationship on purpose.** Elevate the relationship over time from contact to collaborator to trusted advisor. Maintain the relationship through changes and keep investing so the advantage compounds over time.

The Amasian Way calls us to strategically build and maintain relationships to build allegiance and increase our power.

VOICE OF EXPERIENCE

As a volunteer mentor and career coach, one of my favorite things is watching a relationship evolve over time. I have had a mentor-mentee relationship that evolved into a peer and friend relationship. When we get together, we can oscillate between coaching and collaboration. Sometimes, the tables even turn, and I become the mentee, asking for observations and feedback.

That shift happens because the relationship grows over the years. She grew, gained my respect over time, and I was humble enough to recognize that the dynamic changed. If I had clung to the hierarchy of the original relationship, I would have missed out on years of meaningful collaboration. And now that she has become a career coach herself, I can lean on her to help me navigate career inflection points.

This relationship is also strategic because she is deeply academic and curious. She loves to study organizational and people dynamics. Over the years, she built a vast network of mentors, peers, and thought leaders. She has proven to be someone I gladly invest time in. I respect her insights and feedback. I benefit from what she learns and the access she has built through her network.

Relationships are not finite games. They grow and evolve. I have peers from my early career who are now executives and can provide substantive advice, opportunities, and business. I have retired mentors who can still help connect me with funders for my philanthropy efforts. You never really know where relationships can take you over time.

RELATIONSHIPS AND EXPOSURE

In an earlier chapter, I referenced Harvey J. Coleman's formula for success: PIE (Performance, Image, and Exposure). Harvey breaks down success as follows: Performance (10%), Image (30%), and Exposure (60%). I argue that these percentages shift over the course of your career. I agree that performance is table stakes, no matter which role you hold. Your success must be based on substance. You will be better positioned to gain advocates if you have high performance and high potential. We also discussed the importance of managing your professional brand (image).

If you subscribe to Coleman's formula, then exposure is the most important factor (60%) in your professional success. Exposure describes the visibility of your contributions to key decision-makers. Connections and relationships are key to your exposure because they carry your brand promise into rooms you are excluded from. Even if you believe you have autonomy and agency, you will still be discussed in rooms where you are not present. Even the CEO's performance is discussed by the board's executive committee in the CEO's absence. Strategic relationships are even more important for ensuring your brand promise is championed behind closed doors. I know that my career has been lifted and damaged in this context. When my strategic relationships and exposure are strong, I do well. When they were weak, not so much.

Bottom line: Strategic relationships are not "office politics." Build allegiance the right way, and your influence scales.

ALLYSHIP

Not all workplace relationships need to be formed with specific strategic objectives in mind. In fact, most professional connections may not be overtly strategic yet can significantly influence one's success and development. Establishing meaningful personal relationships with colleagues and clients contributes to a more fulfilling work environment, reducing feelings of isolation and fostering collaboration.

Allyship remains crucial in the workplace, just as it was during our school years. From a young age, we're taught social skills and soon discover individual strengths. Generally, introverts value a few close friendships, whereas extraverts consider many acquaintances as friends.

Allyship comes in various shapes. Sometimes, allies are colleagues working alongside us on similar tasks, offering mutual support as teammates striving to improve together. At other times, allies come from different departments, providing a safe environment to share or vent away from our immediate teams. Allies at work truly become friends—they step up when we need help, lift us up with encouragement, and inspire us to surpass our limits. Through their support, allies foster our sense of belonging and empower us to thrive.

In the context of inclusion, allyship involves recognizing that minorities must navigate an imperfect system. These allies may differ from us in appearance and background; however, they demonstrate genuine empathy for our challenges and are committed to offering assistance. During my formative years in a predominantly Caucasian city, community, and school, my sense of belonging and ability to thrive were greatly influenced by the presence of supportive allies. These included peers who respected my differences, their parents who fostered inclusive attitudes, and faculty and staff who provided extra guidance when I was still acquiring English proficiency.

I know people who are afraid to interact with people different from them for fear of being made fun of. For example, someone I knew felt comfortable only among other Indian nationals because she knew she would not have to worry about people not understanding her due to her Indian accent, or about having her English corrected. While she was open to interacting with people who were not Indian, she was too afraid to do so. I helped her see that diverse interactions might actually help her break down the language barrier, as they give others a chance to better understand her accent and, at the same time, help her improve her English.

I also know people who are always skeptical and less open to allyship in all its forms. I am just going to say it out loud. If you have reservations about others because of their race, culture, ethnicity, or any other form of diversity, you will be less likely to gain universal allyship. It is not lost on me that the monolithic Asian descriptor actually includes people who may not appreciate each other. It is really difficult for you to ask others to be inclusive of you and be your ally if you are not inclusive of others yourself. To gain allies, you also need to be an ally to others.

Allyship is also about mutual effort. I remember when a senior partner questioned his colleagues about how they manage client relationships. He asked, "Consider your clients—when did they last invest in you? Or are you constantly investing in them—maybe treating them to expensive steak dinners—without seeing any new business in return?" While this example may seem overly transactional, the message resonated with me. Both at work and in our personal lives, some people tend to only take without ever giving back. Is that really the kind of person you want by your side? When you think about those you consider allies, ask yourself: what have you done for them recently?

Yes, allyship can be strategic. But you should also place value in the allies who give you the feels. They can boost your aura and amplify your zone of psychological safety. They can help to improve and gain momentum for your ideas. They can affirm and broadcast your brand promise.

VOICE OF EXPERIENCE

It was freshman year in college. My two Caucasian roommates and I shared a tiny square-shaped dorm room. It was Valentine's Day, which is also my roommate Jeff's birthday. The three of us and Jeff's girlfriend celebrated all night. At midnight, the three of them suddenly got up and left the room. To my surprise, they returned performing a dragon dance, wearing a makeshift dragon head and sheets for the body. They pronounced that it was the Lunar New Year! I had never been away from my family for the holiday before. They were trying to make me feel at home.

I have been very lucky growing up with many non-Asian allies. However, I know that luck is an abstract concept that can result from intentionality. I grew up in a Caucasian-majority world. Other than my relatives, almost everyone I knew was non-Asian. I made friends nevertheless. A high-school English teacher wrote in my college recommendation letter that he observed I fit in with every crowd, from athletes to intellectual to artistic students. I was open to being friends with everyone and anyone. My childhood experiences made me very comfortable working across diverse groups of people.

Things are different for my kids now. Their schools have been majority Asian American. This meant they never had to hang out with kids of other races or ethnicities if they did not want to. They would have to be intentional about having a diverse group of friends. I have witnessed recent immigrant children stick together. I get that it is more comfortable from a language and interest perspective. No doubt, I would also be tempted to do that if I were in their situation instead of the one I grew up in.

I have also observed similar patterns in the workplace. I worked in Munich, Germany for six months, and the American firm consultants socialized separately from the Dutch and German firm consultants. I found myself bouncing back and forth between the groups and even learning a few common Dutch and German phrases in the process. Because of this, I stood out to the project's partners.

Regardless of skin color, cultural background, or ethnicity, I have found that professionals who can work easily with diverse groups rise through the ranks faster than those who are reluctant to do so. Many executives are sent on expat assignments to gain global experience.

I believe strongly that you must be open to allyship in all of its potential forms to benefit from it. The more you pick and choose, the smaller your universe of allyship becomes. I also strongly believe in the journey I've experienced, from the era of "racial tolerance" to "diversity, equity, and inclusion," and that the best way to gain diverse allies is to embrace differences. I love learning cultural traditions, listening to global music, and tasting exotic flavors. And I *love* cheeseburgers and my Caucasian American allies. There, I said it. There is no togetherness in discrimination of any form, including reverse discrimination. Together, we are stronger.

Bottom line: Allies help us be more than we can be on our own. To gain universal allies, we need to be universal allies.

THE AMASIAN WAY calls us to become universal leaders and allies to ALL people.

Put this into action: Consider how many colleagues you interacted with today. How diverse was the group? This is the lens through which you see your world. Now consider the interactions you had over the past week. How much did that change your lens? The more your lens relies on a single-color filter, the less of a universal leader you will be. Who might you begin interacting with to broaden your lens?

The AAPI Lens

Soft skills, such as communication, influence, and relationship-building, have often been framed as a gap for AAPI professionals, especially in workplace cultures that reward visibility, directness, and self-advocacy. In many AAPI upbringings, humility and harmony are strengths. The issue is not the values. The issue is the translation.

Many of us were taught to do good work, keep our heads down, and let results speak for themselves. In Western work cultures, results still matter. But results that are not understood, repeated, and sponsored often get under-credited.

You do not need to raise your voice to be more effective. You do need a voice. Your voice and the voices of those who advocate for you. You need to become clearer, more intentional, and more strategic.

Here are two common cultural friction points that show up in communication and relationships:

1. **Contextual communication (high-context vs. low-context).** In many Western workplaces, low-context communication is the default. People expect the point early, the ask is clearly stated, and the rationale is in a clean line of logic. In many AAPI contexts, communication can be more high-context, with more implied meaning based on history, hierarchy, tone, and shared understanding. When you use high-context communication in a low-context environment, you may be misread as unclear, hesitant, or unprepared.
2. **Conflict resolution vs. conflict avoidance.** Harmony is a strength until it becomes silence. Avoiding conflict

can reduce short-term friction, but it can also delay decisions, bury misalignment, and quietly damage performance. Amasian Leaders learn to engage conflict with discipline: clear issue framing, respectful tone, direct asks, and follow-through.

The practical reframe is this: *clarity is not aggression, and advocacy is not arrogance.* They are forms of leadership stewardship.

THE CAREER STAGE LENS

Early Career (Build Clarity and Reps)

- Practice "For what, to do what, so what?" in every meeting and email.
- Ask one clarifying question per meeting, even if you think you already understand.
- Find your voice in a meeting by summarizing decisions and next steps at the end.

Mid-Career (Become Promotion-Ready)

- Convert performance into a narrative: outcomes, metrics, and stakeholder impact.
- Build two advocates: one in your direct chain, one outside it.
- Start using a repeatable structure: point, proof, ask.

Senior Leader (Scale Influence and Systems)

- Influence through alignment: pre-wire key stakeholders before formal meetings.
- Build coalitions, not just relationships. Define the "yes path" before you ask.
- Sponsor others publicly. Your influence grows when you make other people stronger.

Career Transition (Increase Agency and Signal Value)

- Treat every conversation as a business case: clarity, relevance, and next step.
- Ask for specific help: introductions, perspective, feedback, or opportunities.
- Build advocates early. Transitions accelerate when someone credible says, "This person delivers."

CHAPTER SUMMARY

As an Amasian Leader, you will not win on competence alone. You win when competence is *understood*, *trusted*, and *championed*. Communication and relationships are what turn your performance into momentum.

Key takeaways:

- Know the purpose of your communication: For what? To do what? So what?
- Plan important conversations. Clarity is a performance advantage.
- Know your audience: demographics, personality, and agenda.
- Presence and delivery skills amplify credibility, especially when the stakes are high.
- Relationships are not optional. They are multipliers.
- Advocates matter. Credibility earned through showing up and moving scales faster when others champion your impact.
- Strategic relationships are not "dirty politics." They are alignment, alliance, and execution.

The Amasian Way calls us to inspire others to take action and build strategic relationships that amplify our value and impact.

JOURNAL ACTIVITY: PUTTING IT ALL TOGETHER—ASK FOR A PROMOTION

Prepare for a conversation with your supervisor where you ask for a promotion.

1. **Outline your message.**
   - Your position (what you want)
   - Supporting points (impact, results, readiness)
   - Your ask (what decision you want and by when)
2. **Build a question tree.**
   - List the likely questions and objections your supervisor may ask
   - Write your best answers using clear proof points
3. **Practice.**
   - Practice the discussion alone. Record yourself and self-critique.
   - Role-play with one person and ask for direct feedback.
4. **Map your advocates.**
   - Identify three people who can strengthen your promotion case.
   - Write exactly what you need from each (feedback, sponsorship, visibility, introductions).

Reflection Questions

- What part of communicating and influencing feels most natural to you right now?
- What part feels most difficult, and what will you do to improve it?
- How would you flex your message if your supervisor is direct, analytic, or relationship-focused?
- Which influencing method do you want to experiment with next, and why?
- What insight or feedback did you get from your practice partner?

Discover More

- Call to action (CTA) and message structure resources (conversation templates, interview response formats, executive summary patterns)
- Maslow's hierarchy of needs; Knowles' andragogy
- DISC personality framework (Dominance, Influence, Steadiness, Conscientiousness)
- "I Have a Dream" (Dr. Martin Luther King Jr.)
- "Be the change you want to see in the world." (often attributed to Mahatma Gandhi)

SO WHAT

Communication, influence, and relationship-building are not "soft." They are career leverage. If technical skill is your engine, these skills are your steering wheel and your fuel line. Without them, you may still move, but you will not move on purpose.

As AAPI professionals, these skills can feel awkward because many of us were rewarded for silence, obedience, and humility. You do not need to abandon those values. You need to upgrade how you show them: clarity, conviction, advocacy, and strategic relationships.

Your next move is simple: pick one high-stakes conversation in the next two weeks. Map it. Practice it. Then recruit one advocate who will help your results travel when you are not in the room.

LOOKING AHEAD

Next chapter, we grow. Communication and relationships create momentum. Growth is what you do with it: expanding capability, taking bigger reps, and leveling up your impact on purpose.

CHAPTER 6

Grow

In the last chapter, we established the discipline of doing the work that matters: clarify the "so what," commit to a point of view, and then move. The most strategic way to move is to move towards growth. Growth does not have to be about upward mobility. You can gain quite a bit by moving laterally and broadening your experience. The important thing is to grow in reps, depth, and breadth while you move.

This chapter is about the capability that underpins sustainable momentum and growth. The kind of growth that shows up in results is how you evolve yourself, develop others, and help an organization adapt fast enough to stay relevant.

I recently helped my son complete a growth mindset module to start sixth grade. It was refreshing to see kids introduced to the concept so early, because it's a topic we talk about at work all the time. Usually, we start talking about it after we've already been humbled by a new challenge. The core truth is simple: our success is limited less by talent than by our attitude and effort toward learning and improvement.

I often coach people not to peak at their last success. I cannot help but roll my eyes internally (I would never do a real one in front of someone; that would be rude) when someone starts reciting achievements from decades ago. I see you, Ivy League graduates who still announce your alma mater as if it were a current performance metric. It was an amazing achievement. But as Janet Jackson once sang, "What have you done for me lately?"

Today, a growth mindset is a sought-after leadership quality because change is happening so quickly that companies need leaders who can keep up and help them become the disruptor rather than the disrupted. It is surreal to see how quickly the list of "dominant" companies changes, and how many household names fade when they stop adapting. Leaders need to grow themselves, grow their teams, and grow their organizations. They need to lead people through transitional change and transformational change.

Here's where we're going in this chapter:

- **Grow yourself.** How belonging, thriving, and a growth mindset create the conditions for taking risks, learning quickly, and recovering from setbacks.
- **Grow in the moment.** How to pace your development, avoid the trap of chasing titles, and protect your work-life-and-me balance so you can sustain performance.
- **Grow others and organizations.** How leaders develop talent, influence without formal power, and become credible change agents when the stakes get real.

The Amasian Way calls us to grow with intention and purpose, in the moment, and in the direction the world is moving.

GROW YOURSELF

Belonging and Thriving

Have you ever seen a box-shaped watermelon? It is literally molded to grow into that shape. The same is true for careers: our growth is influenced by what nurtures us, and by how we choose to nurture ourselves. If fear, isolation, and hesitation are the container, we will eventually hit a ceiling. But when we feel a sense of belonging and stop self-limiting, we give ourselves permission to thrive. And thriving is what gives us the courage to test, learn, develop, and grow.

At a Diversity Committee meeting, a colleague asked, "Have you heard the phrase that diversity is being allowed to go to the dance, and inclusion is being invited to the dance?" Another colleague added, "Belonging is when you feel so comfortable you can decide whether you even want to go. And if you do go, you don't feel pressured to dance." That landed for me. You cannot feel the freedom to thrive and grow if you are in fear of judgment or of being disinvited. That is the feeling of not belonging.

When you feel belonging, you stop running the exhausting background process of self-monitoring: *Am I allowed to be here? Did I earn this seat? What is the "right" way to act? Am I an imposter doomed to be found out?* You are freer to be authentic. You do not have to code-switch to survive the room. For many AAPI professionals who have been conditioned to be agreeable, deferential, and low-friction, belonging can be the difference between quiet competence and visible leadership.

Bottom line: Belonging is performance infrastructure. It reduces the fear and increases your willingness to take smart risks and grow.

Belonging naturally fuels thriving. Thriving is the confidence to stretch and try something before you feel fully ready. That confidence accelerates learning. It also makes you more resilient, because you are not interpreting every setback as a verdict on your worth. You are thriving when you believe you can grow from failure and that the people around you will not punish you for being in progress.

Now, it is easy to blame others when you do not feel a sense of belonging or believe you cannot thrive. Many people do. But relationships, whether one-to-one or one-to-group, are a "two-way street." You cannot control how welcoming a culture is, but you can control how you show up inside it. You must open yourself to others without bringing antagonistic assumptions or self-doubt.

If you walk in with a "DTA—don't trust anyone" attitude, you will struggle to belong. If you are so fearful that it feels like you are walking on a thin glass floor the whole time, you will interpret every signal as a reason to retreat. A closed-minded attitude will also lead to confirmation bias that helps you justify your skepticism.

So, start here: be open to the possibilities. Assume positive intent until evidence proves otherwise. Show up as you wish. Then find allies. Whether it is kids on the first day of school or contestants arriving on *Survivor*, most people's first move is the same: they look for allies. There is strength in numbers. Belonging to a small group often becomes the bridge to belonging in the larger one. And building allies gives you practice and confidence in expanding your network. When you feel comfortable in your own skin, you are ready to thrive. When you thrive, you are ready to grow.

Belonging creates safety. Thriving creates momentum. Growth mindset turns that momentum into capability.

The Growth Mindset

Growth mindset is a concept popularized by psychologist Carol Dweck. At its core, it is the belief that your knowledge, skills, and abilities can improve through learning, deliberate practice, and repetition. People with a growth mindset treat challenges as training data that helps them get better.

The opposite is a fixed mindset: the belief that capabilities are static. When a fixed-mindset person hits a challenge, they often interpret it as a verdict, such as "I'm not good at this," and they either avoid the work, disengage, or quit. A fixed mindset also shuts down curiosity. When you are not open to learning and improving, you cap your own growth long before the job ever does.

Behaviors can reveal whether someone has an open or fixed mindset. For example, when a child tries something unfamiliar, you can notice their mindset by observing how readily they persist or how quickly they give up when faced with difficulties.

The Amasian Way calls us to adopt a growth mindset so we keep improving, keep learning, and keep turning challenges and setbacks into fuel.

Qualities of a Leader with a Growth Mindset

Leaders with a growth mindset tend to:

- **Believe in self.** Confidence in their ability to improve through learning, development, and reps.
- **Embrace challenge.** Willingness to step into difficulty and treat it as skill-building, not a threat.
- **Stay persistent.** Grit to persevere despite obstacles; refusal to tap out at the first setback.
- **Learn from feedback.** Ability to extract useful signal from coaching, critique, and experience.
- **Be driven by others' success.** Motivated rather than threatened by other people's wins.
- **Collaborate to improve.** Commitment to grow with others and bring people along.

VOICE OF EXPERIENCE

Growth is the one thing we can all look back on and recognize. Every one of us has faced something hard and gotten through it. The move is to reuse those "I've done hard things before" memories as proof when the next obstacle shows up.

Here are the "receipts" I pull from when I need courage on demand:

- **Taking risk.** I remind myself that I hang-glided in Brazil and did the Sky Jump off the Stratosphere in Las Vegas.
- **Making a speech.** I remind myself that I have delivered keynotes at Harvard University, in Prague, and in Dubai.
- **Facing a momentous task.** I remind myself that I have shoveled through multiple blizzards in 2013 and 2014 and worked as a short-order cook in Faneuil Hall during tourist season.
- **Embracing major change.** I remind myself that I moved from everything I knew in Hong Kong and that

I have started over each time I left one company for another.

- **Making hard decisions.** I remind myself of the medical decisions I have had to make for my children at their birth.

I'm confident that you can recall plenty of moments where you've managed anxiety in your past. Finding reassurance in past victories reminds you that you have succeeded before, and that facing new challenges will lead to further growth.

I watch my kids face challenges every day and choose between a growth and a fixed mindset. Whether it is math homework or a new school year, I see the same pattern: fear shows up first, and quitting feels tempting. Then they push through it.

One metaphor I use with them often is video games. They do not quit because a level is hard or a final boss fight takes multiple tries. They experiment, learn the pattern, adjust, and run it back. That is a growth mindset in its purest form: *reps without shame.*

Sure, people are naturally more persistent about things they enjoy. But the lesson transfers. The logic behind gamification and serious games is to take what makes games engaging (progress, feedback loops, challenge, reward) and apply it to learning design. Adults and kids learn better when the experience makes a challenge feel like progress rather than punishment.

DEVELOPING GROWTH HABITS: A GROWTH MINDSET PLAYBOOK

Like all leadership skills, a growth mindset is not something you *have*. It is something you *practice*. The more you consciously choose growth over a fixed mindset, the more it becomes a reflex.

For some people, growth orientation was modeled early. For others—especially those conditioned to avoid mistakes, seek certainty, or protect their "face"—a growth mindset requires more intentional, repeated reps. Either way, *you do not "arrive" at a growth-mindset. You train yourself to get there.*

Here is a practical playbook to cultivate a growth mindset.

- **Reframe.** When you notice fixed-mindset thoughts ("I can't," "I'm not good at this," "This is going to expose me"), reframe the challenge into a benefit. Ask: *What* *will I gain by getting better at this?* Every time I step outside to shovel, I tell myself, "This is good for my health." It does not make shoveling fun. It makes the effort useful. That is enough to keep moving.

- **Focus on incremental gains.** Immediate gratification makes long projects feel unbearable. Break the work into milestones you can see and celebrate. During our monthly team meeting, we acknowledge progress toward our annual revenue and operating plan. Acknowledging incremental achievements will build momentum that drives further progress and growth.
- **Replace "failure" with "lesson."** Failures are not final. They are feedback. If you are playing the long game, setbacks are tuition. Athletes miss shots. Golfers miss putts. Musicians miss notes. They do not retire after a bad attempt. They adjust, learn, and keep playing. I tend to own part (sometimes all) of the blame and force myself to reflect on what I will do differently next time.
- **Ask for feedback (and learn how to receive it).** We can draw on the experience and wisdom of those who have been there. "Feedback is a gift" gets repeated because it is true, *but only if you open it.* Not everyone delivers feedback well. The only thing you can control is how you receive it. I try to cut through noise: feelings, perceived agendas, and defensiveness. I extract the signal I can use to improve.
- **Surround yourself with people who want to grow.** Mindsets are contagious. If you spend time with growth-minded people, you will learn how they respond to obstacles by watching, copying, and adapting. My parents paid attention to who we hung out with for a reason. They knew habits transfer. My kids watch other gamers play because they learn how people solve problems. If we surround ourselves with people who celebrate growth, then we will naturally be pulled in the same direction.

- **Be curious.** If curiosity is the engine, then a growth mindset is the steering wheel. When you are willing to learn, you will grow. Resourcefulness and external perspectives take you beyond what you can solve alone. I have become intentional about using generative AI to pressure-test my thinking before I default to my first answer. For example, I will bring a hypothesis and use "what if" prompts to model potential outcomes.
- **Reflect (without sugar-coating).** Reflection turns experience into capability. If you do not reflect, you repeat. Structured reflection shows up everywhere, for example, after-action reviews (AARs) in fire service and military, annual performance reviews, and audit reports. I advocate being brutally honest and sticking to facts when reflecting on setbacks or doing root-cause analysis. Sugar-coating or personal blame prevents improvement. I also advocate learning and moving on rather than succumbing to analysis paralysis or conducting a root-cause analysis just to deflect blame.
- **Be kind (to yourself and others).** People do not improve under constant punishment. Kindness is not softness. It is a performance strategy. Replace "I suck at this" with "I will get better with practice." Reinforce progress. If people become afraid to acknowledge their failures, they learn to hide rather than learn. I have seen long-term damage when people are punished or humiliated over mistakes. Psychological safety enables learning.
- **Set learning goals alongside performance metrics.** Performance outcomes matter, but learning goals are what you control. Pair them.

  For example, improve relationship management skills while increasing managed account sales. Even if you miss the performance goal, you can still gain skills that improve future performance. I ask my team to name a performance goal, then break it into learning and operational activities that make it achievable.

- **Lead a growth culture.** If you lead people, you are a culture designer, whether you admit it or not. Model growth. Share your journey, including setbacks, so people learn how to recover, not just how to win.

  Create a safe place to be curious, to test, to learn, and to exchange coaching. My children's coding program does this well. Kids coach other kids through the same challenges they just solved. That is a learning organization in miniature.

  Jensen Huang, Nvidia's CEO, described how he managed societal biases growing up as an immigrant teenager in Kentucky. He motivates his employees to accept "pain and suffering," believing it builds both character and resilience. Huang's journey started at Denny's, where he washed dishes and cleaned toilets. Nvidia also encountered major hurdles before finding success repurposing gaming graphics chips to what is now essential AI technology.

  A growth mindset is a motivator because it produces observable progress over time. It is not about pretending something is easy. It is about refusing to let *you* be the barrier. Fixed mindset has momentum, too. Quitting can become habitual. And yes, we have all quit things before. Some of those choices are fine. You tried spicy food once, hated it, and never ordered it again. That is not a character flaw.

Bottom line: Adopt a growth mindset more often than a fixed mindset, especially for what matters.

VOICE OF EXPERIENCE

A crucial part of developing a growth mindset is choosing to be positive. It sounds simple, but it is not equally easy for everyone. I actively work on this every time I encounter a new challenge. I remind myself: *choose to be positive.* B positive is not only my blood type but also my mantra.

When you choose to be negative, you give doubt room to expand. Negative thoughts, such as unhappiness, victimhood, and regret, start to fester and pull you into a downward spiral. You develop a bias that only notices the worst parts of the situation. It goes from bad to worse, from difficult to impossible, from unlucky to hopeless. Most of us know someone who does this reflexively and gets upset at the slightest challenge.

When you choose to be positive, you give yourself hope, and hope creates movement. You gain momentum with each step forward. You build energy with each piece of the puzzle solved. You pull from past wins to reassure yourself that you can get through this, too. And you cheer yourself and others to "add oil." (Cantonese phrase of encouragement similar to "keep going.")

Boston's 2004 Red Sox playoff run is a reminder of what collective belief can do. The team was down three games to zero against the Yankees, and the city rallied behind one word: "Believe." That positive energy was rewarded with a historic comeback and, ultimately, a championship that ended an eighty-six-year drought.

I am still a practitioner here. I try to be positive. But there are times I start with a negative attitude. As a New England sports fan, I can assume the worst and feel pleasantly surprised when things work out. But real life is not a game. When you lose a job as the sole breadwinner, hear a cancer diagnosis, or lose a loved one, staying negative does not help you move or grow. In dark times, choosing positivity is a difficult but necessary discipline for yourself and those around you.

Each time I face a challenge, I choose to be positive. Even when negativity creeps in first, I regain composure and choose positivity. A positive mindset helps me stand up, move forward, and grow. When we let negativity win, we stay down and stop growing.

The Amasian Way calls us to choose to be positive no matter the odds against us.

Bottom line: A growth mindset is the decision you must make the moment you want to quit.

JOURNAL ACTIVITY: ARE YOU GROWTH-MINDED?

Think honestly about how you show up at work and in life. Score each statement using: 1 = Never, 2 = Sometimes, 3 = Always.

Growth-minded behaviors (move toward)

_______ When the tough gets going, I get going. *(I become more determined.)*

_______ I reflect and learn from my mistakes.

_______ I seek feedback and coaching.

_______ I am compassionate with myself when I make mistakes.

_______ I celebrate progress.

_______ I help others through setbacks.

Fixed-minded behaviors (watch for)

_______ When the tough gets going, I tap out. *(I quit.)*

_______ I am hard on myself and others over failures.

_______ I get overwhelmed by big challenges.

_______ I get frustrated when I do not see results immediately.

_______ I easily "fall off the wagon." *(I quit commitments early and often.)*

Reflection Questions

- Which two "move toward" behaviors are strongest for you? What evidence do you have?
- Which "watch for" behavior costs you the most under pressure?
- What is one habit you will practice for the next fourteen days to shift your score?

GROW YOURSELF IN THE MOMENT

Picture a person's growth needs as they move from single life to marriage and family. That shift often requires stronger relationship skills, learning to cohabitate, and upgrading from a studio to a larger home. If the couple goes on to have children, they will need to develop parenting skills, support their children through adolescence, and increase their capacity. As they become grandparents, they grow again, this time into a different kind of guide and stabilizer.

Life keeps upgrading the requirements for growth. Your career does, too.

Once you have developed a growth mindset, the next step is to *plan your growth intentionally*. As your responsibilities expand from individual contributor to manager, you will have more opportunities to grow others alongside you. As you become a leader, you will be expected to cultivate growth across your organization and shape the conditions that enable development.

Bottom line: Growth is a cadence. The question is whether you can grow without rushing past the moment you are in.

Career Growth in the Moment

As we discussed earlier, a critical starting point for development is believing you *can* and *must* get better. A curious, growth-oriented mindset is what keeps you learning instead of coasting. Your purpose, ambition, and conviction fuel the discipline to keep improving, especially when the work gets repetitive or the progress feels slow.

Earlier, we created a leadership development roadmap based on your purpose, goals, and an assessment of the gap between your current state and your desired future state. Use that roadmap as a structured guide to plan your learning and performance growth.

Re-run those assessments periodically. Your starting point changes as you grow. Your target changes, too. And as you move from individual contributor to people manager and beyond, you will need a more sophisticated mix of tools and inputs, including feedback, stakeholder perspectives, and performance data. As your network expands, you also gain access to more coaching, pattern recognition, and hard truths.

VOICE OF EXPERIENCE

I love it when I get asked, "What advice would you give your younger self?" I like it because I know my answer immediately: *pace yourself and grow in the moment*. There are so many things I know now that I wish I understood earlier.

I started my MBA program six months after graduating from college. As an early-career individual contributor, I did not have enough work experience to fully appreciate what I was learning. I wish I had worked longer first, the way most of my classmates did. They brought real-world dilemmas into the classroom. I had to imagine mine.

I also remember how ambitious I was coming out of college. I worked as a call center representative at a financial services company. The policy was that you could not post for a new role until you had been in your job for nine months. I applied the moment I was eligible. I was driven to climb the ladder. I barely took time to perfect my craft. I did not get promoted within nine months, but I did become an assistant vice president before I turned 30, which was uncommon. Even though I was "moving," I was not always "growing." I wish I had spent more time building depth at each step instead of just chasing the next title.

That pattern continued when I went into consulting. In an up-or-out environment, I felt constant pressure to keep up. I became obsessed with proving myself through performance metrics rather than building learning goals. To me, readiness meant consistently delivering the metrics that mattered at the next level. I did not slow down enough to master what I needed for the role I was in, and the role I wanted next.

As a director, my upward momentum slowed. That slowdown taught me something important: growing in the moment became the work. Learning and refining my craft mattered more than chasing the next rung. I started pursuing lateral moves that would expand my capabilities at the same level. Over time, I gained more wisdom and experience, and I stopped measuring success only by title or salary.

The more I took time to hone my skills where I was, the more confident I became. That is also when I overcame imposter syndrome. I was no longer trying to "fake it until I made it." I was building the real capability to do the job. And as accountabilities grew, so did the stakes. Wins meant more. Losses did, too. If I did not stay curious and grow in the moment, the business I served could become less relevant and less competitive.

I got a similar lesson when my kids were toddlers. A colleague told me not to rush the moment, no matter how tempting it was. He could see I was eager for the "next" milestone: walking, talking, the next stage. He said parents who rush eventually wish their kids were still young. He was right. I still miss the chubby cheeks and innocent giggles, but I also love witnessing who they become one day at a time.

That is professional maturity, too. I do not regret my career journey, but I can see it clearly: it would have been better if I had spent more time growing in the moment instead of sprinting to the next thing. For many AAPI professionals, that sprint can be intensified by family expectations, comparison, and the pressure to "prove it."

THE AMASIAN WAY calls us to grow in the moment while we grow in our careers.

Promotion Readiness

The traditional view is that of growing your career linearly by climbing up a specific career path. Each rung of the ladder has competency-based role descriptions and promotion readiness qualities. If your workplace has a traditional talent management scheme, you will want to deliver high performance in your current role and demonstrate the qualities that show you are ready for promotion.

At one of the places where I worked, I participated in performance reviews in which all managers in the group presented their direct reports' performance. The performance results were "ranked and stacked" to fit a bell curve, which then informed performance ratings. When we turned to discuss proposed promotions, we shifted the focus to promotion readiness qualities. It was possible for someone to not be ranked as a top performer but still be determined ready for promotion. Readiness matters more than raw output when the question is, "Will this person succeed at the next level?" For example, a top salesperson who focuses solely on their own performance may not be the best candidate to become a sales manager.

There are two key factors when it comes to promotions. First, there must be a business case for the role. You only really worry about this if you are seeking a promotion into a role that does not currently exist. Assuming the role exists, the most important factor is whether *decision-makers agree that the candidate is consistently demonstrating promotion readiness.* Hiring managers and HR care because they want someone who can hit the ground running rather than taking a chance and having it not work out. The best candidates have already been delivering at the next level, consistently. I remember at least two of my promotions came about because higher-ups were surprised to learn I wasn't already in that role.

What those calibration rooms taught me:

- **Bring your own brand.** Be involved in shaping the narrative of your performance and readiness rather than leaving it entirely to someone else to advocate for you. Your advocate likely has multiple direct reports to present, and key elements of your story can get missed without your input.
- **Know what good looks like.** The more you understand how performance ratings and promotion decisions are made, the more successful you will be at delivering and advocating for the right things. Do your homework and tell a narrative that answers decision-makers' questions without making them work for it.
- **Consistency outweighs flash in the pan.** Calibration conversations usually focus on a defined performance

period. If your amazing work happened outside that window, it may not count. That is why Janet Jackson's question matters: "What have you done for me lately?" Do not peak at one success. That opens you up to a consistency challenge.

- **Your potential counts.** Even if you are not the top performer, being a "quick study" and showing potential often gets noticed. Many organizations use tools like the "9-box" to map performance and potential. Sharing your intent to grow helps you get into the conversation and increases your odds of getting stretch opportunities.
- **Who knows you?** When well-known people are introduced, there is often less debate about their performance and readiness because the room already has a shared picture of them. When your brand (image) is less recognized, you may face more questions because you are an unknown commodity, especially at higher levels. You may need more than one advocate (exposure) who "pounds the table" on your behalf. For many AAPI professionals, this is the moment to stop assuming your work will "speak for itself" and start building visible sponsorship. Turning internal partners and external customers into advocates strengthens your case.

Bottom line: Performance gets you noticed. Image and exposure get you promoted.

Ladder vs. Lattice Growth

Less traditional companies have less structured career paths. They tend to focus more on employee mobility across a career lattice (rather than a ladder), where people can move in multiple directions rather than only vertically. Employees may even be exposed to an internal gig economy where roles are less defined.

Growth and success look different in these environments. Similar to an online role-playing game (RPG), you grow through accumulating experiences and skills, and your success is demonstrated by achievements rather than promotions. Your success criteria shift with this type of work arrangement.

If you are growing through a lattice or gigs:

- **You need your network.** You will be picked for gigs based on your relationships and reputation. The more people who have experienced your impact, the more likely you are to be brought onto a gig. Traditional ladders can require fewer advocates than lattices.
- **You need to be agile.** You will be exposed to different work and management styles in short bursts. You need to adapt quickly. You will have less time to get to know the team and the work, so you must become a quick study. Pay special attention to the value chain: who provides your inputs, who consumes your outputs, and what "good" looks like.
- **You need to be proactive.** You will need to take ownership of your own movement rather than being guided through a predefined path. Define your direction based on the skills and experiences you want to build.
- **You need real results.** You must deliver impact within the gig timeframe. You are not being graded on annual performance alone. Your success becomes a portfolio of outcomes, and your narrative needs to align with organizational goals.
- **You need to show up, repeatedly.** When you are brought onto a gig, you must deliver. You must read the group dynamics and be prepared to step up and lead. I once spoke with a senior executive who told me he gave people a chance to work on gigs with his peers. If the person showed up as an equal, he knew his peers would support that person's promotion to their level. If the person showed up and defaulted into subservience because of the pecking order, he would not promote them.

Bottom line: On the ladder, you climb by readiness. On the lattice, you rise by reputation.

Another way of growing through gigs is to take on volunteer roles. There are often internal volunteer roles that give you exposure to other parts of the organization, expanding your brand and network. There are also volunteer opportunities outside of work that give you leadership roles and experience. Do not sleep on volunteering as a way to accelerate growth. At the same time, do not let volunteering come at the expense of your best performance at work. At the end of the day, it is still extracurricular. Like my mama reminded me in college: "My grades and graduating mattered more than my extracurricular activities."

Work, Life, and Me Balance

Another aspect of personal and professional growth you may not consider early in your career is life. In the 1980s, the concept of work-life balance became a topic in talent management, initially to support women in the workplace during maternity leave and through flexible work arrangements. By the time millennials became the majority of the workforce, work-life balance was more accepted than the traditional 9-to-5 schedule.

Sometimes, health takes an unexpected turn, and we need time off when we should have been delivering on an important project. I once had a senior executive call me out for dialing into a work call while recovering from surgery. She said, "B Jae, there is no need to be a hero here. If you come back too soon and end up regressing and needing more time off, that is worse."

Other times, we go through personal emotional issues. It is not always appropriate to bring our troubles to work, but those difficult seasons can affect our ability to bring our best selves. We have to be forgiving of ourselves when that happens. The first time I did not earn a top performer rating was during a period when I was especially depressed. I did not provide a strong narrative of my performance year to my partner. I was focused on healing, and I did not pay attention to my career growth that year. We cannot ignore our well-being while we are on our career journeys.

When we got married in our late 30s, I knew we wanted to start a family quickly. Instead of continuing down a client-facing consulting path, I moved into an internal learning and development director role. That minimized travel so I could be more present at home with our infant children. It was a difficult decision to make when the next promotion would have meant becoming a partner of the firm. At the time, I did not expect that detour in my career trajectory, but I am grateful it was possible. Looking back, I would not trade that time at home for any increase in salary or title.

My coworkers were also supportive during major medical situations at home. They helped me prioritize important family moments over work ones. Each incident reinforced a simple truth: energy is finite, and in certain seasons, family comes first.

The modern workplace is also more focused on mental wellness. Given my experiences, I advocate for work, life, and *me* balance. As a "sandwich generation" professional, I have elderly parents and young children who depend on me. In that reality, "life" is often more about loved ones than me. That is exactly why I have to strengthen myself physically and mentally at the same time. It means carving out time to take care of myself, not as a luxury, but as maintenance. As AAPI professionals, many of us are family-oriented and will drop almost anything to take care of everyone around us, often neglecting ourselves in the process. We need to absolve ourselves of guilt when we slow down or take a break from growth to rebalance work, life, and me.

In the safety industry, we advocate regular inspection, testing, and maintenance (ITM) of safety systems and equipment. You take care of the thing that protects you. If you neglect it, it may not work properly when you need it, leaving you vulnerable. It is why we bring cars in for routine maintenance too: fix small problems before they turn into expensive failures. Similarly, you should check yourself throughout your career to ensure you are well-suited for growth. When necessary, rest, recharge, and renew. That is how you move steadily instead of getting derailed by something preventable.

I was recently impressed with an early-career professional who recognized a need to take a short sabbatical to recharge after a particularly stressful year. She knew that if she was to keep growing in her career, she needed to take a time-out for introspection, take stock of what she had achieved and learned, and regroup to plan for what was next. She demonstrated a very mature outlook and awareness of the importance of mental wellness for her career growth.

THE AMASIAN WAY calls us to take care of ourselves as we take care of others on our career growth journeys.

JOURNAL ACTIVITY: HOW DO YOU RECHARGE?

Think of ways that you monitor and improve your personal well-being. Check all that apply:

- ☐ Meditation
- ☐ Exercise
- ☐ Regular doctor checkups
- ☐ Therapy
- ☐ Diet
- ☐ Getting away for long weekends and vacations
- ☐ Sabbatical
- ☐ Spiritual or religious retreats
- ☐ Arts and crafts, puzzles, pleasure reading
- ☐ Night out to the movies or theater
- ☐ Night out with friends
- ☐ Other: _______

Reflection Questions

- Do you feel that you are carving out adequate time for yourself?
- How might you spend more time taking care of yourself physically and mentally?
- What apps or software might help you take care of yourself more consistently?

GROW OTHERS AND ORGANIZATIONS

At some point in your career, "growth" stops being something you do only for yourself. It becomes something you enable for others and deliver to the business. That is the pivot from individual contributor to leader.

Here is a way to think about it:

- Management grows people.
- Leading change grows organizations.
- Leaders do both simultaneously.

Growing Others

Think of your favorite manager. What made them a great manager for you? Now think of someone who was less effective. What made that person a poor manager for you? If you manage others today, what would your direct reports say is your strength as a manager? What would they name as your areas to improve?

In *First, Break All the Rules* by Marcus Buckingham and Curt Coffman, the authors reference Gallup research suggesting that many people leave their jobs due to a poor relationship with their manager. That idea later turned into the modern meme: "People leave their bosses, not their companies." I believe the core strength of any organization is its middle managers. Similar to Pilates, the stability of the organization depends on the strength of its core.

When you manage a team, a project, or a change, you help others grow through *talent and organizational development.* Talent management is the continuum from recruiting to retiring (or, when necessary, exiting) an employee. Organizational development is the work of designing and implementing programs and projects that help the organization grow through transitional and transformational change. We will first focus on talent management, then extend to organization development.

Bottom line: If you can only deliver through your own effort, you are still an individual contributor, no matter your title.

What Are You Managing?

If you are a people manager or a project manager, do you have a clear understanding of your responsibilities? Are you sure you understand your accountabilities and responsibilities? Do you know the scope of your authority—for example: delegation limits, signing authority, and decision rights? In any role, you should understand your job description and performance metrics, then revisit them periodically with your manager to confirm expectations as priorities shift.

When you are unclear about your role, you risk confusing your team and creating avoidable mismanagement. Beyond your role description, you also need to understand your organization's Human Resources expectations for managers. In many situations, company policy is shaped by state and federal requirements. For example, if a direct report reports harassment, you likely have specific steps you must follow. Mishandling those steps can create legal, financial, and reputational risk for the organization and for you.

You also need to be credible. As I mentioned earlier, you may not be better at your direct report's job than they are. However, you must understand the work well enough to connect it to the larger operation and explain how it creates value. You should also understand the risks associated with the work and how those risks are managed. Managing risks means minimizing preventable mistakes, failures, and incidents. Respect your team by being curious about what they are doing, what is enabling or impeding their performance, and what support they need from you.

Be honest about where your team needs more management. You cannot claim to be "hands off" and ignore developmental needs, unresolved conflict, or performance gaps. Effective managers are resourceful when they do not know the answer, decisive when a decision is required, and consistent about follow-through. If your direct reports routinely go around you to get what they need, it signals that your role is not functioning as intended.

Finally, learn and use the policies and procedures for managing people and projects. For people, that includes the full talent management lifecycle (hiring, onboarding, goal-setting, feedback, performance reviews, development, and, when necessary, corrective action). For projects, that includes the program- and project-management standards your organization uses. Strong execution is more than checking boxes. It is allocating resources well, setting clear expectations, monitoring progress, surfacing risks early, and growing your team's ability to deliver outcomes that matter.

Bottom line: If you cannot define your decision rights, success measures, and risk responsibilities, then you are reacting, not managing.

The People Manager's Job: Turn Potential into Performance

Managing is not being the best at the work. It is being accountable for outcomes through other people. If you want to grow others, you must move past "being helpful" and become intentional about development.

A practical management framework is this:

- **Set clarity.** Define "what good looks like." Align the work to strategy and outcomes. Remove ambiguity early.
- **Create conditions for belonging and performance.** People do their best work when they feel safe enough to be honest and challenged enough to improve. Belonging is not softness. It is a performance enabler.
- **Coach behavior, not personality.** Feedback should be specific, observable, and tied to impact. Praise progress. Correct patterns.
- **Build capability, not dependency.** Your job is not to be the hero. Your job is to build a team that can deliver without you in the room. If your direct reports are not coachable and you are doing their job for them, then you need to counsel them out.

- **Develop replacements.** If no one can step into your role, you have built a bottleneck, not a legacy. Training successors is not charity. It is leadership.

Bottom line: A manager grows others by giving them clarity, standards, feedback, and reps.

Lifting Others as You Climb

Many AAPI professionals are shaped by cultural and family dynamics that emphasize collective success and responsibility. In some contexts, that "we over me" orientation makes it natural to grow others. As you navigate your career, you will likely manage people directly or indirectly. That shift tests whether you can invest in someone else's growth while still delivering your own results.

Managing people and projects moves you out of the individual contributor mindset and into the leadership mindset. It requires you to think beyond your slice of the work, see the broader system, and influence outcomes through others. That is the point. If you can only be successful by doing everything yourself, you are not leading yet.

One of the earliest management lessons I learned came from working for a selfless leader who was willing to develop me into a peer. At the time, it went against my less-experienced understanding of how the world worked. Why would someone train a future equal? Eventually, I realized this is a core expectation of management: identify talent and help people reach their potential. Unfortunately, I have also met leaders who were more focused on themselves and felt threatened by high performers on their teams.

Growing others became easier for me as I learned more about performance management, promotion readiness, and succession planning. I learned a lesson that sounds counterintuitive but is operationally true: *managers need to train their replacements*. Two phrases helped it click for me: "If you are irreplaceable, then you are unpromotable," and "If they cannot live without you, then they will not live without you." Both point to the same leadership reality. If you want to move, you have to make your role survivable without you. Building bench strength is not optional. It is a growth strategy.

The next lesson was about transferable management skills. Early in my career, I remember being frustrated that I was not confident my manager was better than I was at work. I wondered why I was not the manager instead. Later, I found myself managing functions I knew little about. My direct reports had deeper expertise, and they should have. They benefited from my ability to challenge their work through strategic alignment, operational excellence, and performance improvement. I also managed projects where subject matter experts spoke over my head in meetings. I learned to be curious, learn enough to ask the right questions, and do my job effectively. Managers do not need to be better than everyone they manage. They need to be better at managing: setting direction, clearing obstacles, calibrating performance, and seeing the forest for the trees.

When I first became a corporate trainer, my manager had been a schoolteacher. She noticed my coworker and I were so friendly with new hires that we were meeting them after work for happy hour. She gave us a proverb that new teachers often hear: "Do not smile before Christmas." The point was not to be cold. The point was to establish authority and expectations before trying to build closeness. As a manager, respect comes before rapport. This is especially hard when you are promoted to manage people who were once your peers. You earn trust by being firm and fair first, and then you build depth in the relationship over time.

Finally, my work in diversity reinforced a management blind spot that shows up everywhere. Many people assume that surrounding themselves with similar people makes work faster because it reduces friction. Sometimes, it does. The cost is that it also reduces perspective. Diverse experiences and viewpoints often lead to better outcomes because they broaden how a team sees problems and generates solutions. I also learned that people form opinions about others through stereotypes, past experiences (good and bad), and hearsay. If you are going to help others grow, you have to cut through the reflex to judge quickly.

People are complex; they change over time, and good managers learn to meet people where they are.

JOURNAL ACTIVITY: HOW DO YOU GROW AND DEVELOP OTHERS?

Think of a time when you were responsible for helping someone grow (even if you were not officially their manager).

- What did you do to understand their goals, strengths, and development needs?
- How did you help them get motivated to learn and improve?
- What specific actions did you take to support their growth (coaching, stretch work, feedback, resources, introductions)?
- How did you reinforce progress and good behaviors?
- How did you deliver constructive feedback in a way they could hear and use?

Reflection Questions

- What felt easy for you about helping someone grow?
- What did you enjoy most about it?
- What did you gain from helping them succeed (credibility, leverage, trust, satisfaction, results)?
- What was difficult for you about helping someone grow?
- Why do you think it was difficult (skill gap, time, discomfort, unclear expectations, avoidance of conflict)?
- What is one management skill you will deliberately practice in the next two weeks?

The Project Leader's Job: Turn Strategy into Delivery

Organizations do not "grow" because leaders have good intentions. Organizations grow because projects change how work gets done. Projects build capabilities, fix constraints, reduce risk, improve customer outcomes, and create new revenue.

A project, at its core, is a disciplined promise:

- **Outcome.** What will be different?
- **Scope.** What is in and out?
- **Time.** When will it happen?
- **Resources.** Who will do it?
- **Risks.** What could derail it?

Whether your company uses a waterfall, agile, or hybrid approach, the execution standards remain the same. Strong project leaders make work visible, keep commitments real, and escalate issues early.

Projects are also one of the fastest ways to grow people:

- People gain new skills when they are given ownership of deliverables.
- People build confidence when they ship outcomes, not just ideas.
- People build leadership muscle by influencing without formal authority.

Bottom line: If you want to grow an organization, run good projects. If you want to grow people fast, put them on projects with real stakes.

INFLUENCING WITHOUT POWER

Unlike designated people managers, project managers and Scrum Masters typically do not have direct reporting authority over their project teams. Project team members usually have full-time responsibilities and contribute only part of their capacity to the project. Many are also juggling multiple initiatives with competing deadlines.

That reality makes influence a core job requirement, not a "nice to have." Project leaders must be able to align priorities, secure commitments, remove obstacles, and keep delivery moving without relying on hierarchy. When project leaders lack influence skills, they are reduced to tracking tasks and communicating status. They are not managing outcomes. They are reporting on them.

One reason I enjoyed sharpening these skills through volunteering is that it forces you to practice influence in its purest form. You can build structure and discipline into volunteer work, but you cannot rely on authority to get things done. If it is hard to get busy colleagues at work to complete project tasks, it is even harder to get volunteers to prioritize deadlines. Volunteer projects teach you how to motivate, negotiate scope, and build momentum when the only currency you have is clarity, trust, and purpose.

Bottom line: Influence is the project leader's authority.

THE INTERSECTION: HOW YOU GROW PEOPLE WHILE DELIVERING CHANGE

This is where Amasian leadership becomes distinct: values, strategy, and action. Many leaders talk about development. Fewer leaders build development into the work.

Here is what that looks like in practice:

- **Assign work that stretches, then support it.** Do not "protect" high potentials from difficulty. Difficulty is the point.
- **Name the "so what" of the project.** Tie tasks to outcomes. Tie outcomes to strategy. Tie strategy to careers.
- **Make progress measurable.** Not just effort. Not just hours. Observable behavior shifts and deliverables.
- **Use projects as a leadership gym.** Give someone a workstream. Ask for a plan. Require stakeholder updates. Coach how they communicate. Let them lead, then debrief.

VOICE OF EXPERIENCE

Some of the most valuable career growth I have ever had did not come from a title change. It came from being trusted with outcomes. When someone hands you a project with visibility, you learn quickly. You are forced to think in systems, communicate clearly, and manage tradeoffs in real time.

That is why I encourage you to stop waiting for growth to be granted. Volunteer for the work that changes things. Then use that work to grow yourself and others.

The Amasian Way calls us to grow people through management and grow organizations through disciplined delivery.

GROWING AN ORGANIZATION

Let's switch gears to *organization development*. As a leader, your job is not only to perform inside the system. Your job is to help the system adjust so it can stay relevant and compete.

Ben Franklin popularized the line that the only certainties in life are death and taxes. Over time, people added a third certainty: *change*. That addition exists for a reason. Markets shift. Customer expectations shift. Technology shifts. Companies that do not adjust eventually pay for it.

I recently heard a story about a once-hot retailer that lost relevance when it failed to keep up with changing tastes and shopping behaviors. Eventually, it went bankrupt because it lost relevance. Even after the downfall, the asset is still being traded. Ownership changes hands, but the core lesson stays the same: *timing is unforgiving*.

One of the simplest ways I help people understand digital transformation is to ask them to picture Netflix's pivot from mailing DVDs and Blu-ray discs to becoming a streaming service. Imagine the internal conversations across IT, operations, customer service, finance, and legal. Imagine warehouse teams reacting to a future where the physical disc is no longer the product. Imagine IT teams racing to build infrastructure to deliver content reliably, at scale, with security and uptime expectations that did not exist in the DVD era.

Change is not a nice-to-have. Change is how a company stays ahead of trends and competition. And change is happening faster than ever. Entire industries have had to pivot repeatedly.

Telecommunications moved from pagers to cell phones, then from phones to smart devices. Companies like Amazon and Tesla pushed automation and robotics into work that had been manual. Newspapers and magazines have had to evolve into content businesses rather than print publishers. If living things do not evolve, they go extinct. If companies do not evolve, they close for business.

BE THE CHANGE

Change is necessary for people and organizations to improve and grow. We must be open to changing ourselves before we can lead others to change. When we do not change, we do not grow. When we do not change, we are disrupted or left behind. *The most important aspect of a growth-oriented leader is the willingness to change ourselves and others.*

I recently watched Emmitt Smith speak to a group of facility managers. He spent most of his NFL career with the Dallas Cowboys, earned three Super Bowl rings, and is the league's all-time leading rusher. You might ask, "Why is an NFL legend speaking to facility managers?" Because after football, he built a career in commercial real estate. His message was simple: he translated what he learned in sports into a new arena, and he did it with the help of mentors who told him not to peak at his last success.

Emmitt's story is not the default. Many athletes and celebrities peak early and struggle later. Go to a high school reunion, and you may see it in real time. The most popular person at 17 is not always the most capable person at 37.

We need to continuously evolve. If we had stopped at crawling, we never would have learned to stand. If we never stood, we never would have learned to run. Growth is not optional. It is the cost of staying relevant.

This is one reason I respect the entrepreneurial spirit I have seen across many AAPI communities. In my experience growing up in Hong Kong and later living alongside immigrants in the U.S., I have seen people adapt quickly, build from scratch, and figure things out without a perfect map. That adaptability is a strategic advantage when the environment changes faster than the rules.

At the same time, the forces that shaped many of us can be complicated. Much has been written about strict parenting dynamics across many cultures, including "tiger moms" and "dragon dads." In my household, report cards came with one question: "What did your friends get?" I learned benchmarking early. I learned that praise was not guaranteed and standards were not negotiable. Used well, that pressure becomes drive. Used poorly, it becomes anxiety. Either way, it must be managed.

There is an old Chinese Proverb, "The best time to plant a tree was twenty years ago. The second best time is now." It means that even if the past is gone, there is no better time than now to start something that gives you future benefits.

At some point, you either pivot toward the new or become irrelevant. The automobile replaced horse-drawn buggies. Word processors replaced typewriters. We are watching artificial intelligence reshape how people search, produce, and decide. You do not need to predict the future perfectly. You need to build the reflex to adjust.

As you do your job, stay curious about the forces that could change your trajectory. Tools like SWOT are useful because they force you to scan both internal realities and external pressure. Political shifts, new technologies, industry disruption, mergers and acquisitions, life stages, health, and personal obligations can all change your growth plan. I am not advocating paranoia. I am advocating for awareness so you can pivot with intention rather than react in panic.

The most poetic way of thinking about change in my mind is Mahatma Gandhi's quote, "Be the change you want to see in the world." He called us to step up personally and take responsibility for leading change in ourselves and in others.

VOICE OF EXPERIENCE

I have reinvented myself several times. I went from a call center financial services representative to a corporate trainer. As the field evolved, I became an eLearning specialist. Later, I moved into management and strategy consulting. Even within those roles, I had to keep evolving as new disciplines became table stakes.

Early in my learning and development career, a VP coached me on reinvention. She told me she did not care how people collected credentials. She cared whether they kept learning. She pointed to her bookshelf and said she learned by reading what smart people were thinking, then synthesizing it into a point of view she could apply.

She handed me *Performance Consulting* by Robinson and Robinson and gave me a practical method to learn from business books. Start with the table of contents to understand where the author is going. Skim the chapter openings, headings, and summaries. Look for lists, charts, and diagrams that compress the ideas. Then go deep where it matters.

Two weeks later, I presented what I learned to the team. That book stuck with me because the method worked. When I needed to pivot into eLearning, I repeated the approach. I bought a few books, learned quickly, and applied what I learned directly to real work. That pivot shaped the next phase of my career.

Today, I would modernize that method. I would search broadly, pull a set of high-quality sources, and use a generative AI assistant to synthesize themes and tensions. Then I would do the real work: pressure test the synthesis against my context and decide what I believe.

Two things must always happen for reinvention:

1. You must recognize that the environment has changed.
2. You must be resourceful enough to learn your way into the new.

THE AMASIAN WAY calls us to live in the intersection of curiosity, move, and growth.

CHANGE AGILITY BECAME A LEADERSHIP REQUIREMENT

Over the past few decades, *change agility* has moved from "extra credit" to a core leadership expectation. Change management gained mainstream traction as a discipline in the 1990s. Early on, it was sometimes dismissed as a soft-skill add-on. Then the stakes rose.

Organizations faced complex, expensive, high-risk waves of change, including Y2K readiness, Sarbanes-Oxley compliance, and large-scale technology shifts such as cloud adoption. As more leaders experienced how often implementations stalled when adoption was not actively managed, many organizations began staffing change professionals and embedding change capability within organizational development.

Change management matters because change is not successful when a plan is published. Change is successful when *people behave differently* in the new system. And human behavior is where the friction lives.

A lot of people resist change. Some resist quietly. Some resist loudly. Some resist until the consequences become unavoidable. One short, powerful book I often recommend is *Who Moved My Cheese?* by Spencer Johnson. It uses a simple maze-and-cheese metaphor to show different reactions to change. Some characters explore quickly. Others deny reality and repeat old routines as if nothing changed.

As a change management practitioner, I have seen these patterns repeatedly. People who embrace change and volunteer to be early adopters get a longer runway to learn the new way of working. People who resist the hardest often end up stuck, sidelined, or separated from the organization. One of the hardest consequences I have seen involved eliminating a production staff member who refused to learn the new way. From a leadership perspective, the change was necessary to improve operational efficiency. From her perspective, she had reached her tolerance limit and chose not to adapt.

VOICE OF EXPERIENCE

In my career, I became an early adopter without realizing I was building that brand. As a training professional, I was often responsible for creating and delivering rollout training. Later, as a change management consultant, I also owned stakeholder management and communications.

I worked with subject-matter and process experts who were not training professionals but who helped design change training. They gained a deeper understanding of the change and adopted it faster because they had been involved in shaping it. We also built pilot groups made up of people who would be directly impacted. They were nominated by managers or volunteered. After piloting, those participants often became change champions, training co-facilitators, and on-the-job resources for others.

These roles matter. Trainers, process experts, and pilot participants all get in early. They build competence before the change scales. They become the people others rely on, and they are often recognized as part of the change's success. They are also the first names leadership remembers when the next change comes.

Early in my career, I made it a point to be known as someone who embraces change projects. I supported multiple technology rollouts, including moving call center reps from terminals to PCs, merger-driven process changes, and new business launches. Today, I have a reputation for leading complex change initiatives with cross-functional teams.

If you want to grow in your organization, make it clear that you embrace change. Start by leaning in when change is implemented. Adopt quickly. Ask good questions. Become a resource for others. That reputation increases the likelihood that you will be nominated or invited to the next change initiative.

Yes, that often means extra work on top of your day job. But it is an investment that compounds. Once you are inside a change project, soak up the fundamentals of change management and the mechanics of implementation. That is how you move from "participant" to "leader" over time.

THE AMASIAN WAY calls us to be change agents and grow into change champions and leaders.

TRANSITIONAL CHANGE VERSUS TRANSFORMATION CHANGE

Like most things in leadership, change comes in different sizes. *Some changes are transitional. Some are transformational.* If you misdiagnose which one you are in, you will either over-engineer a simple shift or under-resource a high-stakes reinvention.

Transitional change

Transitional changes are *specific*, *incremental*, and *linear*. They usually have a finite outcome and a clear due date. Leaders tend to be more prescriptive because the destination is known. The impact on people is moderate, and the risks are generally manageable.

A simple example is daylight saving time. In the week leading up to the change, reminders start showing up from multiple sources. You might set digital reminders. The night of the change, you get nudges again (and yes, sometimes your mother is the most reliable notification system). At the "cutover" hour, some clocks update automatically. The next morning, you check what was updated correctly and what was not. You fix what you missed. In project terms, you just ran a clean cycle of *communication*, *cutover*, *verification*, and *remediation*.

Transformational change

Transformations are a different animal. They are *complex*, *nonlinear*, and *identity-shifting*. There are more moving parts, more ambiguity, and more dependencies. The "how" is not always obvious, even when the "why" is.

If you have immigrated, you already understand transformation. Moving from one country to another is not a single change. It is a chain reaction across systems, habits, relationships, and identity. Even after you "arrive," there is a long runway of change still ahead: housing, school, transportation, language, credentials, cultural norms, and rebuilding community.

Transformational change carries higher stakes because the consequences of failure are larger. People also resist transformations more because the pivot is deeper. You are not simply adopting a new tool or process. You are learning a new way of operating.

The Amasian Way calls us to be leaders of transitions and transformations to evolve our organizations.

JOURNAL ACTIVITY: ARE YOU A CHANGE CHAMPION?

Think of a recent change at work. Describe the change:

- What problem was it trying to solve?
- Why was it urgent?
- What were the benefits for the organization?
- What were the benefits for you to adopt it?
- What would happen if you did not change?
- What specifically changed for you (tools, process, expectations, behaviors)?
- How did you learn the new way?
- What motivated you to change?
- What motivated you to keep going?

Reflection Questions

- Did you volunteer to help with the change? Why or why not?
- Would you describe yourself as someone who helped lead the change, or someone who was led through it?
- What is one small action you could take this week to be a visible change champion?

CHANGE MANAGEMENT CRASH COURSE

Change management has become a core business discipline over the past two decades. Entire libraries of thought leadership now exist, spanning psychological and data-driven approaches. Change leadership is closely related to and highly sought after. *Before you can lead change, you need to understand how to manage it.*

In my experience, change is most likely to succeed when the following *seven elements* exist together:

1. **Change vision.** You must inspire stakeholders to change. The vision should align with the strategy and be simple enough to repeat. It should communicate urgency and outcomes while appealing to both rational and emotional motives. A change vision is designed for broad relevance rather than for a narrow audience.
2. **Urgency for change.** There must be a credible reason to act now. Being specific about the consequences of inaction matters as much as describing the "art of the possible." Urgency should be concrete and believable, so people pay attention rather than tune it out. The "burning platform" concept exists for a reason. Common drivers include competition, regulatory changes, financial health, incident response, and technology disruption.
3. **Change objectives and key results.** Benefits should combine concrete targets with motivating ambition. Stakeholders need specific outcomes to pursue, not generic intent. For example: "By replacing our current system, we will improve efficiency, reduce costs, and strengthen security. We will also enable better forecasting and decision-making. We expect meaningful profit improvement over the next several years."
4. **Leader sponsorship.** Senior leaders must align behind the vision, urgency, and objectives. They need to prioritize resources and consistently reinforce the change through strategic communication. At launch, they rally stakeholders to adopt the new. After launch, they sustain momentum, remove obstacles, and celebrate wins.
5. **Stakeholder involvement and representation.** Engagement begins in discovery and continues through design and implementation. When people believe they were represented at the table, they are more confident that their interests were considered. When they believe change was designed in a vacuum or decided in an "ivory tower," they become skeptical and resistant. Representation requires real listening, not symbolic attendance. Representatives

must engage their constituents, listen actively, and bring feedback into the change design.

6. **Stakeholder alignment and buy-in.** Alignment means stakeholders comply. Buy-in means they commit. Buy-in is stronger but more fragile. Stakeholder commitment can drift during the change lifecycle. This is not a "set it and forget it" appliance. You need an active stakeholder management plan and consistent follow-through.
7. **Change management program.** Like project and program management, change requires an accountable core team that monitors progress and manages risk. Change impacts the operating model across strategy, structure, policies and procedures, technology, and talent. Effective programs coordinate across workstreams and functions. They integrate stakeholder management, communication, and training so people are prepared to change, not merely informed that change is happening.

Changes in the workplace happen so frequently and quickly now that it feels like we are constantly managing them. There are many great change management frameworks and methods. I encourage you to spend time to learn more about change management. You can begin by researching *Kotter's 8-step Process for Leading Change* and the *Procsci ADKAR® Model.*

VOICE OF EXPERIENCE

Culture can make or break change. I have watched organizations without a strong change culture struggle through both transitional and transformational shifts.

I worked in an organization that invested significant capital in world-class systems but failed to realize its objectives and key results. The common thread was not the technology. It was culture. Even though the organization's stated values called for a growth mindset, many people remained committed to doing things the way they had always been done.

I have also seen a recurring pattern in system implementations: organizations insist they are unique and therefore require highly tailored solutions. In reality, "out of the box" functionality is often good enough to improve performance. The bigger obstacle is the time, identity, and pride people have invested in current processes. Giving them up feels like losing competence and control.

In one implementation, leadership allowed each division to configure the system as it saw fit. The outcome was a fragmented deployment. Departments used the same tool in incompatible ways. Customizations that helped one group created friction for others. The system failed to deliver one of its most basic promises: a single source of truth for shared data. The problem was not a lack of technical capability. The problem was governance and a change program that did not coordinate the operating model across functions.

In another case, the organization incurred significant rework costs because the initial deployment excluded critical functions and deviated too far from standard functionality. The more you customize beyond the "out of the box," the higher your total cost of ownership. Vendors update their platforms regularly, and every customization increases the complexity of testing, remediation, and upgrades. In this case, the project team insisted on rewiring the new system to mirror existing workflows. Senior leadership had already identified this as a cultural risk. It still happened. A stronger change program would have detected and managed that risk earlier through stakeholder alignment, governance, and clearer "non-negotiables."

These examples reinforce a simple truth: *the seven elements work together*. When one is missing, the probability of success drops. When multiple are missing, failure becomes a matter of time. The opportunity cost of the time and effort to get a change back on track is originally intended time-to-growth.

A DEEPER DIVE INTO STAKEHOLDER MANAGEMENT

To manage stakeholders effectively through change, you must first *study them*. Identify the stakeholders and explain what the change means to each group. This is typically captured in a *stakeholder inventory*.

Next, identify the stakeholders who influence their groups. When you understand key influencers in terms of their buy-in, their influence level, who they represent, and who influences them, you can manage them intentionally and leverage them appropriately.

Before you draft a stakeholder management plan, answer these four questions:

1. Who is impacted, and how?
2. Who can accelerate adoption, and who can block it?
3. Who influences those influencers?
4. What does each group stand to gain or lose?

VOICE OF EXPERIENCE

During my first change management consulting project, a reorganization in the client's IT department triggered a significant change among key stakeholders. A new leader joined the stakeholder group, and she had the power to influence roughly one-third of the target population for the change.

The project came to a halt. The new leader had not been brought onboard, was not bought in, and had concerns. We could not move forward until we addressed them. We recruited her division head, along with colleagues already aligned, to bring her up to speed, answer her questions, and help her reach a decision that would allow the program to proceed.

I have seen many change efforts stall when a key stakeholder feels left out or is not kept up to date in a timely way. A stakeholder inventory, influence-and-impact mapping, and RACI diagrams are not administrative paperwork. They are risk controls that ensure the program includes the right parties.

Mishaps in stakeholder management can shift someone from an advocate to a detractor, sometimes overnight. Change projects can be derailed due to stakeholder mismanagement leading to unforseen extra time, effort, and funding.

STAKEHOLDER MANAGEMENT PLAN

Once you have an inventory and a clear understanding of stakeholder groups and influencers, build a *stakeholder management plan* to improve adoption through relationship management, communication, and training.

The plan should specify:

- *What* activities will occur
- *Who* owns them
- *When* will the activities occur
- *Which* audience does each activity serves

Examples include:

- Executive sponsor update meetings where the change leader reports progress, risks, and decisions needed
- Pilot team training for end users who need to learn new tasks
- Strategic messages from the executive sponsor in advance of cutover to reinforce urgency, celebrate early wins, and sustain momentum

Change Communication Plan

The *change communication plan* is a core component of stakeholder management. Map the stakeholder inventory to the *RACI framework* to determine who needs what type of communication and how often.

Most communication plans include three message types:

1. **Strategic.** Leader-delivered messaging that aligns the organization and inspires change
2. **Operational.** Project status, progress, risks, issues, and decisions for accountable and responsible stakeholders
3. **Tactical.** Practical direction for end users about what to do differently, when to do it, and how to do it

A communication plan should include:

- **Message type.** Is it strategic, operational, or tactical in nature?
- **Author.** Who drafts the content?
- **Messenger.** Who delivers it?

- **Message.** What are the key points?
- **Audience.** Who will receive the communication?
- **Delivery method.** How will the communication be sent to the audience?
- **Owner.** Who is accountable for delivery?
- **Target date.** What is the planned delivery date?
- **Status.** What is the status of the communication (not started, in progress, or completed)?

While strategic communication (such as the change vision) is designed for broad relevance, your communication plan should also include tailored messaging. Targeted communication enables leaders and influencers to address the real questions their stakeholders are asking. Relevance improves alignment. Clarity improves buy-in.

Align Communication and Training

Communication must be coordinated with training. The following elements should stay consistent across both:

- **Change brand**. Name, color, font, imagery, and other signals that clearly identify the change.
- **Change vision.** A simplified statement of where you are going and why
- **Urgency for change.** A credible reason to act now.
- **Change OKRs.** Metrics that matter, what "good" looks like
- **Performance change.** New accountabilities and metrics, plus reinforcement and consequences tied to adoption

When communication and training reinforce the same story, the audience is more likely to engage and learn. This also aligns with adult learning principles, including WIIFM ("what's in it for me") and the need to understand why training matters to the job.

VOICE OF EXPERIENCE

My most successful training projects tied to change management were the ones where the training team was engaged early. When the training function is brought in at the beginning, it can translate change intent into learning outcomes, performance expectations, and practical reinforcement.

Here is what "early engagement" looks like in practice:

- **Use change communications to shape learning.** Leverage the change vision, urgency, and OKRs to author training objectives and the course overview so training reinforces the same narrative leaders are communicating.
- **Get into the test environment.** Ensure the training team has access to test environments so they can learn and experience the new workflows firsthand.
- **Design UAT with learning in mind.** Support the instructional design of *user acceptance testing* (UAT) so test scenarios reflect real work, not just system features.
- **Build materials from the test scripts.** Develop training and performance support tools (job aids) using UAT scripts and scenarios so the content mirrors what users will actually do.
- **Turn pilots into multipliers.** Train pilot participants to serve as adjunct facilitators and on-the-job resources who can support adoption within their teams.
- **Sustain after go-live.** Post-rollout, partner with champions to monitor adoption and build additional resources to address friction points, common errors, and evolving questions.

I have learned that change management is not "just communications" or "just training." It is a well-crafted change program paired with a meticulously designed stakeholder management plan. That combination should inform communication and training so both are designed to enable people to change successfully.

The Change Playbook

As a quick recap, you need to apply rigor and structure to leading and managing change. This includes:

1. Ensuring that *change elements are in place to align the organization* on the urgency of change, expected outcomes, how change will take place, and executive sponsorship.
2. Key stakeholders are identified and a *stakeholder management plan* is created to help them navigate their unique change journeys.
3. A *change communication plan* is in place to set clarity, provide updates, inform cut over, and sustain momentum for all stakeholder groups.
4. *Training and ongoing support* aligned with stakeholder and communication plans help users adopt changes effectively.

GROWING ORGANIZATIONS THROUGH TRANSFORMATIONS

As discussed, transformational changes are more complex and harder to manage than transitional changes. If an organization is not ready for transformation, it can be difficult to get it there quickly. While executives must sponsor and champion transformations, you do not have to be an executive to lead them. Transformations affect the organization at every level, and everyone plays a role in their success. They are also long and arduous.

I once worked with an HR leader who kept a chart on her wall showing a continuum of change readiness. In almost every conversation, she would point to the chart and describe where she believed the organization was on its digital transformation journey. She often joked that the first few years were all "fits and starts" because people were in denial and not fully onboard.

Here are five things to keep in mind as you lead your organization through a transformation.

1. **Tie it all together.** Transformations are often a combination of multiple transitional change projects. People prefer stability. Eventually, everyone hits a threshold for change fatigue, the point at which they cannot

absorb another "new thing" without losing energy or engagement.

To reduce fatigue and improve coherence:

- Pace the changes so you do not overwhelm audiences with endless waves of disruption.
- Connect each change to the larger program so the organization can see the forest, not just the trees.

2. **Build conviction and commitment from the top team.** Every top team leader must communicate from the same script and model the behaviors required for transformation. Any visible fragmentation at the top will slow adoption, increase skepticism, and set the transformation back.
3. **Cultivate a growth mindset and culture.** In *The Fifth Discipline: The Art & Practice of The Learning Organization*, Peter Senge describes five disciplines that help organizations continuously learn, improve results, and foster innovation. These concepts reinforce the growth mindset that is necessary to embrace transformation. The more leaders prioritize, support, and model learning and adaptability, the less resistance the organization will show when the transformation becomes uncomfortable.
4. **Transform the whole organization.** Transformations are meant to become permanent. Once the organization shifts, it cannot keep one foot in the old world and one foot in the new. Policies, procedures, governance, and enabling functions must stop reinforcing old behaviors and start supporting the new ones.

   People also need to see that the transformation is not optional or reversible. The sooner that becomes clear, the sooner adoption moves from debate to execution.
5. **Sustain momentum.** Celebrate milestones and realized benefits. Positive reinforcement sustains energy and motivation over a long journey. Keep the transformation and its progress visible in strategic communication. Engage stakeholders regularly, answer questions clearly,

and follow through on feedback. Use success stories to show what is possible, and do not allow lagging adoption to slow the overall pace.

BE THE DRIVER OF GROWTH

Knowing what motivates you to grow will help you learn to develop others and organizations. The combination of operational complexity and the psychology of motivation calls leaders to consider people, process, and technology when navigating both transitional changes and organizational transformations.

In your growth journey, you will need to motivate yourself to constantly and strategically make moves to help you grow. As a manager and leader, you will need to motivate others to grow and change. The larger your scope of responsibilities, the wider your net of influence needs to be to successfully bring others along.

You must lead by example. No one will follow the lead of someone who lacks the mindset and ability to grow and change. You must embody the conviction of your change vision for others to believe in it and believe in your leadership.

But conviction is not enough. You must leverage the communication and connection skills to influence others to believe in the change themselves and take action. You must use rigorous change management techniques to achieve alignment, increase adoption, and drive growth across your teams and organization.

The Amasian Way calls us to be cerebral and empathetic when growing an organization.

AAPI LENS

For many AAPI professionals, "Grow" is not just a career aspiration. It is a cultural contract. We are often raised to pursue excellence, avoid bringing shame to the family, and keep pushing even when we are exhausted. That drive can be a competitive advantage, but it can also create two quiet risks: perfectionism that turns learning into fear, and self-sacrifice that turns growth into burnout.

This chapter reframes growth as something more sustainable and more powerful. Belonging enables thriving. Thriving fuels learning. And learning compounds when you stop treating setbacks as proof you are not enough and start treating them as data that helps you improve. A growth mindset is about refusing to let fear, isolation, or fixed identity cap your trajectory. For AAPI leaders in particular, growth also means expanding beyond "doer excellence" into influence, sponsorship, and change leadership, while staying rooted in values like community, humility, and lifting others as you climb.

THE CAREER STAGE LENS

Early Career (Individual Contributor)

Your growth is about building foundational skills, learning how work really works, and developing the habit of feedback. Focus on repetition, coaching, and small wins that compound. Build belonging intentionally by finding allies and mentors, not by waiting to be invited.

Mid-Career (Manager/Senior IC)

Your growth becomes two-dimensional. You must grow your own capability while developing others. This is where many people stall: they keep optimizing for performance metrics while neglecting learning goals, relationship capital, and change agility. Manage your energy and protect "me" time so growth stays sustainable.

Senior Career (Leader/Executive)

Your growth is increasingly measured by what you scale: culture, systems, talent pipelines, and transformation outcomes. Your effectiveness depends on leading transitions and transformations with both rigor and empathy. You are no longer just proving yourself. You are building an environment where others can thrive, and where change becomes repeatable.

JOURNAL ACTIVITY: PUTTING IT ALL TOGETHER—GROW THROUGH CHANGE

- Learn about the Kübler-Ross Change Curve Model.
- Reflect on how the curve shows up for you when you must learn something new.
- Reflect on how the curve shows up for your team when they must learn something new.
- Reflect on how the curve shows up when your organization is going through a major change.

Reflection Questions

- What helps you move from resistance to experimentation faster?
- What is one action you can take to reduce uncertainty for your team this month?
- What is one change lever you can pull to accelerate adoption in your organization (sponsorship, clarity, training, incentives, champions)?

CHAPTER SUMMARY

This chapter was about building the mindset and habits that make growth repeatable. Stay curious. Reframe obstacles into learning. Practice growth until it becomes reflexive. Take care of yourself so you can sustain the journey. Grow others by managing well and grow organizations by leading projects and change with both discipline and empathy.

Key points to remember:

- **Belonging drives thriving, and thriving fuels growth.** When you feel safe and supported, you take smarter risks, recover faster, and learn more.
- **Growth mindset is a practice, not a personality trait.** You can train it through deliberate habits: reframe, seek feedback, reflect, and celebrate incremental gains.

- **Grow in the moment.** Ambition without pacing creates shallow capability and unnecessary burnout. Master the level you are on while preparing for the next.
- **Careers move like ladders and lattices.** Traditional promotion paths reward consistent readiness; modern mobility rewards network, agility, proactivity, and measurable impact.
- **Work, life, and me balance is part of professional maturity.** If you neglect maintenance, you eventually pay for breakdowns. Sustainable growth requires recovery.
- **Growing others is a leadership multiplier.** Great managers develop talent, build trust, hold standards, and create conditions for people to perform and learn.
- **Growing organizations requires change capability.** Successful change blends vision, urgency, OKRs, sponsorship, stakeholder inclusion, alignment, and a managed program.
- **Stakeholder management is not optional.** Inventory stakeholders, map influence, plan communication and training, and manage buy-in throughout the lifecycle.
- **Transformations require pacing and reinforcement.** Tie projects together, sustain momentum, and make the new way irreversible through systems and culture.

DISCOVER MORE

- *Growth Mindset* (Christopher G. Moore and Robert J. Glasgow)
- *Who Moved My Cheese?* (Spencer Johnson)
- *Leading Change* (John Kotter)
- Prosci ADKAR Model
- *The Fifth Discipline* (Peter Senge)

SO WHAT

Whether you *level-up* or *glow-up*, you are progressing. Growth is not motivational. It is operational. If you want sustainable momentum, you must grow yourself, grow others, and help your organization adapt faster than the environment changes. Build belonging, cultivate a growth mindset, pace your development, and use projects as the gym where people and capabilities are built. Then volunteer for the work that changes things, because that is where growth compounds.

The Amasian Way calls us to stay curious, move with change, and grow, so we can help others and our organizations do the same.

LOOKING AHEAD

Growth builds capability. Leadership is how you turn capability into outcomes through people. The next chapter, we will focus on leadership.

CHAPTER 7

Lead and Serve

In the previous chapter, we focused on growth. Growth is about building capability through reps. Leadership is when that capability has to show up in public, under pressure, and with consequences.

Amasian leadership is not about earning a title. It is about converting competence into followership and impact, especially when it is uncomfortable.

I like to describe leaders as either Leaders with an uppercase L: those with designated accountability to lead, and then leaders with a lowercase l: those who lead from their position regardless of role or title. That distinction matters at work. There are Leaders with formal accountability, decision rights, and consequences attached to the role. Then, there are leaders who see what needs to happen and help drive it forward anyway. Santa Claus is the official Leader of operations at the North Pole. Yet on one particularly stormy Christmas Eve, Rudolph led. The title did not change. The moment did.

Many companies talk about leadership in their recruiting literature. They say they want leaders. They insist everyone is a leader. The reality is that most organizations are still pyramid hierarchies. Most people are part of the workforce, not the leadership layer. Yes, you can lead from any position. Leadership is not tied to titles. At the same time, if you hold a leadership title, you cannot opt out of leading. You are accountable for outcomes through other people.

On your career journey, lowercase-l leadership is how you earn the right to uppercase-L roles. You learn. You build skill. You practice influence. You deliver. Over time, you get trusted with a larger scope, harder decisions, and higher stakes.

Now I am going to say something controversial about the "everyone is a leader" idea. Not everyone can be a leader, and not everyone wants to be. Some people are perfectly content to be followers in some situations, or in most situations. And if everyone in a company is trying to lead all the time, no one is left to execute. You have probably attended a meeting when there were too many captains and no one was rowing. Nothing got done.

There is another hard truth. Some official Leaders should not be followed. Title and competence are not the same thing. Unfortunately, people often follow charisma instead of qualifications, and organizations pay the price later.

Some people avoid uppercase-L roles because of the burden they carry. Leadership is a spotlight. It amplifies both the good and the bad. Some decisions are emotionally taxing, such as restructurings that cost people their jobs or the discontinuation of a passion project that no longer makes strategic sense. When things do not go your way, the scrutiny can be severe. When things do go your way, the gratitude rarely matches the effort.

That said, if you have the ambition, conviction, and skills, you should contribute them. Lead yourself, lead others, and lead what matters. Even if you do not aspire to be an executive, if you have the ability to lead, do not wait to be asked. Step up from your position.

Bullies win in the school yard because no one steps up to oppose them. Projects fail at work because the right person did not step up to lead when things began to go badly. If you have the right stuff, you have a responsibility to use it. Not perfectly. Not constantly. But deliberately, when it matters.

Nicholas Murray Butler, president of Columbia University, delivered a 1931 speech that remains a challenge. He described three groups: the few who make things happen, the many who watch things happen, and the overwhelming majority who have no notion of what happens. Whether you rise is shaped by your choices, your environment, and your learning.

The Amasian Way calls us to show up, step up, and lead what matters.

Here is where we are going in this chapter:

- **Define leadership as behavior, not a title.** What followership is, how it is earned, and why competence alone is not enough.
- **Lead yourself first.** Discipline, self-management, and decision habits that make you credible when the stakes rise.
- **Lead with strategy.** How leaders prioritize, make trade-offs, and stay anchored to a north star instead of living in reactive "whack-a-mole" mode.
- **Build influence on purpose.** How to move outcomes through stakeholders when you do not have formal authority.
- **Lead the Amasian Way.** How to synthesize humility with advocacy, diplomacy with clarity, and stability with smart risk.
- **Lead to serve society.** How to give back and pay forward by lifting communities and society with your leadership skills.

Are People Born to be Leaders?

I believe leaders are not born. They are made. Not by luck, but by the paths they choose, the effort they invest, and the support they accept along the way.

"But what about kings and queens?" Yes, monarchies have birthright appointments. Even then, they are groomed before they take the throne. And when they lead poorly, they still answer to citizens, institutions, and foes. Title may be inherited, but leadership is still learned.

I watch a lot of NBA games, especially the Boston Celtics. Commentators will say a player "makes the difficult shot look easy." What they mean is: the work happened earlier. Elite players practice obsessively so execution looks effortless under pressure. Leadership is the same. Some people appear "natural" because they have put in thousands of reps in decision-making, communication, relationship-building, and recovery after failure. The work is what makes it look like talent.

Some people develop leadership skills consciously. They plan their development, seek mentors and coaches, pursue stretch assignments, and keep sharpening their approach. Others build leadership skills without realizing it. They emulate leaders they admire, borrow techniques, and eventually make those techniques their own.

I see that in my own life. My friends once joked that I never have a conversation with a stranger. They said it as if I had instantly become friends with people I had just met. My wife still laughs that bartenders and servers will tell me their life stories as if we have known each other for years. The truth is, I am fairly shy and meeting people is not always comfortable for me. Early in my career, I worked in a call center and handled around one hundred calls a day with strangers. Over time, those communicating with strangers and relationship-building reps became a reflex. I still use the same principles I learned in that first job out of college when I meet someone new.

Volunteering has been another "leadership gym" for me. I have become a better leader at work because volunteering put me in situations where I had to step up and lead without formal authority. That is also why I keep doing it. Right now, I am building a new set of reps in board service by serving on boards of directors and advisory boards. Over time, I want to give back and increase my impact through board leadership in retirement.

There are many ways to build leadership capability. Here are the ones I recommend most:

- **Be planful and purposeful** about formal leadership development, not only informal learning.
- **Perform at a high level in your current role** so you can lead from your position and earn credibility.
- **Engage your stakeholders** and ask how they experience you. Then act on the feedback.
- **Network consistently** so you can learn from other leaders and let them experience your leadership in real time.

- **Volunteer to practice** so you can build influence, decision reps, and follow-through before you ever get the title.

For early-career professionals, leading from your position is how you build your brand.

Bottom line: Leadership capabilities are built, not bestowed. If you have conviction and you put in the reps, you can develop into the kind of leader people choose to follow.

FIRST, YOU MUST LEAD YOURSELF

My biggest enemy is myself. I often wonder what I could have been if I had applied myself more. I know the greatest among us are obsessive. Some Olympic champions spend most of their waking hours perfecting a talent just to compete in events that last seconds or minutes.

I do not have that level of motivation. Not even close. I am a major procrastinator. I swore to myself I would write this book when I became a dad, as a gift to my children. They are almost teenagers now.

Here is what I have learned the hard way. We all choose where our energy goes. Not all of us want the lifestyle that comes with chasing to be "the best." That lifestyle is probably one without chicken wings and noodles, which is a non-starter for me. Obsession comes with sacrifices, and those sacrifices are real.

I also do not want the Amasian Way to become a philosophy that says, "If you cannot be the best, do not bother." I have come to admire the idea of the "infinite game." The goal is not to win once. *The goal is to keep improving.* Many of us talk ourselves out of effort because we assume we cannot beat the people who are wired for obsession. That story is convenient and often wrong. If we all commit to being better than we were yesterday, it benefits ourselves, the people around us, and the communities we serve. When enough people stand up, bullies stop winning. You do not need to be the toughest person in the room. You just need to move.

At the same time, I want to honor reality. Sometimes, it is absolutely the right decision to pull back. I have seen incredible leaders step away to care for aging parents or ailing spouses. I have seen people step aside from work to battle cancer. We all have seasons. Your attention needs to go where it matters most. Sometimes, you need to recharge so you can fight another day.

Wherever you are, whatever your situation, the first step toward leadership is leading yourself. It might sound obvious, but it is the foundation. I have to use self-discipline to show up, move, and grow. I must set expectations for myself the same way I would for someone I lead. If I expect others to have a growth mindset, I need to exhibit one. If I expect others to embrace change, I need to champion it.

A common notion in self-love is, "You cannot love others until you can love yourself." Similarly, you cannot lead others until you can lead yourself.

> *The Amasian Way calls us to drive ourselves to be successful and to improve upon those successes.*

To lead yourself, you need to proactively drive your own success. You need a purpose. You need a roadmap. You need curiosity. You need to show up, make a move, and grow. Leaders do not leave their career growth to chance or to others. They keep improving so they can carry greater responsibility without breaking.

Bottom line: Leaders stay in the driver's seat of their own success, especially when the road gets hard.

Think and Act with a Strategic Mindset

A strategic mindset is one of the clearest separators between leaders, managers, and individual contributors. Leaders are disciplined about focusing on the right thing at the right time for the right reason.

Have you ever felt like you spent your whole week putting out fires? Do you feel stretched because everyone is pulling you in different directions? Some days, work feels like a long game of whack-a-mole, except the moles are priorities that keep popping up faster than you can respond.

Strategic thinking is what keeps leaders from living in a permanent reaction mode. Tactical execution and emotional intelligence matter in the moment, but strategic thinking protects the mission. It keeps your decisions aligned to vision and long-term outcomes, not just the loudest request of the day. For many high performers, this is a hard shift because they are trained to solve what is in front of them. Leadership requires you to see beyond it, anticipate macro shifts, and adjust before the organization pays the price.

The path toward a strategic mindset starts with critical thinking. As you grow in your career, you learn to evaluate situations with more than instinct. You learn to ask better questions, test assumptions, and pick frameworks that help you think clearly under pressure. Business programs teach many models. The value is not in knowing the names. The value is using them to make better decisions consistently.

STRATEGY TOOLSET

Here are a few tools I turn to regularly.

1. Break the Right Rules

There are many strategic thinking tools out there. Try them on real problems at work or while volunteering. Keep what works. Discard what does not. Follow the rules when the rules produce the outcome you want. Break the rules when they limit your thinking and when you can justify the tradeoff.

Asking "What if?" is not a creativity exercise. It is a strategic move. It keeps you from being trapped inside other people's assumptions.

2. Two-by-Two Grid

When you are overwhelmed, a two-by-two forces clarity. Pick two variables that matter, and plot options. It immediately shows you where to focus and where to stop over-investing.

Example 1. Frequency vs. Impact

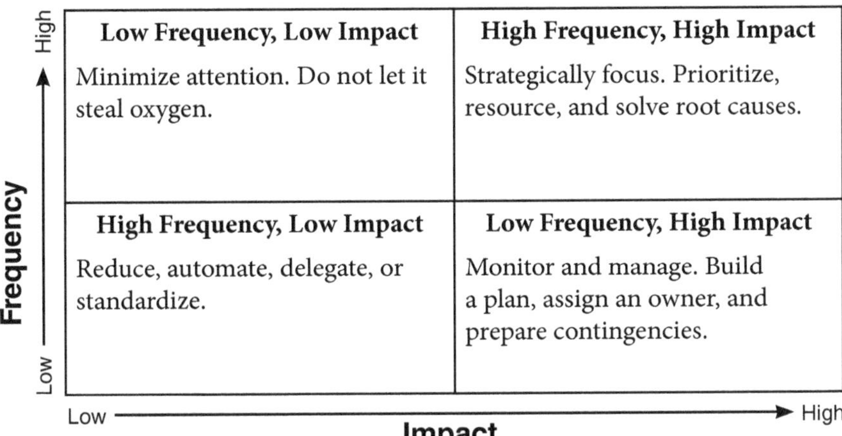

Example 2. Investment vs. Value

Investment (Low → High)	Low Value	High Value
High	**High Investment, Low Value** Avoid. This is where careers go to die.	**High Investment, High Value** Strategic capital investment. Fund it, plan it, govern it.
Low	**Low Investment, Low Value** Decline politely. Do not clutter the roadmap.	**Low Investment, High Value** Low-hanging fruit. Move fast.

Value: Low → High

You can swap the axes based on the decision:

- Risk vs. reward
- Urgency vs. importance
- Growth vs. market share
- Capability vs. performance

3. Serenity Prayer as a Focus Tool

This may sound like an unusual strategy tool, but it is one of the most effective ways to reduce wasted energy.

God, grant me the serenity
to accept the things I cannot change,
the courage to change the things I can,
and the wisdom to know the difference.

When a challenge hits, I remind my team to separate:

1. What we control
2. What we influence (directly or through others)
3. What we cannot touch

Then we act accordingly. We build a plan for what we control, a strategy for influence, and a workaround for what we cannot change. This is how you avoid burning a week arguing with gravity.

4. Hypothesis-Based Problem Solving

Consultants often use this approach because it is efficient. Instead of boiling the ocean, you start with a best-guess answer, then test it quickly with data and analysis. You prove or disprove the hypothesis, refine, and repeat.

I once taught this method and used a personal analogy that was funny but true. When I started dating my wife more than a decade ago, I made the hypothesis that I would marry her. Then I gathered "data" over time to prove or disprove it. Happy to report that we have been married for nearly fifteen years and have two amazing children.

5. Is the Juice Worth the Squeeze?

One of my bosses used this phrase constantly, and it is a strategic filter disguised as a casual question.

As a product line owner, I must sort through passionate ideas all the time. Some are well thought out. Many are not. Sometimes, people are simply shooting from the hip in the first iteration of an idea. As a leader, your job is to prioritize and invest limited resources in the decisions that will create the greatest value. You cannot chase every shiny object, idea, or trend.

So, ask:

- What investment is required (time, money, talent, political capital)?
- How will we pay for it, and how will it pay back?
- What do we stop doing to make room for it?
- What is the cost of doing nothing?

Fiscal discipline is not cynicism. It is leadership.

6. Rose, Thorn, and Bud

I love this exercise from Design Thinking workshops because it forces honest critique without turning into a fight.

Participants illustrate an idea visually (like a movie poster), then do a gallery walk and use three labels:

- **Rose.** What is strong and worth keeping?
- **Thorn.** What concerns you and why?
- **Bud.** What has potential, and what would make it better?

It trains teams to step back from enthusiasm, pressure-test the idea, and improve it quickly.

Five Moves to Strengthen Strategic Focus

Maintaining strategic focus becomes increasingly important as your leadership responsibilities expand. It is essential to rise above daily operational details and avoid becoming entangled in minor tasks.

1. **Follow the north star.** Keep decisions aligned to vision, mission, and purpose. Ask hard questions to ensure resources flow to what matters most.
2. **See the forest.** Keep the bigger picture in view. Individual performance serves team performance. Team performance serves organizational performance. Evaluate trends over time, not just this week's noise. Be aware of how your competition and the industry are moving.
3. **Model scenarios.** Lay out best-case, worst-case, and most-likely outcomes. Identify causes, effects, and levers.

Learn from history inside your organization and from patterns outside it.

4. **Write the acceptance speech.** Define "what winning looks like," then work backward from the story of success to the roadmap that makes it real.
5. **Get a check-up.** Use tools like SWOT, PESTLE, Business Model Canvas, and Balanced Scorecard to pressure-test your strategy and adjust before reality forces you to.

People want to follow someone who takes them toward something more meaningful than getting things done. A strategic mindset lifts leaders out of the weeds, reduces the churn of fleeting wins, and turns effort into momentum toward an enduring purpose. For mid-career professionals, these tools will help lift you from being a problem solver to a strategist.

JOURNAL ACTIVITY

"What keeps you up at night?" is a question consultants often use to surface what is truly top of mind for clients. I also like the question, "What gets you out of bed in the morning?" because it reveals what leaders care about and where they are willing to place big bets.

If you want to build a strategic mindset, study what senior leaders are worried about, what they are excited about, and what they are measuring. This is one of the fastest ways to raise your thinking from tasks to outcomes.

ACTIVITY

Research and read the latest CEO surveys from one or more strategy and management consulting firms, such as McKinsey, Bain, PwC, Accenture, Deloitte, KPMG, or EY.

As you read, capture:

- The top themes leaders are prioritizing
- The risks they are managing
- The capabilities they are building
- The metrics or outcomes they emphasize

Reflection Questions

1. What are the top three things CEOs are concerned about or passionate about right now?
2. Why do those priorities matter to them, and what is at stake if they get them wrong?
3. Where does your work directly connect to those priorities? Be specific about outcomes, not activities.
4. If you were asked the same questions, what would be top of mind for you, and why? What would that reveal about your strategic focus?

Bottom line: Leaders earn followership by focusing attention and resources on what matters most, and by making it clear why it matters.

BUILD INFLUENCE ON PURPOSE

Another key leadership capability is influence. Leaders influence whether they intend to or not, because the title creates implied authority. Before you have that authority, you must earn movement through credibility, communication, and relationships. That is why chapter 5, "Communicate and Connect," matters. Leadership is where you apply those skills under higher stakes.

As you move into more senior roles, the stakes rise, and the stakeholder map expands. Misalignment becomes expensive, especially in transformational work. More stakeholders also mean more agendas, more trade-offs, and more ways for your work to be diluted or blocked. If you want to lead large initiatives or organizations, you must become deliberate about influence.

AAPI professionals often have a natural advantage here. We are practiced at reading context, navigating opposing values, and building harmony. Where many of us fall short is owning the influencer role. We make space for unspoken words and assume the work will speak for itself. In Western workplace cultures, clarity and directness are not optional. A leader is accountable for alignment, and alignment rarely happens by accident.

Five Influence Moves That Create Followership

Influencing skills require clarity, trust, and transparency. Here are five moves that help increase your influence over others.

1. **Align everyone on the "so what."** Be explicit about urgency, objectives, and success measures. Name the consequences of inaction and what "winning" looks like.
2. **Make decisions transparent and translated.** Explain the decision and rationale in plain language. Translate what it means for each stakeholder group so they can act, not just nod.
3. **Give credit where it is due.** Share wins and spotlight contributors. Humility builds trust and increases followership, especially when pressure is high.
4. **Use an influence multiplier.** Build coaches, advocates, and allies who can amplify the message and model the behavior. This is not dirty politics. It is how large groups mobilize.
5. **Practice presence and likability.** Charisma is not a personality type. It is a skill. Your presence can show up in meetings, writing, video, and hallway moments. If people do not trust you or enjoy working with you, influence becomes harder.

If influencing does not come naturally to you, do not avoid it. Bring forward the chapter 5 skills, and put in targeted reps:

- **Rep 1: Clarity.** Get to the heart of the "so what" and keep it as the north star.
- **Rep 2: Point of view.** Take a declarative stance. Conviction is part of the leadership signal.
- **Rep 3: Tradeoff.** Negotiate, compromise, and move past impasse. Progress beats perfect.
- **Rep 4: Ask for support.** Make the business case, and ask directly for commitment, resources, or a decision.

- **Rep 5: Advocacy.** Help people choose the decision you are advocating by making the benefits, risks, and path forward unmistakable.

Bottom line: You prove your influencing skills in leadership moments, when outcomes, followership, and your brand promise are on the line.

MODERN LEADERSHIP

In the years that I have been involved with leadership development, I have noticed two categories of leadership capability:

- *Evergreen qualities* that remain valuable across eras
- *Emerging qualities* that rise because of work, technology, and cultural change

For many AAPI professionals, "emerging" skills can be where the friction shows up most, because they often require higher visibility, sharper advocacy, and a more public point of view than we were conditioned to practice early in our careers.

Evergreen versus Emerging Leadership Capabilities

During a visit to the global headquarters of a financial services organization, I observed a striking juxtaposition between traditional and modern workplace environments. One floor exemplified conventional executive practices, featuring private elevator access, enclosed offices, and decision-making processes conducted in seclusion. In contrast, another floor embodied contemporary standards with transparent glass walls, leaders positioned centrally in an open workspace, and an emphasis on visible, accessible leadership. This experience served as a metaphor illustrating that effective leadership encompasses both enduring traditional qualities and innovative approaches aligned with current expectations.

Here are some examples of evergreen versus emerging leadership qualities.

Evergreen Leadership Qualities	Emerging Leadership Qualities
Integrity and business ethics	Trust and transparency
Communication	Transformation leadership
Emotional intelligence	Innovation and disruption
Vision and strategic thinking	Experience design mindset
Adaptability and resilience	Data-driven decision-making
Decision-making	Agile and design thinking fluency
Relationship building and networking	Diversity, equity, inclusion, and belonging leadership
Business acumen	Mental wellness leadership
Executive presence	Digital and AI fluency
	Influence through platforms and networks

This is not an exhaustive list, and it will not remain static. Over time, "emerging" skills either become evergreen or are replaced by the next set of demands as the world evolves.

Leaders also need to flex across multiple generations in the workforce, with differing preferences for feedback, communication style, and what "trustworthy" looks like. And as remote and hybrid work becomes normal, many employees expect more visibility and more context from leaders who once relied on proximity to communicate credibility.

Leadership expectations will keep evolving. That is why it is not enough to "be good at your job." If you want to lead at the next level, you need to keep investing in the fundamentals while deliberately building the emerging skills that make followership possible in today's environment.

The following explores next-level leadership in the modern corporate environment.

Constant Disruption

At the turn of the millennium, change management became a mainstream discipline. Over time, change leadership matured into a durable capability. Meanwhile, the scale and speed of change increased. Many organizations now experience overlapping transformations with less time to absorb each one.

Next-level leaders aim to disrupt rather than be disrupted. They move with agility, make decisions with imperfect information, and build confidence through momentum. They accept that progress is often messy, and they know how to steady the organization while still pushing it forward.

Reimagined Work

Today's workforce faces a new wave of work redesign. Technology continues to change how work is performed, and generative AI has permanently altered research, content creation, and decision-making.

Next-level leaders treat technology as a lever for rethinking work, not merely improving it. They start with "What if?" They test, learn, and iterate. They do not wait for certainty before taking thoughtful action.

Experience Continuum

Customer experience pushed organizations to redesign products and services around the end user. Now, employee experience is shaping the people agenda, and experience design thinking is spreading across work more broadly.

Next-level leaders think about experience as part of performance. They recognize that better-designed experiences reduce friction, increase adoption, and strengthen retention, which ultimately improves outcomes.

Trust and Transparency

Leaders operate under constant scrutiny, and trust is harder to maintain when information moves fast and narratives form quickly. People expect clarity, visibility, and consistency.

Next-level leaders manage trust as an asset. They communicate with discipline, stay visible, and bring others into the "why" behind decisions. They protect their credibility by aligning rhetoric with results.

How Leaders Are Skilling Up

Leaders are responding to these demands in different ways. Some build technical fluency to lead their businesses differently. Others adopt new ways of leading people. Some do the deeper internal work to strengthen how they show up.

Examples of how leaders are changing behaviors and skilling up:

- Defining a leadership purpose and point of view
- Immersing themselves in agile and design thinking
- Expanding networks to innovate with others
- Curating knowledge to stay relevant
- Building focus practices to reduce noise and increase clarity
- Redesigning work environments to support creativity and performance
- Becoming early adopters of new technology
- Crowdsourcing ideas from flatter organizations
- Investing in communication, presence, and stakeholder influence
- Building multi-generational personal boards of advisors

These attributes are already showing up in succession planning and leadership selection processes. The goal is not to discard the fundamentals. The goal is to keep moving as the world moves. For senior leaders, this is how you scale trust through systems and transparency.

Bottom line: Evergreen skills help you earn trust. Emerging skills keep you relevant. Next-level leadership requires both.

VOICE OF EXPERIENCE

My Chinese family name is 謝, which means "thanks." It is a constant reminder for me to be grateful. Gratitude leadership is an emerging trend in which leaders intentionally express appreciation.

When I reflect on my career, I am grateful for the journey and for the people who traveled it with me. I am grateful for the joy of the high points and for the lessons they taught me from the low points. I agree with the quote "luck is when preparation meets opportunity," often attributed to Seneca. I am grateful for those who made me aware that I needed to prepare, those who helped me prepare, and those who gave me opportunities.

Early in my career, I was not always grateful. I was often eager to leap to the next thing. Over time, I became more mindful of the moment, the weight of my accountabilities, the people I impact, and the support I receive. I learned to pause and recognize that progress is built one rep at a time, and that gratitude makes the reps easier to sustain.

I regularly give shout-outs to recognize achievements. I try to reward those who contributed to the team's success. I do not claim someone else's ideas as my own, and I aim to give credit where it is due. Celebrating accomplishments and practicing gratitude together is the first agenda item in our year-end team meetings, because it reinforces what we value.

I am also grateful for the leadership roles I have been entrusted with. Leadership is not just about personal wins. It carries accountability for results and responsibility to people. Even small leadership decisions can shape someone's experience at work and their belief in what is possible.

I am also grateful for new challenges. Recently, I took on a new product area and had to learn an entirely new landscape. That kind of learning is uncomfortable at first. Over time, I have learned that gratitude fuels courage because it helps you treat the unknown as an opportunity rather than a threat.

The Japanese phrase said before a meal is *Itadakimasu* (いただきます). It means "I humbly receive." I think leaders should carry that posture. Grateful leaders are more grounded, more human, and more aware of their impact on others. People can feel it when gratitude is real, and it changes how they experience your leadership.

JOURNAL ACTIVITY: THE RENAISSANCE LEADER

1. Research several sources to identify:
   - A list of traditional evergreen leadership qualities
   - A list of emerging leadership qualities
2. Use generative AI to create a short self-assessment that evaluates your understanding of both lists.
3. Reflect on your current leadership brand against both lists. Identify:
   - What you already demonstrate with proof
   - What you need to develop next
   - Where are you avoiding discomfort instead of building reps

Reflection Questions

- How do these qualities show up in your work today, and where are you currently underusing your voice?
- Which two emerging skills matter most for your next career move, and why?
- Where do you need more practice, coaching, or feedback to close the gap?
- What is one change you will make this week that will be visible to others and measurable by outcomes?
- How does this change how you lead on Monday?

Bottom line: Fundamentals build trust. Modern demands test relevance. Leaders who keep learning keep leading.

BECOME AN AMASIAN LEADER

I think I have always leaned toward leading. Before I stepped into my professional career, I had plenty of experience leading others. From a young age, I was outspoken. I held student government roles. Other kids looked up to me. In high school, I was a student leader and a part-time supervisor at the restaurant where I worked on weekends and in the summer. I mentored underclassmen. In college, I managed food services, served as a resident assistant (RA), and became vice president (VP) of several student organizations.

Those early reps mattered. I learned real skills and some tough lessons the hard way. So, when I began my career, I was already setting my sights on climbing the corporate ladder and leading others.

You cannot lead for the first time when you are called upon to do so. Leading others requires practice. Recently, I spoke to my daughter's fourth-grade class about leadership, and I told them this: leadership is a habit before it is a title.

When your friends are sitting around wondering what to do, that is a leadership moment. When the teacher asks for a volunteer, that is a leadership moment. I have seen many potential leaders shy away from opportunities because they never formed the habit of stepping up. Every time a kid decides to go with the flow, they are conditioning themselves to follow. Every time a kid steps up, they are reinforcing the reps that make leadership feel natural later.

Western leadership qualities may have been easier for me because I grew up in America (from age ten) and because my father was a "ham" with a microphone. That gave me an advantage. At the same time, I can see how certain Western leadership expectations were harder for me because of my Eastern cultural influences.

That tension is not a weakness. It is the work. It is also where the Amasian advantage is built.

East versus West

Let's revisit some differences between traditional Eastern and Western business philosophies. These are not absolutes. They are patterns many of us have encountered.

Western (often emphasized)	**Eastern** (often emphasized)
Individual achievement is highly visible and rewarded.	Collective success and harmony are prioritized.
Disruption and risk-taking are celebrated.	Stability and long-term endurance are valued.
Innovate by reimagining and reinventing.	Improve by enhancing what already works.
Flex quickly across new perspectives and trends.	Respect proven track record, tradition, and wisdom.
Transform by breaking from the past.	Steward by strengthening and nurturing what exists.
Direct communication, clarity, and advocacy.	"Save face" dynamics, diplomacy, and relationship protection.

Navigating Your Fusion Identity

Your Eastern and Western cultural influences can pull in opposite directions. Many AAPI professionals are raised to be humble, risk-aware, and diligent for collective success. Yet school and work cultures often celebrate people who step up, speak with confidence, take credit, and advocate visibly.

The path forward is not choosing East or West. The path forward is synthesis.

1. **Notice the tug-of-war.** Name where it shows up for you: speaking up, disagreeing, self-advocacy, visibility, decision-making, and conflict.
2. **Know how you can flex.** Decide where you will lean into diplomacy and where you will lean into directness.
3. **Build your fusion qualities.** Combine the strengths of both influences into leadership behaviors that deliver results.

Fusion Qualities that Create Amasian Leadership

Your multicultural identities enable distinct abilities that are less accessible to those with a single dominant cultural background.

Western	Eastern	Fusion (The Amasian Way)
Individualism	Collectivism	**Servant leader with a point of view** who aligns people to a shared outcome
Disruption	Stability	**Crafty sailor** who takes calculated risks and navigates uncertainty with discipline
Imagination Engineering	Performance Enhancing	**North star navigator** who tests new routes while staying accountable to outcomes
The Unknown	The Proven	**Renaissance leader** who reframes wisdom for new contexts and new stakeholders
Transform	Steward	**Agile steward** who modernizes systems while protecting what must endure
Direct	Subtle	**Impactful rhetoric** that blends clarity with diplomacy to move decisions forward

Convergence and divergence

I am from Hong Kong. Growing up in Hong Kong in the '70s, I was raised to believe Hong Kong was far ahead of mainland China in business and modernization. In the late 2000s, I visited mainland China to embrace my cultural heritage. My first stop was Shanghai. When the city came into view, my jaw dropped. It felt bigger and more modern than I expected. Today, megacities across China reflect the pace of economic development and innovation.

It would be dated to treat Eastern and Western corporate cultures as extreme opposites. Many global companies operate across both contexts, and leadership expectations are blending. The key is knowing where cultures are converging and where they still diverge.

Areas that are converging:

- **Technology and innovation.** AI, digital platforms, and automation are accelerating everywhere. Digital and AI fluency is now a leadership requirement, not a niche skill.

- **Results and performance pressure.** Short-term outcomes matter, and long-term bets matter. Leaders are judged by delivery and trajectory.
- **Talent expectations.** Across regions, employees are pushing for meaning, flexibility, development, and a healthier relationship with work.
- **Competitive intensity.** Startups disrupt faster. Mature companies tighten execution. Both demand leaders who can focus and move.

Areas that still diverge (in many contexts)

- **Span and layers.** Many Western organizations aim for flatter structures and challenge norms more openly. Many Eastern contexts retain more deference and top-down authority.
- **Control and risk posture.** Some Eastern business environments remain more controlled and risk-aware, while Western environments may be more tolerant of iterative test-and-learn approaches.
- **Communication dynamics.** In many Western settings, "no" is explicit. In many Eastern settings, "no" may be indirect to protect relationships or preserve face.
- **Duty versus purpose.** Eastern contexts may emphasize duty and obligation more strongly, while Western narratives often emphasize purpose and individual choice.

The convergence can be strongest in technology-driven industries. The divergence can remain stronger in more traditional sectors. Either way, AAPI professionals often experience the same underlying tension: you are expected to perform with discipline and lead with visibility and influence.

Amasian leadership

AAPI leaders need to understand what is converging and diverging, lean into their multiple identities, and translate across audiences without losing their point of view.

Trailblazing AAPI leaders have already challenged the "model minority" box. They have proven that AAPI leadership is not only possible but also differentiated. They often lead with substance and outcomes, supported by business intelligence (BI), not just charisma. They unite opposing positions by synthesizing perspectives and aligning decisions to what matters.

Leaders like Jensen Huang, Indra Nooyi, Sundar Pichai, Andrew Yang, Vera Wang, Kristi Yamaguchi, and Dwayne Johnson have expanded what people imagine when they picture AAPI leadership and influence. They changed narratives through results, visibility, and conviction. They have remodeled the "model minority." They proved that we can lead and add value rather than be diligent, subservient contributors.

Amasian Superpowers

You are Amasian because you are inclusive and flexible. You have grit. You can be bold and brilliant while staying grounded in purpose and collective good.

> *The Amasian Way leans in on our propensity to outwork, outsmart, and outlast everyone else in the room.*

Your Amasian leadership superpowers are not despite your roots, but because of them. Your roots are enriched by both Eastern and Western nutrients. You bring guts, grit, heart, and smarts. You keep moving when others give up. You keep evolving when others fade into the status quo. You lift people toward a higher purpose while others lose followers chasing personal gain.

Turning Your Fears into Fuel

I would not be me if I did not name the reality of trying to lead while carrying fear. Is this the right time to step up and stand out? If what feels at stake is your status in America, your career stability, or your family's security, is it worth the risk?

Fear can activate our most risk-averse default reflexes: keep our heads down, do not rock the boat, do not make waves.

Beyond anti-immigrant sentiment, there is also backlash toward anything associated with diversity, equity, and inclusion (DEI). Being known as a DEI champion, or simply being visible as a leader with a diverse background, can invite lazy narratives. You may be called a "DEI hire," as if your results were not earned.

These fears are real. The mistake is letting fear become your strategy.

AAPI communities have faced discrimination and exclusion across American history. Even in recent years, many AAPI professionals have watched hostility rise during moments of national stress, including during the COVID era. I will never forget seeing AAPI doctors and nurses go to work with purpose and courage, despite the risk and the noise around them. They turned fear into fuel. They stayed on mission.

THE AMASIAN WAY calls us
to channel our fear of discrimination
and rise to lead with even stronger conviction.

Here are five ways to channel fear without pretending it is not there.

1. Name it, flip it, and work it.

- **Name the fear.** "If I stand out, I will become a target."
- **Flip it into a controllable aim.** "If I stand out for measurable results and dependable leadership, I increase the odds that I am valued and protected."
- **Work it.** Collect proof. Track outcomes. Document impact. Build a results narrative you can communicate clearly.

Start small. Build competence and confidence together. Progression is the point.

2. Own your brand.

You are more than someone else's label. Build your brand around outcomes, not opinions.

- Put a spotlight on your *talent*, *merit*, and *results*.
- Make your work legible. Make your decisions visible.
- Let your narrative travel faster than the rumors.

3. Earn it twice, then say it once.

Promotions and expanded scope always come with questions. Performance, readiness, relationships, and fit will be debated somewhere, even if you never hear it.

You cannot control other people's doubts. You can control your proof.

- Have your case ready with *indisputable results* and clear behaviors that show you are already operating at the next level.
- Ensure success criteria are explicit and discussed early, not retroactively.
- Accept what you earned without apology, and without arrogance.

4. Change the game with allies and leverage.

To give in to anti-Asian hostility is to validate it. To lead with results and relationships is to challenge it.

Every life you impact is one more person whose experience of AAPI leadership becomes real rather than theoretical. Allyship helps you become a defying presence, not a hidden conformist. Build allies before you need them. Then borrow and share leverage with purpose.

5. Evolve your leverage, not just your anxiety.

Fear about visa status or job security can become a trap if it pushes you into invisibility.

Knowledge is power.

- Understand the rules and constraints you operate within.
- Build optionality through in-demand skills, credibility, and a portable portfolio.
- Increase your vitality so your organization has a reason to fight to keep you.

People use therapy to work through fear because fear does not disappear on command. It changes through repetition. Just as you cannot fix anxiety in a day, you cannot overcome the fear of discrimination all at once. Put one foot in front of the other. Start small, gain momentum, then go bigger.

This book has been clear from the beginning. The Amasian Way is not the easy route. It is hard work. When fear is in the air, it is easy to default back to "model minority" habits: stay quiet, work hard, hope you are not noticed. That is how you end up back under the bamboo ceiling.

I would rather remodel the model minority into the Amasian Way.

At worst, you always have a choice. Lead elsewhere. Bruce Lee returned to Hong Kong when Hollywood was not ready for him. Jeremy Lin took his talents to the Chinese Basketball Association when the NBA was not ready for him. If your fear becomes reality, you still have choices. Leaving and starting somewhere new is a common chapter in many leadership journeys, whether it is opportunity, misalignment, or circumstance.

Some days, you are the windshield. Other days, you are the bug. Either way, keep moving. When one door closes, another opens. Get up, move, and step into the open door.

YOU, THE AMASIAN LEADER

The Amasian Leader is one who has navigated and synthesized Eastern and Western cultural influences into a fusion leadership style.

Here are attributes that often show up in the Amasian brand. These archetypes are not labels. They are behavioral cues you can practice and prove. Yes, this list is intended to be fun and meaningful.

Name	Description
Tenacious D	Defense wins championships. You grind, you endure, and you motivate others with work ethic and discipline.
Crouching Tiger, Hidden Dragon	Quiet champion. You lead with substance, not attention-seeking. You advocate for the collective, not just yourself.
Family Switchboard	You bridge differences and connect people. You translate across perspectives and mobilize action by appealing to what matters to each audience.
Bamboo Scaffolding	Strong, flexible, resilient. You can weather storms without breaking, and you operate with pragmatic budgets and sensible plans.
Nine-Tailed Fox	Strategic, resourceful, and politically fluent. You read the room, build alignment behind the scenes, and move when the votes are already there.
Tortoise	Long-game leadership. You plant seeds, stay ready and steady, and build enduring success instead of chasing quick wins.
Gemini Uplifter	You bridge dual identities through curiosity and communication. You create alignment and lift people through change.
Value Hunter	You pursue the "so what." You demand substance over fluff, challenge smoke and mirrors, and use data to model and test decisions that create sustainable value.
Banyan Tree	Deep roots. Integrity, gratitude, loyalty, and authenticity. You connect networks and bring people together for a higher purpose.
Remodeled Minority	You broke the mold. You are an upstander with a voice. You communicate with impact, influence decisions, and own your narrative.

Bottom line: You, the Amasian Leader can bring a different and needed type of leadership to the Western corporate culture.

VOICE OF EXPERIENCE

In many ways, I assimilated into American culture long before I decided to recapture my Chinese heritage. Still, being Chinese American is a visible diversity. People who do not know me may see me as a minority and assume I am an immigrant. I am proud to be both.

People who know me often forget those labels because my personality and performance come through first. I grew up in a city with very few minorities, so most of my close friends are Caucasian. To them, I am just one of the guys. Sometimes, they do not remember I am Chinese American until they hear me speak Cantonese around my parents.

In school and at work, I have rarely been singled out as a minority or immigrant unless I chose to step into that arena by leading ERGs or serving on diversity committees. One time, after I presented to a senior leadership team, my well-intentioned manager told his peers, "Isn't it great that he was able to do this in front of a completely white leadership team?" It was awkward because up to that moment, the only thing that mattered was the vision and business outcomes I was there to drive. But I cannot choose when I want to be seen for my diverse background. It is always there, visibly. As uncomfortable as the moment was, I was still grateful that he attempted to "see me."

I thought long and hard about this while writing the book. People's experiences of me often exceed their perception of me as a minority or immigrant. While I do want people to see the adversity that can come with those parts of my identity, I also know I have worked hard to build a brand narrative anchored in performance and image.

I admire Dwayne Johnson's endurance and drive. He is half Samoan and half Black, but you do not hear people discuss his background unless he chooses to make it part of the story, such as when he brings Polynesian cultures to the world through entertainment. I am not "the Rock." But I understand the principle. I am rarely reduced to my identity in day-to-day work because I have built a reputation around results. I am not naive, though. I know I will not be in every conversation about me, and I cannot control other people's agendas. What I can control is my choices, my proof, and my options. If I discover that a place is no longer right for me, I have a choice.

I believe the Amasian Way is about becoming the best version of yourself, including your multicultural superpowers, and becoming your own exceptional Asian American Pacific Islander leader. Your talent and impact become your brand promise and narrative. Your diverse background is a strength, not a crutch. Your success is not because of a handout. It is because you put in the work, delivered results, built the right relationships, and led with substance. That journey is valuable whether diversity is celebrated or debated.

The Amasian Way calls us to rise above the systemic and bias challenges to lead as our best authentic multi-cultural selves.

SERVE AND LEAD SOCIETY

Earlier, I asked you why you want to lead. Here is a reason that belongs near the top: *lead society and serve the greater good.*

The final step on the Amasian Way is serve and lead society. Whether you are just beginning, on the path, or at the end of your journey, you can contribute your time and talents to the greater good of society.

Service is leadership with the ego turned down, and the purpose turned up. When you serve, you are not negotiating for status or attention. You are contributing because it matters. You lift others without keeping score.

The Amasian Way calls us to be leaders who give back and pay forward through volunteering for the betterment of society.

Service can show up at work and in your community:

- Advocate for fairness and respect from any seat.
- Mentor, coach, or sponsor someone who needs a lift.
- Lead volunteerism and normalize giving back.
- Serve through ERGs, boards, nonprofits, or civic work.

Service as Your Brand

Service should be additive to your brand, not a replacement for performance. If your job performance is subpar, volunteer impact will not save the narrative. Your performance brand needs to lead the story. Then service strengthens it by expanding your reps, credibility, and influence.

I have lived that loop. Ascend Global Leaders expanded my professional network beyond networking and gave me leadership roles I use at work every day. Serving on the BCNC board broadened my view of local community needs and strengthened my board-level leadership skills. Service builds capability, capability increases impact, and the loop keeps compounding.

I have found that my professional and leadership brand combines both my career and volunteer experiences. The resulting combination yields a much larger multiplier than it does on its own. My service brand has meant more to recruiters. My career brand lends credibility in my volunteering.

The Career and Service Ecosystem

By serving and leading in your community, you apply your knowledge and experience to volunteer work. In turn, volunteering helps you develop new skills that can benefit your career. This creates a positive cycle of growth that enriches both your professional life and your volunteer efforts.

Service has returned more gifts than I can count:

- **Societal:** real impact for people and community
- **Personal:** purpose, gratitude, and perspective
- **Professional:** leadership reps you cannot get from a job alone, including influence without authority, stakeholder alignment, networking, and governance

I have shared many examples of how my volunteering contributed to my leadership skills along the way. One caution: serve with pure intention. If you serve to be admired, protected, or rewarded, it will eventually show. Service is often thankless, and it requires consistency between what you advocate and how you behave.

Most importantly, the network I have built through my volunteer outlets contributes to my career, and vice versa. You are the natural synergy between your work and volunteer networks. When you build a network for one purpose, you are automatically building the network for the other.

As you advance and take on leadership roles, your whole career and service network prosper together. Every success you achieve positively impacts each part of that ecosystem.

VOICE OF EXPERIENCE

In 2008, I attended my first Ascend National Convention. I was teaching a class on Networking 101 on behalf of my firm who was sponsoring the event. I had never been a part of anything like this convention. Ascend Global Leaders, as it is known today, is North America's largest non-profit organization focused on professional and leadership development of Pan Asians. Even though I worked at one of the Big Four firms, I had never been in a room filled with thousands of people who looked and sounded like me, an AAPI professional. The keynote speakers, presenters, and panelists were seasoned professionals who offered authentic advice drawn from their careers.

Up until this point in my career, I had avoided affinity groups for AAPI professionals because I was convinced that I had gotten really far without any help based on my immigrant minority status. This convention changed my life. Not only did I find the content valuable, but I was also amazed by how many younger professionals were there, eagerly soaking up all the lessons. They were not looking for handouts. They needed help. Ascend Global Leaders was there to meet their needs.

When I returned to Boston, I joined Ascend's New England chapter. Given my experience in learning and development,

I quickly became part of the executive team responsible for professional development programs. Eventually, I became the chapter's president. Today, I am still active with Ascend both locally and nationally. I have built a fantastic network over the past fifteen-plus years, and I remain connected with many people I mentored. For me, that Ascend National Convention was my calling. I became convinced that I needed to be better and I needed to help others like me to be better.

THE AMASIAN WAY is placing hope in yourself, above all, so that you can lead yourself, others, and society to be better.

Find an outlet to provide service for others that aligns with your purpose. I have been very impressed by the people in my network who are intentional about how they give back and pay it forward. One colleague intentionally shifted his volunteering from professional to community settings to bring his gifts to those who were less fortunate. Another wanted to focus on gender equality beyond race and ethnicity. My cousin focuses on the Boston Chinatown community, while my wife focuses on our local one. There is no one right answer as to who and how you serve. The point is to serve. Imagine the good we could do for our communities if we all spent one day per month serving them.

Bottom line: There is no shortage of societal and community needs where you can make a difference. Start today.

JOURNAL ACTIVITY: SERVANT LEADERSHIP

Choose one service lane for the next 90 days:

- One opportunity at work
- One opportunity outside work
- One opportunity that supports the AAPI community

Reflection Questions

- Why this lane, and why now?
- What skill will you contribute, and what skill will you build?
- What will "impact with proof" look like in ninety days?

The AAPI Lens

For many AAPI professionals, leadership is complicated by a quiet tension. We are often rewarded early for reliability and execution, then later expected to demonstrate visibility, influence, and decisive advocacy. That shift can feel unnatural if you were conditioned to avoid risk, protect harmony, or let the work speak for itself.

This chapter reframes leadership as a practiced set of behaviors, not a personality trait. You can honor humility and collective success while still leading with clarity, presence, and a point of view. The Amasian advantage is synthesis. You can translate across audiences, combine diplomacy with directness, and use evidence and outcomes to earn trust in rooms where charisma is often overvalued.

If this feels uncomfortable, that is not a sign you are unfit to lead. It is the work. Leadership is built through reps, especially the reps that stretch you.

THE CAREER STAGE LENS

- **Early career:** Practice lowercase-l leadership. Take ownership, communicate the "so what," and ship visible outcomes. Build your leadership brand through reliability plus initiative. Gain experience by volunteering.
- **Mid-career:** Shift from high performer to multiplier. Lead through others, prioritize strategically, and build influence across stakeholders. Protect your energy so

leadership is sustainable, not just impressive. Practice and lend your skills by volunteering.

- **Senior career:** Your leadership is measured by what scales. Culture, systems, talent pipelines, and a community of leaders. Increase transparency, sponsorship, and strategic clarity. Make other people's success repeatable. You can be a servant leader by giving back and paying forward for your community.
- **Career transition:** Use leadership as proof, not a claim. Build a portfolio of outcomes, a clear narrative, and a credibility lane that reinforces performance rather than replacing it. Volunteer and service can support your narrative, but your results must still lead the story.

CHAPTER SUMMARY

This chapter reframes leadership as a capability you build through reps, not a title you inherit. Lead from any seat by stepping up with clarity and follow-through. Start by leading yourself, then widen your impact through strategic thinking, modern leadership skills, and the discipline to be seen. The Amasian leader earns trust through substance, aligns people across differences, and uses influence to move what matters.

Key points to remember:

- Leadership is behavior before it is a title. Followership is earned through trust and results.
- Leaders are made through reps. Practice, coaching, and deliberate development create "natural" leadership.
- Strategic mindset separates leadership from management. Focus is a discipline. Choose what matters and choose what to stop.
- Modern leadership requires both evergreen fundamentals and emerging skills, including digital fluency, change agility, and transparency.
- Amasian leadership is fusion. Combine diplomacy and directness, humility and advocacy, stability and innovation.

- Leadership gets tested when it is uncomfortable. Use friction as data, then move anyway.
- Serve society and communities by sharing your talents and network.

JOURNAL ACTIVITY: PUTTING IT ALL TOGETHER

Revisit this question from your very first journaling exercise: Why should anyone follow me?

Record your answer on video (two to three minutes). Address how you will lead yourself, others, the organization, and society. Compare this to your original answer.

Reflection Questions

- What changed between your first and second video?
- What would you add to your Amasian leadership brand promise now?
- Choose one skill to learn, practice, and demonstrate in the next 30 days? How will you assess your progress?

Discover More

- Growth mindset as a leadership operating system (Carol Dweck)
- Change leadership fundamentals: urgency, coalition, momentum (John Kotter)
- The learning organization and systems thinking (Peter Senge)
- CEO Surveys: what leaders prioritize now (McKinsey, Bain, PwC)
- Design Thinking: "Rose, Thorn, Bud" as a critique tool for ideas and decisions

SO WHAT

Leadership is not a promotion. It is a practice. If you want to be trusted with bigger scope, lead from your seat now. Communicate the "so what," make decisions visible, and deliver proof.

Do not wait until you feel ready. Readiness is built by doing the reps. The leaders who rise are the ones who step up before they are asked.

Looking Ahead

Next, we will revisit the key concepts of the Amasian Way and help you get underway on your own journey.

CONCLUSION

Your Amasian Way

We have been on a long journey. We explored leadership concepts through an AAPI lens, naming the opportunities and pressures that often come with multiple identities. Along the way, we returned to one idea again and again:

Your brand promise and how people experience you can outshine stereotypes and unconscious bias.

You cannot control every room, every narrative, or every gatekeeper. But you can control your development, your decisions, and your reps. You can discover the strengths of your multiple identities, invest in skills, practice under pressure, and lead strategically with intention.

This final chapter is not about learning more. It is about mobilizing what you already learned.

THE "SO WHAT" OF THIS BOOK

You are unique because you have the synergetic strength of multi-cultural influences that set you apart from other leaders. Your diversity is your strength. You need to dive deeper to understand those strengths, how to develop and lean into them, and make them your undeniable *Amasian leadership experience.*

Here are the key points of this book:

1. *Discover* the strengths of your multiple identities and cultural influences.
2. Be *planful* and *purposeful* in your development, and bring others along to hold you accountable and help you adjust your path. Study the game.

3. *Learn*, *develop*, and *practice* continuously to improve your skills.
4. *Show up* brilliantly and *move* boldly to attract others to your brand.
5. *Influence* others to change for the better and build a *network* of advocates.
6. Continuously *grow* and improve yourself, your team, and your organization to stay relevant and competitive.
7. Bring traditional and emerging leadership qualities to *lead* yourself and others to the new.
8. *Serve* society for the betterment of everyone.

That is *the Amasian Way*.

FINAL REMINDERS THAT KEEP YOU MOVING

You do not need perfection to begin. You need reps.

Doctors, lawyers, and consultants call what they do "practice" for a reason. Improvement is the point. The infinite game is not about winning once. It is about staying in motion and getting better over time.

Here are the reminders I want you to carry into Monday:

1. **Choose courage when it is easier to "lie flat."** Do not avoid difficult things when doing them is the right thing to do. Work smarter, not harder. But do not confuse comfort with strategy. Step up when it matters. Own your narrative. Get back up when you fall. Lead change instead of letting change happen to you.
2. **Protect the *work*, *life*, and *me* balance so you can sustain the climb.** Work and life will pull you in competing directions, especially with multiple identities. Find your work, life, and me balance. Schedule breaks on your calendar so that you do not burn out or flame out.
3. **Stay positive and manage your energy.** Attitude matters. Conviction gives you fuel when the road gets steep. Negativity drains energy and shrinks your options. Choose to spend your energy positively and strategically.
4. **Run ITMI on yourself.** Treat yourself regularly with inspection, testing, maintenance, and investing (ITMI).

Get feedback. Adjust early. Fix small problems before they become big ones. When maintenance is not enough, invest to level up for an increased scope.

5. **Get in the game as a player-coach.** Stay close to the work and to the people. Roll up your sleeves when needed. The credibility and empathy you gain from "playing" make your leadership real.
6. **Stay curious so you stay relevant.** Work will change. If you stand still, you will be left behind. Keep learning, reading, watching, listening, and testing. Curiosity is career insurance.
7. **Grow with the "Virtuous Cycle."** Share your leadership experience with a wider audience to gather valuable feedback and insights that can help you further refine and strengthen your leadership skills.
8. **Let others in and help.** We are stronger together. Build a personal board of advisors. Grow your network. Do not let pride and humility get in the way of asking for help. Mentor others. Create "ride or die" colleagues by being one.

YOUR AMASIAN "BE ATTITUDES"

Use these as mantras, especially when at high-stakes moments:

- **Be self-aware.** Know your drivers, limits, and patterns. Seek feedback. Manage wellness.
- **Be authentic.** Bring your integrated self. Spend energy on progress, not performance.
- **Be kind.** Kindness fuels trust, mental wellness, and collective success.
- **Be a strategic problem solver.** Prioritize what matters. Build the case. Test, learn, and follow through.
- **Be in the moment.** Do fewer things well, focus on the big rocks. Do not be a distracted driver.
- **Be a player.** Study the game, run a game plan, win, then elevate the game.
- **Be curious.** Synthesize perspectives and build something new.

- **Be ready.** Practice so that opportunity does not surprise you.
- **Be resilient.** Learn fast, recover faster, and keep moving.
- **Be bold and brilliant.** Take calculated risks. Advocate with substance. Own your narrative.
- **Be real.** Stay awake to bias and inequity. Navigate smart channels. Remember that you have choices.

THE AMASIAN EXPERIENCE

This is where I want to land the plane.

People need to see you and experience you. You are who they should remember.

- Your Amasian brand promise consistently delivers value and impact.
- Your Amasian leadership experience is the "wow" feeling of following your lead.
- Your Amasian brand draws everyone to you.

You do not need to be the loudest in the room. You need to be the most consistent. You need to build a record of outcomes and a pattern of leadership behaviors that people trust under pressure.

TAKE YOUR NEXT STEPS

Thank you for reading this book. If you did the journal activities, you already have your raw material. If you did not, do not punish yourself. Start now.

After that, use this simple plan to move forward:

Your next 7 days

- Write your Amasian brand promise in one sentence. Make it your computer login passphrase to help you remember it.
- Identify one leadership rep you will practice this week (visibility, advocacy, decision, influence, feedback).

- Make one outcome visible. Document the proof.

Your next 30 days

- Ask for targeted feedback from three stakeholders: "What should I start, stop, continue?"
- Choose one skill to build with reps and proof.
- Create one moment of leadership that is uncomfortable on purpose.

Your next 90 days

- Deliver one meaningful outcome that strengthens your narrative.
- Build one mentor, sponsor, or ally relationship that increases your leverage.
- Choose one service lane and create impact with proof.

Thank you for reading this book. Thank you for being Amasian. I appreciate you.

Now is the time for you to go on your leadership journey and let everyone experience your Amasian Way.

Afterword

Everything I knew as an immigrant has changed. When I was growing up, there were just a handful of Chinese kids at my school. I was the only Chinese student in my high school class of 1990. Today, my town and my high school have nearly 50 percent of their students who are Asian.

I am a child of the '80s, well before political correctness, "woke," and cancel culture. I experienced a lot of overt racism and unconscious bias. I was a minority wherever I went. It is hurtful to think back to those days, when the words used to describe diversity were "racial tolerance." Americans took pride in encouraging one another to tolerate minorities, especially those who assimilated and became Americanized.

It did not take me long for me to realize how difficult it was to be different when I first immigrated to the United States. I went from being one of many Chinese kids in a Hong Kong Catholic all-boys school to being one of a few Chinese kids in a Caucasian-majority public co-ed school. I was dealing with all sorts of new feelings and experiences. While teachers were excited to show me off to my classmates as a new and different child, most of the other kids were less curious and more demeaning. At that point, I thought I had no choice but to fit in and not draw attention to my diverse background to avoid being teased. Of course, it is difficult to hide my skin color. As a 10-year-old boy, I was desperate to fit in.

At one point, I pointed at a small group of Chinese kids on the school bus, which included my cousins, and declared to my white American classmates that I was not a "chink" like them. "Chink" was about the most derogatory term for an Asian that I had been called numerous times. To this day, I cringe when I think about that incident and simultaneously feel shame and sympathy for my younger self.

The portrayal of Asian enemies in numerous Vietnam War movies made it a hostile environment for my younger years. I vividly recall walking home from school in the seventh grade, bleeding from an ice ball thrown across the street at my head. The kids who threw the ice ball yelled, "Go back on a boat to where you came from!" I yelled back, "I came on an airplane!" while wiping the blood off my forehead, as if that made any difference.

Because there were so few other Chinese kids besides my cousins, I ended up befriending mostly Caucasian American kids. I was lucky to have had a few close friends who helped me navigate my new home in America. Their families were also very kind to me. My closest friend's parents were Lithuanian immigrants themselves. We bonded over our "immigrant song." These friends, who are still like brothers to me today, made it much easier for me to adjust to my new life in America.

One of my other best friends, Tim, and I were in the cafeteria in high school. He told me, "I never think of you as Chinese." It was 1990. I had been an immigrant for eight years. I felt validated. It was great to know that I finally fit in. I was so proud to have fully assimilated into an American.

I was so wrong, and I did not know it yet.

Even though I was well-liked in college and rarely faced overt racism, I was regularly reminded that my belonging was conditional. Most of the time, I was treated like any other American student, but there were moments when cultural lines hardened. One friend's parents rejected me because of my background and pushed us apart. Another friend, after eating at my parents' home, later mocked our traditional Chinese dishes to others on campus.

I was living in two worlds. I was either an insider among Americans or among the Asian community, or I am an outsider to both. I kept switching my identity to fit in, but there were still times when both groups dismissed me because I was simultaneously too Americanized or not Americanized enough.

In my senior year of college, I had the opportunity to attend a retreat with several minority resident assistants and school counselors. We spent the day exploring concepts of diversity. I vividly remember an African ritual that helped us see how each person contributed their individuality to a greater community.

Each of us poured a glass of water into a shared pitcher and then received a glass back. It symbolized that when we contributed our diversity, we received something greater in return. Like the idea of a melting pot, but with a different meaning. The word I came away with that day was "celebrate." We celebrated racial differences. For the first time, I could visualize a world beyond tolerance.

Fast-forward to 2010. I was a director at one of the Big Four accounting firms when I began volunteering with Ascend Global Leaders, the largest nonprofit organization dedicated to developing North America's AAPI leaders, professionals, and students.

Ascend became the family I never knew I needed. Through mentors and the community, I began reflecting on my earlier experiences differently. I realized I no longer wanted to dismiss the Chinese part of my identity. Although college taught me to appreciate many cultures, I had hidden my own. After becoming involved with Ascend, I recognized how deeply my Chinese culture had influenced my decisions, actions, and leadership instincts. By suppressing or not acknowledging this part of me, I was not whole. Instead, I was unsuccessfully code-switching rather than being congruent and showing up as my best self.

Today, while there has been progress in diversity, equity, and inclusion, many of the patterns of discrimination remain disturbingly familiar. Over the past decade, xenophobia against Chinese people has steadily risen. Political narratives, trade wars, espionage rhetoric, and media portrayals have reinforced the idea of China as an enemy. That rhetoric increases animosity toward Chinese Americans.

During the COVID-19 pandemic, that hostility reached a new high. The result was a resurgence of systemic prejudice, unconscious bias, microaggressions, racist rhetoric, and hate crimes against all AAPI communities. It did not matter whether the individual was Chinese, Japanese, Korean, etc. Hate extended to all AAPIs because those who held racist views saw all Asians as the same. My 8-year-old daughter once told me that a boy in her class said, "I do not like Asians." The elderly and children were attacked in public. The community feared for their lives.

I am typically treated with respect and kindness among people I know. In public, I am seen and treated for my visible diversity—the color of my skin and the slant in my eyes. Although I am fluent in English, I am often treated by someone as a foreigner with a language barrier. Once, I paused to think of the answer when asked for directions, and heard the person repeat his question more loudly and slowly, in a derogatory tone. The people who know me are not the ones who judge me by my appearance. That realization reminded me how futile it was to try so hard to fit in. I was never going to erase how others initially see me.

You cannot control how people see you. You cannot control why they judge you. You can control how people experience you.

I no longer obsess about things that I cannot control. Instead, I chose to help people experience me by showing up, acting with kindness, leading with substance and empathy, and learning, growing, and improving myself and others. The more people experience me, the fewer people will judge me without knowing me.

I recently had a conversation with Tim. Among other things, we talked about that incident in the cafeteria. He said, "Oh, I didn't mean I don't think of you as Chinese because you reminded me of a white dude. I mean, you are B. Jae! You are *you*!" It dawned on me at that moment that my successes in life and in my career were never about whether I was assimilating into American life. My work, life, and relationship successes result from how others experience *me*—the *me* who is an unapologetic amalgamation of my life's experiences, choices, and actions. People who knew me associated me with how I made them feel and what I did for them.

I came to realize that sustained experience eventually becomes a personal brand. When what people experience from you is clear, consistent, and valuable, it begins to supersede the stereotypes and assumptions attached to identity.

That realization became the foundation for this leadership framework: the Amasian Way. It is about becoming the ultimate version of yourself and delivering an undeniable experience.

Throughout my career, colleagues and associates have consistently remembered me, often recalling our interactions years later and expressing a willingness to reconnect and offer assistance when needed. Their recollections center on the impression I made during our professional encounters. For this reason, I make it a priority to ensure that every interaction is conducted thoughtfully and reflects my desired professional and leadership brand.

My childhood experiences closely parallel those of many Asian immigrants I have encountered throughout the years. Likewise, my adult life in America mirrors that of numerous second- and third-generation AAPI individuals who often struggle to identify with commonly held stereotypes.

Recognizing the impact of both Eastern and Western influences on my perspective, choices, and behavior has been transformative. Although I initially resisted acknowledging it, I am now keenly aware of the stereotypes others may attribute to me without personal knowledge or experience. These epiphanies now significantly contribute to how I think, act, and lead as an AAPI professional.

Around ten years ago, I delivered a keynote titled "My Journey from Purpose to Impact," where I shared how I discovered my purpose at the time: to make people happy. Over the years, my sense of purpose has shifted from transactional to transformational. Now, my purpose is to "lead and help others lead."

I am excited about the positive impact and influence that you and other Amasian leaders will bring.

About the Author

Bartholomew Jae (謝思穎)—known as B. Jae among friends and colleagues—moved from Hong Kong to Quincy, Massachusetts, with his parents and two brothers when he was 10. Raised in both Chinese and Catholic traditions, B. Jae lived in America from age 10 into adulthood.

B. Jae has over thirty years of experience as a business leader specializing in leadership, talent, and organizational development. B. Jae has had the privilege of working with global Fortune 100 companies on transformational projects. He has delivered keynote addresses and participated in panels worldwide.

After graduating from Bentley College, he began as a registered representative at Scudder Investments, later shifting into a training role and rising to assistant vice president at 29. After Scudder, B. Jae helped launch a start-up in the eLearning sector, starting as an instructional designer and advancing to VP of products and production. In the mid-2000s, he began consulting with PwC, eventually transitioning to an internal leadership role in learning and development so he could spend more time with his young children. He later joined Accenture's strategy consulting practice before moving on to lead training and certification at the National Fire Protection Association (NFPA).

Today, B. Jae resides in Quincy with his wife and two children, close to his parents, and regularly volunteers his time, expertise, and resources to his local community, church, and the Asian American community. For over thirty years, he has served as a lector at Sacred Heart Parish in Quincy. He has been involved with Ascend Global Leaders for more than fifteen years, including multiple terms as president of the New England chapter. Additionally, B. Jae supports recent immigrants through his service on the board of directors for the Boston Chinatown Neighborhood Center.

www.ingramcontent.com/pod-product-compliance
Ingram Content Group UK Ltd.
Pitfield, Milton Keynes, MK11 3LW, UK
UKHW062310290726
14090UKWH00018B/983